Catholic Culture in the USA

GW00360851

Catholic Culture in the USA

In and Out of Church

John Portmann

continuum

Continuum
Continuum International Publishing Group
The Tower Building   80 Maiden Lane
11 York Road   Suite 704
London SE1 7NX   New York NY 10038

www.continuumbooks.com

British Library Cataloguing-in-Publication Data
A catalogue record for this book is available from the British Library.

ISBN: HB: 978–1–4411–6359–2
      PB: 978–1–4411–8892–2

Library of Congress Cataloging-in-Publication Data
Portmann, John.
  Catholic culture in the USA: in and out of church/John Portmann.
    p. cm.
  Includes bibliographical references (p. 189) and index.
    ISBN 978–1–4411–6359–2—ISBN 978–1–4411–8892–2   1. Catholics—United
States—Religion.   2. Catholic Church—United States—Customs and practices.
I. Title.

  BX1406.3.P67 2010
  282'.7309045—dc22

                                                      2009014176

Typeset by RefineCatch Limited, Bungay, Suffolk
Printed and bound in Great Britain by
CPI Antony Rowe, Chippenham, Wiltshire

To my parents,
Catholics through and through

Contents

Acknowledgments

Many thanks to my editor Kirsty Schaper, who expressed enthusiasm for this project from the outset. Vanessa Ochs carefully read the proposal, when the project involved a comparison between cultural Catholicism and cultural Judaism, and offered helpful comments. Although I eventually dropped the chapters on Judaism, I profited from her erudite perspective. Cecelia Moore and Anthony J. Carroll, S.J. read the entire manuscript and improved it with several important suggestions.

Daniel Ortiz, the pride of St. Polycarp Catholic School in Louisville, Kentucky, provoked me to justify this project. Various newspaper articles would prompt him to remark at least once a year on how distant the Catholic Church seems to him; in the process, he leavened this book.

Over the years, hundreds of Catholic friends and strangers have offered to me their personal—even intimate—accounts of growing up Catholic and one day finding themselves far from the church. I have sometimes felt like Alfred Kinsey, although I elicited religious histories, not sexual ones. I am grateful to the many people who have introduced me to Catholic culture.

Foreword

When a biologist identifies a rare bird in some faraway swamp, describes its habits and graces it with a name in the taxonomic charts, it makes news. John Portmann's *Catholic Culture in the USA* should be even more newsworthy because it identifies a hitherto unlabelled species which exists at hand, in broad daylight: "Cultural Catholics." The activities and habits of individual members of the species are anything but uniform and Portmann offers a necessary and valuable "natural history" of the varied behaviors.

The very idea of "Cultural Catholic" is novel and controversial. While the term locates a social reality, it is not at all clear that the species "Committed Catholics" would recognize such folks as Catholics at all, at all. There are a host of alternate terms which have been used in the past for individuals less-than-Catholic: "ex-Catholics," "former Catholics," "lapsed Catholics," "cafeteria Catholics"—how about just "bad Catholics"—and most recently there is the class of "recovering Catholics." As to the last designation, Portmann's principal claim is that most Catholics never "recover." They may miss Mass, scorn the sacraments, write screeds denouncing everyone from the Pope on down, but somehow they continue to resonate to something distinctly "Catholic." The persistence of Catholic sensibility well after one has abandoned ritual and opted out of this or that piece of the moral catechism is a conceptual puzzle in its own right. It is also a significant practical problem for the official church.

One can appreciate the conceptual puzzle of "Cultural Catholic" by comparing the term to "Cultural Jew" which has somewhat more currency. Judaism in fact and in significant commentary is not a religion of belief, orthodoxy, but a religion of practice, orthopraxis. One can, it has been argued, jettison all sorts of supernatural claims on up to a belief in God, and still identify as Jewish by carrying on the moral practices at the heart of Judaism: care for the widow and orphan, compassion for the poor. Added to moral injunction there is a strong genealogical reality to Judaism. The great modern Jewish theologian, Franz Rosenzweig put it this way: "The belief [of the Jew] is not the content of a testimony, but a product of reproduction. The Jew, engendered a Jew, attests his belief by continuing to procreate the Jewish people. His belief is not in something, he is himself the belief." (*The Star of Redemption*, Notre Dame, 1970, p. 342). A Cultural Jew may not be observant beyond attending synagogue on High Holidays but he or she persists in a deep generational loyalty to the Jewish people and their tragic history. Even support of the state of Israel may be sufficient for cultural self-identification.

One can define Cultural Jew with some clarity but similar strategies don't work for Cultural Catholic. As Portmann maintains, something of the "supernatural" is necessary for the Cultural Catholic. No one remains a Catholic who simply adheres to Catholic moral teaching; there has to be some supernatural ingredient. One may be a cultural Jew because of support of the state of Israel, no one is a cultural Catholic because of support of the Vatican City. On the contrary, it is precisely disagreement with what is often proclaimed from the Vatican that drives many cradle Catholics out of Sunday service and manifest Catholicism.

In the course of his study, Portmann ranges over a number of customs and practices in which a Cultural Catholic may participate while at the same time being anywhere from absent to antagonistic to official Catholicism. European customs like processionals and carnival which, while not mainstays of normal American Catholicism, have always existed in ethnic communities within the United States. With the growth of the Hispanic population of Catholics, processional activity will probably become more frequent. It may not be not clear whether enthusiasts who mount or cheer on these processions are expressing religious or ethnic attachment. Portmann is probably correct, however, that even a bystander can grasp something out of the ordinary as the Statue of the Virgin is carried shoulder high down the public street.

More important for locating cultural Catholics is noting whether they participate in the three great life-change sacraments: Baptism, Marriage, and Funerals. Whatever one's skepticism about salvation from sin, maybe one ought to baptize the baby "just in case." Even a secular bride may desire a "church wedding" as a mark of solemnity and celebration. (Then, grandparents would be offended if the proper blessings are not attended to.) Funerals: Finley Peter Dunne, the author of the famous Mr. Dooley stories, when asked if he were a Roman Catholic always replied "No, I'm a Chicago Catholic." (Being myself from Chicago, I am inclined to think that Chicago Catholic and Cultural Catholic overlap.) Dunne left specific instructions that he have a modest funeral. It was, however, a grand and lengthy affair at St. Patrick's in New York. A friend quipped after the ceremony, "Peter spent more time in church today that he ever did in life." And that can be said of many Cultural Catholics. Birth, love, and death seem to compel special sacramental moments and no matter how lapsed, choosy, or ex, occasional Catholics rejoin the church even if it is only to make a final exit.

It is one thing to be distant from Church practice, it is quite another to be a dissenter. Portmann offers a short history of Catholic dissent in the United States. It is in the area of dissent that the puzzle of Cultural Catholic is most manifest. A Christmas-and-Easter Catholic may believe (more or less) but just be bored with Sunday service. The dissenter thinks that there is something definitely wrong with the Church: erroneous theology, moral misdirection, dull liturgy, or abusive priests. Why don't dissenters simply decamp, give up on Catholicism and join some Protestant denomination. But they don't—much to the annoyance of Committed Catholics at EWTN, the Legionnaires of Christ, Opus Dei, and various "conservative" commentators like the late Fr. Richard John Neuhaus. The fact of significant dissent which does not lead to schism is at the heart of the puzzle of Cultural Catholics and fully justifies Portmann's location of the species and his suggestions for understanding the persistence of Catholic sensibility beyond practical indifference and dissent.

In his final chapter, Portmann examines three possible explanations for Cultural Catholics, two are derived from social psychology, and the third examines a Freudian theory of "family romance." The problem with the social psychological theories is, in my judgment, that they are in the end too "rational." The first attempts to calculate the cost-benefit ratio involved in ego-reinforcement from belonging to a group, the second sees Church membership as a way to manage the terror of death. Certainly people do derive ego-reinforcement by attachment to publicly visible organizations like the Catholic Church. Church membership may or may not, however, lead to ego-reinforcement depending one's situation in life. As someone who spent his entire professional life in high prestige secular higher education, I can't say that being identified as a Catholic was exactly ego-reinforcing. Professor of physics would have been more self-enhancing.

As for the notion that Church practice is useful because it balances the cost of present practice against future reward after death, that view is at least heretical. The traditional confessional ritual acknowledged cost-benefit, "I fear the pains of hell" but the real reason was "because I offend thee, my God, who is all good and deserving of all my love." There are costs and benefits for love, but a love based on rational calculation is no love at all. Attachment to Catholic cultural modes despite indifference and dissent needs an explanation as "irrational" as love itself.

Portmann is thus on the right track when he examines—however gingerly—Freud's notion of "family romance" as an explanation for deep impact of Catholicism. The base line of the "family romance" story is most instructive in explaining the "supernatural" element which lingers in Catholic sensibility. Contrast Cultural Jew and Cultural Catholic: it is relatively straightforward to account for Cultural Jew on the basis of family *loyalty*, family *romance* goes farther. In the Freudian Oedipal conflict, the individual is faced with a practical impossibility. The male child is not simply loyal to his mother, according to the standard theory he is sexually in love with her. He cannot attain that goal because the father stands in the way. The child must therefore slay the father. That is also impractical so he seeks to identify with the father. Only it is not the actual limited, flesh and blood father at hand—that one gets slain in imagination. The actual father is overshadowed by an "ideal" father. A similar blending of actuality and "ideal" is present when Cultural Catholics are haunted by the supernatural. The supernatural hovers over the everyday, just as the "ideal" father haunts the actual father at hand in the unstable resolution of the Oedipal complex.

As Andrew Greeley and others have argued, there is a distinctive Catholic *imagination*. Catholic sensibility senses that what is at hand, what is just natural—like birth, sex, and death—has an added dimension that is acknowledged even if only in a fleeting moment at a Corpus Christi processional or attendance at a family wedding. Charles Taylor in his monumental study, *A Secular Age*, suggests a theme song protesting our down to earth, practical, no nonsense age, Peggy Lee's "Is that all there is?" The Cultural Catholic is haunted by the sense that what is at hand is *not* all there is? There is something more which is the "super-natural."

Locating the Cultural Catholic is an interesting conceptual problem, the official Church, however, has a practical problem of winning back the lost sheep. Portmann's view that the essential for Cultural

Catholics is a whiff of the supernatural could be the solution but, in my opinion, such a strategy would reveal a surprising paradox. Cultural Catholics may sense something supernatural in everything from processions to funerals but they do *not* find the supernatural in official Catholicism—and in part they are correct.

The charge that the official Church is actually diminishing the "supernatural" demands careful definition of the term. There are two ways to look at "supernatural." In one understanding, the supernatural is a higher reality replacing our lived "natural" experience. One projects a sort of two-layered view in which "supernature" is like Plato's Forms which exist above us and constitute whatever order there is in our human world of murky change. One flees from nature and change to supernature and eternity. A contrasting idea of the supernatural holds that supernatural and natural are bound together; the natural remains but is deepened into mystery. When Juliana of Norwich saw heaven in a hazelnut, the hazelnut remained its palpable self.

There are two prominent aspects of official Church life which seem to me to be de-supernaturalized: sexual ethics and the Eucharistic liturgy. Portmann properly notes the wide disaffection with official sexual ethics in areas like birth control, homosexuality, and even abortion. Turned off by what are regarded as unacceptable teachings on sex, Cultural Catholics are not all that inclined toward regular Mass attendance and when they go they find the experience lacks a sense of the supernatural.

Given these two ways of regarding the "supernatural," official Church teaching on sexuality tends toward the Platonic. Sex as experienced is replaced by an abstract discussion of gender and procreation that leads on to a sexual ideal and rationally constructed moral theory. John Paul II's series of talks collected and published as *Man and Woman He Created Them: A Theology of the Body* claims to be based on a branch of philosophy called "phenomenology." But it is the very phenomenon of sexuality which seems most lacking in this lengthy and philosophically dense treatise. Sexuality as a *phenomenon* resists full rationality and the ideal. Sexuality presents itself like the second notion of supernatural: a very present natural urge with a dimension of mystery we cannot fully comprehend. One can, of course, regard sex as *just* natural: we couple sexually as part of species behavior. But that is another abstraction and delusion. A rose is a rose is a rose but sex is not sex. In sexuality we are caught up in personal joys and disasters beyond the course of nature, into a mystery we cannot and would not wish to unravel. The very mystery of sex is the source of its power and value. If official Church teaching on sexuality fails to connect with Cultural Catholics, it is because ideal sexuality lacks the very thing that keeps them Catholic, a sense for mystery.

What about the fact that Mass seems to boring to the Cultural Catholic? I would suggest that even there, in the midst of ritual, incense and all, mystery is missed. (The mystery that is missing is *not* the mystery of Latin before the advent of the vernacular Mass!) I offer a minor example: in the Eucharistic sacrifice, the separate consecration of the bread and the wine is a re-enactment of the death of Jesus: the separation of body and life giving blood which is death. There is no problem understanding why symbolic re-enactment of Calvary is at the heart of Christian worship. Immediately following the Consecration, however, we hear the proclamation: "Christ has died, Christ is risen, Christ will come again." What's wrong with that? Nothing at all *theologically*, but as an experience in liturgy, something is missing: recognition of the majesty of death.

We stand before death as we stand before sexuality, caught up in a profound reality which we struggle to understand. Death is final mystery. It is customary at public ceremonies to observe a few moment of silence in memory of a deceased person. The moment of silence recognizes that we stand without sufficient words before death! In the quick liturgical proclamation following the consecration we hurry past the solemnity of death to the resurrection—an even greater mystery. It is as if there was no entombment, no Holy Saturday of utter loss and the silent grave. Whatever the mystery of resurrection and Christ's return may point to, they cannot be allowed to trivialize not only the death of the man Jesus but also, it is claimed, the death of God. How can the proclamation of a death—and the death of God at that!—be boring? But as brushed through in a neat formula it seems to be so. No wonder folks with a taste for mystery stay home and read the paper— which is chock-a-block full of the incomprehensible violence which marks our world.

Catholic Culture in the USA is a valuable work because it highlights the reality of Cultural Catholicism and offers succinct and accurate accounts of its manifestation. As observation of an interesting social reality, it has obvious importance. It should be essential reading for priests and bishops who lead the official Church. Cultural Catholicism is most firmly rooted in the lives of "cradle Catholics," many of whom emerged from the thick Catholic culture or parochial schools, compulsory mass attendance, frequent confession, and sacramental galore.

Today that confined Catholic world has dissipated. The Catholic sense and place of the supernatural is attenuated, but the supernatural will not and cannot vanish from human consciousness. There is too much mystery from birth to sex to death to ever lose the sense that the world is "uncanny." So be it, how will an official Church which, in my judgment, has denatured mystery in overly rationalized ethics and deductive theology capture the free-floating supernatural which persists. If it fails to do so, official Catholicism will shrink and Cultural Catholic will be an endangered species. Take heed.

Dennis O'Brien

Preface

My interest in cultural Catholics stretches far into the past. As a kid, I wondered why a number of our Catholic neighbors never bothered to go to Mass, apart from Christmas and Easter. Catholicism seemed more of an occasional hobby to them than the organizing life force it was for my own parents. Before I had a word for it, I knew what a cultural Catholic was—someone who was raised Catholic and so appreciates the rituals, ceremonies, community, values, and self-identification of being a Catholic. They have associated morality with their Catholicism because the two were taught hand in hand during their upbringing, and this association remains even if they don't see eye-to-eye with the Catholic Church on every issue when they get older.

I found more evidence of this phenomenon in college, when well-meaning Catholic friends would sometimes scoff at me for going to Mass. Other examples, taken from television newscasts and the newspapers, suggested themselves in time. In the American presidential election of 2004, a small group of bishops told the world that Senator John Kerry of Massachusetts was not a good Catholic and could not receive communion in their dioceses.[1] The candidate for president found himself denounced by his own people, all because he felt bound by conscience to defend *Roe v. Wade*, the 1973 Supreme Court ruling which legalized abortion in some circumstances. Kerry stated that he personally abhorred abortion but that, as an elected official, he could not impose his private moral views on others. Senator Joe Biden, a pro-choice Catholic who ran for president in 2008, largely escaped the fate of Kerry, a fact that suggested that "fake Catholic" was a moving target. What, I wondered, was the difference between a bad Catholic and a lapsed Catholic? And why did members of either subset not just pick up and move to another faith? Was it really a good idea to ban problem Catholics from communion, or would it perhaps be better to view communion as "food for the journey," as Pope Pius X had once termed it? Wouldn't problem Catholics need communion even more than devout Catholics?

Cultural Catholics never struck me as particularly threatening in the first place. With age and experience, I have found myself caring about them more and more. Not only do they deserve a defense, they merit acknowledgment as a bulging class with an appealing identity. Cultural Catholics share deep reflexes and instincts. They tend to play well with others, and they rarely accuse the faithful of other religions of automatic condemnation to hell. Cultural Catholics feel the pull of a certain tide; they do not want to join another religion.

Rather than attempting to construct neat categories and definitions, I emphasize the tentativeness of early twenty-first century Catholicism in the United States. Through an open-ended exploration (rather than a quantitative analysis) of cultural Catholicism, I celebrate the faithfulness of an inchoate community. I aim at the same time to communicate something of my own enthusiasm for the sophistication, complexity, and resilience of Catholic culture. Born the day that Pope John XXIII died, I was one of the lucky kids: I only ever encountered loving priests and nuns.

Introduction

Catholic culture pulses through the United States. Films as diverse as *The Bells of Saint Mary's* or *The Godfather* or *The Passion of the Christ* or *Doubt* transport it. Newspapers and journals transmit it, and they run the gamut from the very conservative, such as *The Wanderer* or *Crisis* or *Fidelity*, to the more liberal, such as *The National Catholic Reporter* and *Commonweal*. Local parish centers compete with blogs and specialty Web sites to keep the faithful rooted in the particularity and peculiarity of Catholicism. These sources, and many more, pump a supplementary culture into some American homes before making their way back to Rome, where they may return scarcely recognizable.

I want to illuminate that culture, imposingly vast as it may be. I will focus on the United States, a country known for its ethnic diversity, rapid social change, and creeping secularism. By the year 2030, Catholic culture will have changed significantly, as a result of a cumulative influx of immigrants from Mexico, Central America, and South America. This book only begins to describe the spiritual outlook of cultural Catholics, a largely middle-class, English-speaking, educated group.

In the early 1970s the Catholic way of living changed in a number of ways, almost all of which are immediately familiar to Catholics born before 1960. The Second Vatican Council (1962–1965) transformed Catholic culture in ways still debated in the twenty-first century. In the *Pastoral Constitution on the Church in the Modern World*, a document from Vatican II, the council took up the "proper development of culture" and, in so doing, offered this useful definition of culture:

> The word "culture" in the general sense refers to all those things which go to the refining and developing of man's diverse mental and physical endowments. He strives to subdue the earth by his

knowledge and his labor; he humanizes social life both in the family and in the whole civic community through the improvement of customs and institutions; he expresses through his works the great spiritual experiences and aspirations of men throughout the ages; he communicates and preserves nations of men throughout the ages; he communicates and preserves them to be an inspiration for the progress of many, even of all mankind.

Hence it follows that culture necessarily has historical and social overtones, and the word "culture" often carries with it sociological and technological connotations; in this sense one can speak about a plurality of cultures.[1]

So many sociological studies have been conducted since Vatican II that I don't propose another one here. Rather, I try to interpret those statistics narratively. The remarks I offer are meant to be suggestive, not exhaustive.

Long before political leaders settled on the national borders familiar in the modern West, Catholic culture already thrived. In 2004 then Cardinal Joseph Ratzinger published a small book in which he indicated his conviction that "Europe" was a cultural concept before it became a geographic one.[2] The book, a collection of essays and lectures, noted the painful irony of Europe's cultural ascendancy: by the time that the languages and sciences of Europe had suffused the globe in the twenty-first century, the culture of Europe had stagnated. This concern about Europe's cultural demise partly explained Ratzinger's 2004 opposition to admitting Turkey in the European Union. Ratzinger feared a further dilution of Christian culture would result from an influx of Muslim Turks.

Around this working notion of culture I will focus a necessarily general description of Catholic culture in the United States, a hodgepodge culture largely imported from Europe. To the description I will add the nuance of certain reflexes, instincts, rhythms, longings, and compulsions. I do not believe that what I add to the cultural vignette— informed dissent—conflicts with the spirit of Catholic culture. What will prove debatable is a certain question of emphasis in the snapshot I offer.

The Roman Catholic Church comprises a myriad of particular cultures across the globe; the same is almost true of the Roman Catholic Church in the United States. This book is a sustained reflection on the cultural side of a mega-church in a single, exceptionally ethnically diverse, country. I am guided by the approach Clifford Geertz set out in the 1966 essay "Religion as a Cultural System."[3] Geertz understands by "culture" a "pattern of meanings," or ideas carried in symbols, by which people pass along their knowledge of life. Cultural analysis is for Geertz always a matter of "guessing at meanings, assessing the guesses, and drawing explanatory conclusions."

Many observers in the United States and Western Europe have noted both the frequency of lay disagreement with Rome and declining levels of parish involvement; this cultural uprooting and drifting away has led to an increasingly crowded destination. Catholics who migrate to this spiritual place frequently make their own life decisions, sometimes dissenting outright from the Church and other times filling in the large spaces where the official church gives no instruction or ignores specific details. New inventions and technological developments test the intellectual ingenuity of conflicted believers, who keep one foot in the secular world and another foot in the vague realm of Catholic culture. This new brand of believer shows emotional loyalty more than anything to some Catholic ideal. If there is a problem with these institution-wary believers, it is either that they misunderstand the very possibility of their cultural perch or, alternately, sentimentality—they want the comfort and pride that go with a Catholic identity, but they don't want to pay the price for being a "proper" Catholic—a category that is itself open to dispute.

Today many Catholics and even more non-Catholics view Catholic culture as restrictive: There are just so many things you can't do, particularly in the sexual realm, and so many others which you must do but don't (for example, attending Mass every Sunday and making regular confessions before a priest). In fact, it would be easy to portray Catholic culture as precisely the opposite, that is, fun-loving and progressive. Various scholarly accounts have left that impression. In the aftermath of the Protestant Reformation, some Protestants rejected elements of Catholic culture which today might seem likely to attract young members. Protestants winced at the vigorous affirmation of the human body in paintings, the frequency with which artists depicted the penis of the infant Jesus or the Virgin Mary breast-feeding her young child.[4] Protestants criticized and eschewed carnivals as well, specifically, the unusually jovial celebrations anticipating Lent.[5] Catholics have, beyond that, generally embraced alcohol, whereas some early Protestants, especially Puritans in England, condemned it as intrinsically evil. Even today, some Mormons, Muslims, Baptists, and Methodists will oppose alcohol consumption as immoral—either because alcohol is bad in itself or by virtue of the consequences to which it is likely to lead.

And yet the church seems to appeal to fewer and fewer Americans. That the Catholic Church is in crisis in the United States has become such a commonplace since the 1970s that probably no one would attempt to publish a book on the subject. Already in 1967 Catholics could read a book (by a priest, no less) startlingly entitled *A Modern Priest Looks at his Outdated Church*.[6] There's only so long you can keep this sort of shock fresh and vivid; that day has long since passed, despite the frequent bickering between the conservative and liberal wings of this vast community of American Catholics.

Never before has the Catholic laity felt so confident or courageous.[7] Perhaps in response to the increasing self-confidence and self-assertion of the laity, some Vatican representatives have begun to castigate trouble-makers publicly. Of course, Rome has long known about the threat of heretics and has sometimes excommunicated the "faithful" who had outstayed their welcome. In the twenty-first century, though, it is considerably harder to compel the faithful to do much of anything, including leave. Early twenty-first century bishops in the United States have publicly refused to give the Eucharist to Catholic politicians who vote "pro-choice," even though these politicians may attend Mass weekly and privately condemn abortion. Meanwhile, some Catholics who skip Mass may quake in the shadows of such recriminations. This kind of pressure could push a Catholic away from the fold, but it doesn't always. The staying, the lingering, is what this book is about. Because public excommunication happens so seldom (it doesn't erase a Catholic identity, in any event), and because Catholicism lacks a public degradation ritual, problem Catholics have proliferated.[8]

It is certainly relevant that Roman Catholics in North America no longer live in fear of ecclesiastical authorities. In the tumultuous sixteenth century, especially in England, the future of the Church was far from certain. Eamon Duffy has argued persuasively that the reason ordinary English Catholics participated in stripping the altars of remnants of traditional liturgical practice in the mid-sixteenth century was fear of royal authority.[9] That fear is perfectly understandable in an age in which the church could ruin a person financially and personally. Apart from an excommunication, which happens infrequently in the twenty-first century, it seems unfathomable that the Vatican would punish contemporary Catholics who disagree with the Holy See on, say, the ordination of women, gay marriage, or artificial birth control. The reason why dissident or ambivalent Catholics stay within the Church often has little if anything to do with fear but something to do with genuine faith. Perhaps the very worst that can be said about unorthodox or occasional Catholics is that they display a sort of blind faith—not the faith of peasants, but the instincts of the devout who really do believe in the "core principles" of the Church.

Chief Justice of the Supreme Court John Roberts might qualify as a devout Catholic, as might Mel Gibson, the Domino's Pizza mogul Tom Monahan, or Yale Law professor Robert Bork. Most Americans, whether Catholic or not, are familiar with traditional Catholic concerns, which cluster around the following poles:

- devotion to the Virgin Mary as the mother of God
- the indissolubility of marriage and the inadvisability of marrying a non-Catholic
- the real, literal presence of Christ in the Eucharist
- venial sin (that is, relatively trivial wrongdoing) and (deserving Hell for all eternity) mortal sin
- the necessity of confessing mortal sin
- the immortal soul
- the resurrection of the body
- Purgatory and the point of praying for the souls stranded there
- infallibility and the primacy of the Pope as the successor of Saint Peter
- the role of bishops as successors of the Apostles
- the intercession of the saints
- the reality of Satan, and of demons and angels
- a hostile antagonism toward atheistic communism
- the inadmissibility of contraception, abortion, premarital sex, adultery, homosexuality, and remarriage after divorce
- the inadmissibility of worshipping with non-Catholics
- weekly attendance at Mass, as well as holy days of obligation
- the imperative to avoid meat on Fridays

Such concerns long oriented a Catholic's journey through life. Not so today: Cultural Catholics pick and choose from this menu *but they do not walk away from it*. Devout Catholics may feel toward cultural Catholics the kind of weary disdain specialists sometimes feel toward the dilettante or the rushed tourist who cares more about crossing off items on a list than admiring art or a beautiful cityscape.

Liberal and conservative Catholics have drifted farther away from one another since the 1970s. Intramural bickering sometimes ends in slurs to the effect that someone (usually a liberal) is not a "real Catholic." Each side decries a lack of faithfulness on the other. The underlying problem is often a question of the degree to which Catholic ideals can or should blend with the wider, secular society. The story of making accommodations to modernity is a very old one. According to Elaine Pagels, the notion of Satan springs from Hebrew Scriptures as a device for identifying just this sort of internal threat. Gradually, the line that had divided the Israelites from foreigners came to extend to and include those Jews who—for whatever reason—favored accommodation with the foreigners. In time, "these dissidents began increasingly to invoke the *satan* to characterize their Jewish opponents."[10] Satan was not the distant enemy, but the intimate one. As Pagels points out, it is hardly surprising that early Christians came to view Jews as satanic. Although the word "satanic" may never be invoked by either side in these skirmishes, the point to be taken is that plenty of social groups have grappled with internal divisions before.

In the twentieth century, Freud would classify such disputes as an example of "the narcissism of small differences." From the perspective of a distant outsider, liberal and conservative Catholics may seem to quibble over details. From an internal perspective, however, a piety competition akin to sibling rivalry ends by not only hurting feelings but nearly stripping concerned parties of a core identity—"Roman Catholic." In terms of evolution, we can expect not only distinctly new faith groups to pop up on the American horizon but also imaginative innovations of old faith groups to pop out of the past.

This book introduces a new term to describe a bulging class of Catholics who are not entirely orthodox: cultural Catholics. Sociologists and pollsters have tracked this unwieldy group since the late 1970s, and scholars have tried to make sense of a barrage of statistics in books such as Father Andrew Greeley's *The Catholic Imagination* (2000), Michele Dillon's *Catholic Identity* (1999), and Thomas Groome's *What Makes Us Catholic* (2003). My book builds on such previous studies and tries to reach higher by defending Americans who yearn to remain in an extended Catholic family despite often thoroughgoing ambivalence about that family.

Cultural Catholicism isn't so much innovative as it is suspended in air; cultural Catholicism seems to wait for the institutional Church to modernize itself, particularly with regard to sexual ethics and gender roles. In terms of cultural evolution, cultural Catholicism has frozen itself pending a future thawing, when the Church will have made further accommodations to modernity.

In the attempt to distinguish those who follow Catholic rules diligently from those who don't, it is important to remember the possibility of simple boredom, temporary or chronic. When Montaigne visited Rome in the late sixteenth century, he made a point of attending both a circumcision ceremony inside a home located in the ghetto and Sabbath services in a synagogue there. He observed that the Jews "pay no more attention to their prayers than we do in ours, talking of other affairs in the midst of them and not bringing much reverence to their mysteries."[11] That they were bored did not disqualify them from the ranks of Roman Jews, Montaigne understood. That so many Roman Catholics across the United States also feel bored in church takes little away from their identity as Catholic. Many Americans never stop to think of their identity as an American, but that hardly means they never will.

The amorphous subset "cultural Catholicism" might include non-believers. If a person raised as a Jew were to become atheist, it seems unlikely that he would land in the same mental spot as a person raised as a Catholic who then became an atheist. The supernatural worldview in which a Catholic had been steeped would set him or her apart from an atheist raised as a Jew, or a Protestant for that matter. Whether secular Jews are more likely to be atheists than cultural Catholics remains to be seen, but it is not so difficult to find even Orthodox Jews who claim to be atheist. A sociological study such as Michele Dillon's *Catholic Identity* makes clear the deep-seated belief in God of most Catholic dissidents and, if you will, occasional Catholics.

Although I acknowledge that American Catholics increasingly express their faith in ways having little if anything to do with dogma, I have found little evidence in sociological surveys that Catholic culture, writ large, was as detached from belief in God as Camille Paglia asserted in the mid-1990s: "The religion and the family culture are completely intertwined. You can see it there. There's a respect for the mother; respect for the family, that's your identity. And it doesn't matter whether in your heart you believe in God or not."[12] The extent to which cultural Catholicism involves atheism exceeds the scope of this book. While there is certainly no necessary connection between the two, I think it best to follow Paglia's lead and move on to other questions. Certainly, some Jews will openly admit that they do not believe in God but continue to follow religious rules for communal or social reasons. That may happen in Catholicism as well, but I believe it is important to recognize the crucial role of dissent in the Catholic sphere. Plenty of sociological surveys have shown that "lapsed" or "problem" or "occasional" Catholics genuinely disagree with certain tenets of Church teaching; this disagreement troubles them because they still believe in God and they still wish to remain part of the Catholic Church.

One of the advantages of Paglia's phrasing is the way in which it avoids drawing a line in the sand between "good" Catholics and "bad" Catholics. Even model Catholics may sometimes disagree with a Church teaching and even lapsed Catholics may sometimes feel terrible guilt over insufficient devotion to the rules. The question of believing in God should draw together all those people (even non-Catholics) who, like some of the greatest saints, understand what it feels like to doubt. Even a conservative theologian such as Michael Novak may acknowledge the widespread persistence of doubt. In *No One Sees God*, he asserts that the line of belief and unbelief runs not between opposing communities but down the souls of us all.[13]

One might question where cultural Catholics come from. Despite numerous polls and sociological data about the preferences and instincts of post-Vatican II Catholics, we lack a precise account of when and how Catholics stopped attending Mass every Sunday, stopped defending the pope, stopped thinking of the faith as the essential anchor of their lives. That said, it should not seem far-fetched to conclude that most cultural Catholics are "cradle Catholics." Data might show that those who convert into the faith exhibit less ambivalence and dissent than those mature Catholics whose parents educated them in the faith. This is to say that one doesn't *convert* to cultural Catholicism; one almost *graduates* into it (some might say "progresses").

Catholic culture anywhere will tend to reflect local or regional attitudes and customs. Atheism in the United States arouses more public distrust and fear than in the United Kingdom or Scandinavian countries, which means that cultural Catholics in the United States will be less likely to profess atheism or, perhaps, even to adopt such beliefs. Although talk of "cultural Catholicism" may itself be relatively new, scholars have known for quite a while that the American experience of Roman Catholic faith would differ from the experience of, say, a Brazilian or an African.[14] This much is obvious; what is less obvious is how the shadow culture could overtake the institutional church in the life of an individual Catholic.

In the early twenty-first century, cultural blending and cross-fertilization is more evident in America than it has ever been before. It is fine to be culturally different, and ethnic diversity is lauded in schools and workplaces. In 2004, Samuel Huntington pointed to an ominous identity crisis in America. At a time when relatively homogeneous cultures and nations were becoming more unified, countries made up of diverse ethnicities and multiple languages were in danger of weakening.[15] While "subnational identities" among ethnic and other groups were enjoying a robust tightening, the overarching identity of "American" sputtered and foundered in ambiguity. If Huntington is correct, American Catholics struggle on two fronts in the early twenty-first century: both their country and their church are muddling through an identity crisis. The Church's identity crisis is hardly news, but the combination of the two challenges bears noticing. Catholics who embrace (often unreflectively) secular culture also find themselves scrambling for an interpreter.

The relegation of distinctive Catholic activity to the private sphere helped Catholics to assimilate, but also to disappear. While Protestant Americans before the 1970s may not have explicitly hoped for the disappearance of a Catholic subgroup, they may have approved of the idea of social fusion (into mainline Protestantism). After the French Revolution, various Enlightenment thinkers openly hoped that Jews especially but also pious Catholics would abandon their respective distinctive practices and therefore become more committed to France. Catholics did not disappear in nineteenth-century France, nor did they disappear in twentieth-century America. But "cultural Catholics," as I call them, are pressing on social boundaries in ways worth exploring.

Tension between secular and ecclesiastical forces is hardly new, which is not to say that this tension is the same in all lands. Virtually every society in which Catholics live will represent a variation of the broader pattern: Catholic nucleus surrounded by local color. The danger to be avoided was that the Catholic Church would become an Australian institution in Australia, a Brazilian institution in Brazil, and an American institution in America. Even worse was the danger of assimilation, after which the ecclesiastical commitment of Catholics would presumably be more aesthetic than spiritual, or a soppy indulgence of nostalgic sentimentality.

It might be thought that conservative and liberal Catholics in the United States now constitute two separate churches, but I don't see it that way at all. It was the nineteenth-century sociologist Emile Durkheim who saw the power of ritual to unite people who do not share beliefs.[16] Rituals such as the Mass and religious processions helped bring about social solidarity then and now—especially in the case of baptisms or weddings or funerals. Catholics of all stripes and sizes express allegiance through ritual.

Durkheim's insights pervade my analysis. Durkheim recognized, as I do, that the symbols employed in ritual can hold diverse and even conflicting meanings for the same individual. Borrowing from other theorists, the historian David Kertzer has contended that human thought processes "do not require resolution of such conflict, nor any necessary consistency in symbolic use."[17] Think of a Catholic viewing, say, a crucifix or a statue of the Virgin Mary. In the face of the first, a believer may feel consolation (because Christ died for that believer, as well as the rest of humanity) or suffering (because of the physical and emotional horrors Christ endured) or even regret over anti-Semitism (because some Christians blamed the death of Christ on Jews and used the crucifix to galvanize hatred of Jews). In the face of the second, a Catholic may feel love for an enduring ideal or shame over having failed to overcome sexual temptations in the way that Mary did.

Just as an individual may perceive his personality to shift and sway regularly, so can we expect categories such as "devout Catholic" and "cultural Catholic" to do the same. We should refrain from attributing permanence to a Catholic's theological convictions, since these convictions are neither consistent nor held with equal force over the course of even a decade. What Durkheim has helped us to see is that Catholics (although he was not talking specifically about Catholics) are not so much engaging in "make-it-up-as-you-go-along theology" as wrestling with the complexity and uncertainty of symbols. As Catholics of various sorts try to discern the norms of conduct and of success in their local communities, the ambiguity of the symbols on which Catholic rituals hinge emerges as a great benefit. Catholics will interpret symbols differently, and Catholics will disagree among themselves on those interpretations. It is ritual and family-feeling which will keep Catholics together; it is ritual that will keep cultural Catholics Catholic.

Dissent has become one of those rituals. Although some Catholics do dissent ritually in groups (think of, for example, Catholics for a Free Choice or Dignity or perhaps even the Democratic Party), most of this dissent happens accidentally—over the backyard fence, on the subway, at the office coffee station. There are so very many cultural Catholics in America now that running into one can hardly qualify as a surprise. They are legion, and they recognize one another when they meet. As a group, they have no interest in organizing a splinter organization. Instead, they either lash themselves for not being more pious or sigh in the resignation of watchful waiting; "The Church will eventually change for the better," they might say to one another.

The ritual of the Mass brings together Catholics who hold disparate views on several important moral issues. The Mass is only the most obvious of rites capable of helping Catholics to feel bound together in a community. Advocating for illegal immigrants or mentoring fatherless children on the weekend or seeking signatures on petitions to overturn the death penalty can enhance a Catholic's sense of solidarity with people he sees at Mass, even if only occasionally. It may seem that these criteria amount to setting the bar rather low, that is, to allowing just about anyone to call himself Catholic. The desire to be counted as a Catholic counts for something worth taking seriously.

The Catholic emphasis on social justice and caring for the most vulnerable members of society could ultimately bring back to the fold many "lapsed" or disenchanted Catholics who have not converted to another faith, out of a sense of futility of ever erasing their Catholic identity. It would be a mistake to portray cultural Catholics as "thinking Catholics" and traditional Catholics as obedient drones. I have too much respect for traditional Catholics even to suggest such a slight. By the same token, it would be wrong-headed to set an analogy between full-time and part-time work: cultural Catholics may spend significant time working out their salvation in fear and trembling. Instead of veiling contempt for cultural Catholics behind terms such as dilettante, dabbler, or amateur, we should remember that even the amateur loves what he does.

Chapter 1

Who Are Cultural Catholics?

Who are cultural Catholics? And who cares? A cultural Catholic is someone who wants to be Catholic but feels the Church gets in the way. The United States holds different kinds of cultural Catholics, for example:

- Dissenters
- Catholics who may disagree with elements of official teaching, but who don't wish to engage in public protest
- Catholics with low levels of religious intensity
- Catholics with little or no education about their faith and spotty Mass attendance but who relish Catholic identity.

The tug of practice, tradition, and community keeps millions of Catholics tethered to the Church. Official doctrines—of which there are many—may have little to do with the spiritual commitments of cultural Catholics. Americans may walk away from political parties or places of employment when they can no longer support underlying positions; Americans do not, however, cut ties with their families over intellectual disputes except in the most extreme of cases.

An analysis of dissent often fails to predict Catholic behavior. Such analysis cannot explain, for example, why Catholic reform groups have never been able to mobilize the grassroots, despite polls showing overwhelming support for their positions. Nor can such analysis explain why both John Paul II and Benedict XVI enjoy high approval ratings across all ideological categories of American Catholics, even though many of those Catholics reject some of the most prominent teachings of these popes.

Cultural Catholics are everywhere. They have become a powerful social force in the United States, which is not to suggest that America has a monopoly on cultural Catholics. The roster of personalities in Kerry Kennedy's book *Being Catholic Now* (2008) indicated not only the spectrum but also the social importance of cultural Catholics.[1] Television personality Bill Maher could be called a cultural Catholic. He had a Catholic father and a Jewish mother and was raised Catholic (taught by nuns who told him he'd go to hell for leaning on the pew in front of him during Mass) for his first thirteen years. Although he believes God has chosen him to destroy religion, he was still Catholic enough to agree to contribute a chapter to Kerry Kennedy's book. Best-selling author Frank McCourt is a cultural Catholic, disaffected from the tradition but completely shaped by it. The nuns at her school told the actress Susan Sarandon that she had an "overabundance of original sin" and, just before she believed she was about to have a vision of the Virgin Mary, Sarandon realized she didn't want it.

The list goes on. As their numbers increase, cultural Catholics merit more and more attention. Who dislikes them and why?

Cafeteria Catholics

Objections to occasional Catholics cropped up within two decades of Vatican II's end. Concerned that an entire nation had grown complacent about its Roman Catholicism, Pope John Paul II visited France in 1980 and asked, "France, what have you done with the promises of your baptism?"[2] In effect, the pope accused the French of sliding into cultural Catholicism, agnosticism, or sloth. In 1984, Cardinal Joseph Ratzinger, the head of the Sacred Congregation for the Doctrine of the Faith, lambasted all those Catholics who pick and choose among doctrines to believe.[3] The metaphor of customers in a cafeteria, choosing what to eat from a smorgasbord of offerings, denigrates cultural Catholics. James P. McFadden, then president of the National Committee of Catholic Laymen, once lamented the nuisance of cultural Catholics: "You don't need to be Catholic to be Catholic anymore. If you dissent, you don't get out. That's the problem. Martin Luther looks like a prince compared to these people because he knew when it was time to go."[4] Who were "these people"? What did they want and what exactly was wrong with them? Part of the challenge of rebutting conservative critics stemmed from the vastness of the category coming into view in the 1980s. It wasn't just Catholic dissenters who came in for blame but also, by extension, the lazy.

It's not uncommon to hear Catholics in Mass praying for their lazy or indifferent brothers and sisters; bringing "lapsed" Catholics back to Mass strikes me as a perfectly reasonable goal. When Pope Benedict XVI stepped into his new post in 2005, he listed "filling the empty churches of Europe" as one of his foremost goals. Attentive Catholics understood right away that he wanted what various priests in different American churches had long urged Catholics to pray into reality.

The institutional Church bears some of the blame for having alienated cultural Catholics. Here follows one of many examples: Shortly after Benedict XVI ascended to the papacy in 2005, the Jesuit editor of *America* magazine was forced to resign. Before becoming Pope Benedict XVI, Cardinal Ratzinger had set in place an investigation of Father Tom Reese, who had supposedly published too much dissent in his magazine. After the news of Reese's departure was made public, the editors of *Commonweal* wrote: "If the moderate views expressed in *America*, views widely shared by the vast majority of lay Catholics, are judged suspect by the [Congregation for the Doctrine of the Faith], how is the average Catholic to assess his or her own relationship to the church?"[5] It seemed clear to some attentive American Catholics in 2005 that the new pope did not like the faithful to be critical, to pick and choose in the sacred sphere.

Back in 1984, Benedict had blamed the "cafeteria" phenomenon on the Second Vatican Council (1962–65). Shortly after this groundbreaking and "liberal" event concluded, a Swiss priest started the ultra-conservative Society of St. Pius X to try to fight the changes of Vatican II. We should note at the outset that conservatives no less than liberals are guilty of "picking and choosing" when it comes to Catholicism. The very existence of the Society of St. Pius X speaks to the level of traditional Catholic opposition to what I term "cultural Catholicism," as do the well-publicized efforts of a pizza mogul named Tom Monahan to erect both an orthodox Catholic university ("Ave Maria University") and a "Catholic town" near Naples, Florida.[6] It could be argued that cultural Catholics come from the right every bit as much as from the left, but this would surely misrepresent the headcount.

Although one might object that dissent is dissent (Jesus said that those who are not with you are against you), it does seem expedient to distinguish here between the hard- and the soft-core. Part of the problem with defending "problem Catholics" is the idea of integrity, including as it does an appealing sense of wholeheartedness. It is very tempting indeed to think that our parents and close friends love us without qualification, but many of us will concede that we at times dislike our parents and best friends. I take this realization as a healthy step toward maturity, not a tragedy. By the same token, I find Catholics critical of their church interesting and deserving of sympathy. The other problem Catholics, the lazy, also interest me; I call these disparate groups "cultural Catholics." A burgeoning category indeed, cultural Catholicism would require much more than a single book to explain.

Part of the problem in throwing a conceptual rope around this bulging group is definitional: how wide a lasso do we need? The moniker "cultural Catholic" stretches over at least two very different categories—the dissident and the slothful—which themselves threaten to slide out of the lasso.[7] Beyond that: Even rule-following Catholics should technically qualify as cultural Catholics. Rule-following Catholics are doctrinally obedient Catholics *and* cultural Catholics, if we take "cultural Catholic" in the widest sense, that of including people who follow or enact Catholic culture outside of the Church. I think it analytically prudent to exclude from the group "cultural Catholic" the devout who aim to follow most rules. I emphasize that the category under discussion lacks hard edges; fog surrounds it, and I try merely to cast some light on the terrain.

Various obstacles prevent a sharp demarcation between cultural Catholic and apostate. It would be naïve to suppose that Catholic dissent only began in the late 1960s or only happened in North America. The automobile likely had an enormous impact on the Catholic pastoral system: Long before Vatican II, many Catholics were likely driving to inconveniently located parishes in order to hear a priest say what they liked. Our own gullibility will determine how likely we are to accept historical accounts of Catholic piety. We should refrain from attributing too much significance to a Catholic's set of theological convictions, since these are neither consistent nor are they equally developed and strongly held. As I try to argue for the possibility of a dissenter with her heart in the right place, it would be foolish to take so simplistic a view of the Catholic past. Or the present: it would be equally naïve to assume that conservative Catholics today agree with *all* the rules. However we resolve the romantic lure of nostalgia, the social shift in Catholic attitude toward rule-following holds significant implications for how we understand descriptions from other centuries about the rules, origin, and cultural meaning of Catholic identity.

Why stretch the category "Roman Catholic" to such tenuous lengths as to include the cafeteria variety? The Church could profit immensely from the social criticism and intellectual refinement on

offer. Throughout the United States, a growing number of young
people—but not only young people—proclaim themselves "spiritual
but not religious." Sociological studies suggest that what is happening
in other religions is taking place in Catholicism as well: the well-
informed young who intentionally stand on the sidelines may have a
valuable story to tell. For those who wanted to minimize the number
of distinct Christian communities, this move initially appears good
news. For Catholics who wish to blend with other Christian communities, but only on Catholic terms, the news is naturally troubling.
Allowing into the category dissident and slothful Catholics buys the
institutional Church a little more time—either to persuade those in
question to change their minds or, for the Church, to change itself.

In the meanwhile, we can remind ourselves that the category to
which I point has been around for a good while. Cultural Catholics
may see a family resemblance in nineteenth-century "liberal Catholicism." According to Thomas Bokenkotter, "liberal Catholicism was an
entirely new idea" which sprang up early in the nineteenth century. "It
was during this period of its extraordinary revival that the Catholic
Church was first confronted squarely with the momentous question of
how it was going to relate to liberalism—the new political movement that espoused the ideals of the Enlightenment and the French
Revolution." What the liberal Catholics wanted was "a parliamentary
system of government based on a written constitution that would
guarantee personal rights, including freedom of religion."[8] Pope Pius
IX squelched liberal Catholicism with the infamous Syllabus of Errors.

Given how spiritually engaged Catholic dissidents can be, it doesn't
make sense to denigrate them or judge them agnostics. In my view,
Catholics involved in ongoing, earnest protest of one or more Church
policies are practicing their faith regularly. Ultimately, the reason for
including dissidents in the category of cultural Catholics is the impossibility of establishing how much dissidence qualifies you as a problem
(it could be, for instance, that someone has simply lost interest in
confession) and how useful is the distinction between public and private dissent. Very few Catholics ever sign a full-page protest in a major
newspaper, but they may speak loudly enough in a parish meeting to
achieve the same effect. And then there are those whose protest makes
no waves, not even in their own lives. They threaten no one.

I break the unwieldy category "problem Catholics in America" into
three distinct groups, each of which I defend in this book.

Public Dissenters

Some Catholic dissenters do in fact leave the Church, just as Martin Luther and Henry VIII did. Although we may debate whether it's possible to stop being Catholic, those who leave the Church exceed the scope of this study.[9] Public dissidents may or may not themselves be public figures. "Famous dissenters" would be high-profile Catholic public figures whose dissonance, whether publicized or not, causes what might be described as a negative public image for the Church (to the extent that members who criticize the Church can be considered a public threat). For example, Justice Clarence Thomas, while still on the US Supreme Court, published a memoir, *My Grandfather's Son*, in 2007. A Catholic, Thomas criticized the Roman Catholic Church in the book for not being as "adamant about ending racism then as it is about ending abortion now." Note here the difference between a dissenter and a sinner: A well-known priest or bishop caught up in a sex scandal should not be dignified as a dissenter.

This category would include John Kerry and his wife Teresa Heinz Kerry, who disagreed with the Church over whether a pro-life Catholic politician could take a pro-choice stand in office. Earlier, in the 1984 Presidential election, Geraldine Ferraro, a Catholic politician from New York, had landed in trouble with the Church for the same reason. None of these three Americans had launched an open protest of Church policies. On the contrary, the private disagreement of these three Catholics suddenly became very public. The dissent was accidental to the extent that changing the Church—as opposed to accommodating secular challenges and making sense of competing beliefs—was never the goal. And none of the three wanted to leave the Church. What all three wanted was permission to contain their pro-life beliefs within the private sphere.

The same "accidental dissenter" description would also seem to fit John Rock, a Harvard professor and gynecologist, who pioneered the birth-control pill in the late 1950s. As a devout Catholic, he believed that he had circumvented the Church's ban on artificial birth control (*Casti Connubii*, 1933) by preventing ovulation. The Church had opposed any contraceptive device that came between sperm and egg (for example, a diaphragm or a condom), but the birth control pill did not fall into that category (without an egg, nothing could come between sperm and egg). John Rock became a national celebrity in the 1960s; all the while, he expected the Church to endorse the pill and overturn *Casti Connubii*. In 1968, Pope Paul VI delivered *Humanae Vitae*, a ringing condemnation of the pill. Rock never recovered from the shock and grew distant from the Church with which the American public had firmly identified him. John Rock did want to change the Church, which would have updated its moral stance on the basis of a new scientific discovery.

Sometimes a public figure will indeed lash out at the Church, and longstanding private dissent will became deliberately public. Andrew Sullivan, an Oxford graduate who earned a doctorate at Harvard, garnered a national reputation in the United States as an author and as editor of the *New Republic*. On 19 October 2003, he published an Op-Ed piece in the *New York Times* ("Losing a Church, Keeping the Faith") that harshly criticized the Church not only for opposing same-sex marriage but also for supposedly harboring and spreading homophobia. Sullivan went further than the various bishops who, in the same decade, urged the Vatican to allow condoms in Africa, a continent reeling from the AIDS crisis. Those clerics pleaded with the Vatican to see condoms in a new light (as a means of preventing the spread of disease, as opposed to a means of preventing conception). Sullivan threw down a gauntlet—not only asking for change, but castigating the Church sharply. Unlike the clerics who tried to change Vatican policy, Sullivan reached out to the general public to pressure his Church to overturn a policy with which he disagreed.

The Irish singer Sinead O'Connor, to take another example, rose to international prominence in the 1990s. Her career received a significant blow—especially in the United States—on 3 October 1992, when she appeared on the television program *Saturday Night Live* as a musical guest. Toward the end of the show O'Connor performed an a capella version of the Bob Marley song "War." The song portrays war as an appropriate response for victims of racial injustice, child abuse, and other types of cruelty. At the song's conclusion O'Connor brandished a color photo of Pope John Paul II, ripped it into pieces, and exhorted, "Fight the real enemy."

The reaction to O'Connor's protest was swift. Over the next few days the NBC switchboard in New York received thousands of calls, mostly denouncing O'Connor's performance. The network and the show's executive producer, Lorne Michaels, both denied any knowledge of O'Connor's plan and insisted that she had performed the song differently in rehearsal. Catholic groups expressed outrage at the act and called it patently offensive to people of all religious beliefs. NBC never again aired the O'Connor performance. In the resultant media furor, she was booed off stages and heckled by audiences. Many Americans destroyed her records, and various radio stations refused to play her songs.

The O'Connor example is interesting because the Church never had to reprimand her or denounce her action. The public seemed to do that for the Church. On 22 September 1997, O'Connor was interviewed in *Vita*, an Italian weekly newspaper. In the interview, she asked the pope to forgive her. She confessed that the tearing of the photo was "a ridiculous act, the gesture of a girl rebel." She claimed she had acted badly "because I was in rebellion against the faith, but I was still within the faith." She went on to quote Augustine, saying, "Anger is the first step towards courage." (Later, in a 2002 interview with the online journal *Salon*, she declared that she wouldn't change anything about her infamous appearance on *Saturday Night Live*.)

O'Connor's dissent is the most aggressive of the few examples I have offered here. Like Luther and Henry VIII before her, she wanted to hold on to certain aspects of the Catholic tradition. Can this desire alone qualify her as a Catholic? I believe that it can and should. Not every Catholic who criticizes the Church wants to maintain ties with it. Germaine Greer, a well-known feminist, was educated in Catholic schools in Australia and became a professor at Cambridge University. An intellectual celebrity who renounced the Church, Greer advocated rampant sexual freedom for women, trashed marriage and the family, and fulminated against the imposition of Western values on indigenous peasant cultures throughout the world. Although we might try to argue that her Catholic baptism makes her forever Catholic, Greer repudiated nearly every value the nuns taught her as a child. O'Connor qualifies as a cultural Catholic, where Greer does not.

Sometimes an entire group, such as Catholics for a Free Choice, qualifies for the category "Public Dissenters." Although the individual Catholics in such a group may lack a public profile, they join forces to argue that good Catholics may morally advocate a woman's fundamental right to have an abortion. In the 7 October 1984 issue of the *New York Times*, an advertisement sponsored by Catholics for a Free Choice called for open dialog among American Catholics on the issue of abortion. The Vatican commanded the twenty-four signers to publicly retract their statements or face dismissal from their congregations. Catholics who marched in a Gay Pride Parade might also fall into this category, although the open march through a city or town would still be arguably less public than placing a full-page advertisement in America's most powerful newspaper.

We see, then, that public dissent involves opposition to the Church that more or less immediately threatens to undermine a public image. An individual's social status can magnify the dissent, especially if the media are involved. Whether they like it or not, famous or powerful Catholics must pay special attention to the terms in which they discuss their church. That said, the social status of a famous or powerful Catholic should not necessarily prevent him from speaking critically about some aspect of the Church.

Private Dissenters

Private dissent drives this book. Polls capture the large percentage of Americans who self-identify as Catholic but who stay away from Mass, or bless the birth control pill, or who support gay marriage and embryonic stem-cell research. It is sometimes quite difficult to separate this group of Catholics from the lazy or lapsed Catholics (to which I later turn). These private dissenters choose to stay in the Church, even though they receive no obvious political or economic rewards for doing so. Michael Cuneo, among others who study Catholic culture, has puzzled over this question of why: "[I]t's not entirely clear why so many Americans remain actively involved with their church despite rejecting so much of its moral teaching."[10] That we don't know the names of the millions in this group does not detract from the import-ance of the individuals in it. Almost every Catholic is himself a private dissenter at one time or another.

In a best-selling memoir about the emotional difficulties of moving past her husband's death, Joan Didion included a relevant aside that deepened the narrative of grieving. After having much earlier self-identified as an Episcopalian, she wrote: "I did not believe in the resurrection of the body . . . Nor had my Catholic husband."[11] There is an important difference between dissent (often private) and protest (usually public). Didion's husband of several decades was already dead; he was not protesting (nor did she indicate that he ever had done, and he seemed determined to retain a vital tie to the Catholic Church). This incidental detail and the way in which she cursorily works it into the larger narrative leave the impression that disagreement with a central tenet of Catholic theology did not bother her Catholic hus-band, John Gregory Dunne, a well-educated author who had earned widespread success as a public intellectual. Nor should it bother Catholics much.

Most private dissent is, well, private. I have purposely chosen a celebrity as an example to illustrate the obvious point that even public figures have private moments. No one will deny that ordinary people have many such moments. Looking back over the Church's past, a well-educated Catholic today may wince at the idea that a pope approved public executions until 1870—in order to maintain public order. That same pope, Pius IX, introduced anti-Jewish legislation and tried to hold onto slavery by arguing that it could be reconciled with natural law and divine revelation. Catholics today must accept that the history of their people does not always sit well with contemporary sensitivities.[12] In fairness, it must be said that the Catholic Church was not alone in taking stances which would come to be seen as anachronistic. For example, both David Hume (d. 1776) and Immanuel Kant (d. 1804) chose not to extend equality and freedom to blacks.

Dissident Catholics may be embarrassed Catholics who resist associating themselves too closely with a Church that has hurt anyone who belongs to a community they now esteem—for example, Jews. Contemporary Catholics unsure of the Church's standing in the eyes of contemporary Jews may writhe at the thought that the Fourth Lateran Council (1215) excluded Jews from public employment and stipulated that Jews were to live in ghettos; that council also mandated that Jews were to wear yellow stars outside the ghetto. Six and a half centuries later, Vatican I proclaimed a view of the Church's superiority that could leave many cultural Catholics feeling jittery today:

> To the Catholic Church alone belong all the manifold and wonderful endowments which by divine disposition are meant to set forth the credibility of the Christian faith. Nay more, the Church by herself, with her marvelous propagation, eminent holiness, and inexhaustible fruitfulness in everything that is good, with her Catholic unity and invincible stability, is a great and perpetual motive of credibility and an irrefutable testimony of her divine mission.[13] (*Dei Filius*, DH, 3013; ND 123)

History has validated some of the cultural Catholic's hesitations: Vatican II strove valiantly to undo the tone of the message that Catholics enjoy a monopoly on God's approval.

The Right of Christian Initiation (RCIA), a program for converts to Catholicism, prompts interested individuals to think carefully before believing. The Church understands the process may be long and sometimes difficult. As one apologist for the faith puts it:

The Catholic Church recognizes that persons seeking to form their views and consciences through the teachings of the Bible and the Church may find themselves temporarily struggling to understand and assent to a particular teaching. In such cases, one's salvation would not be jeopardized. However, Catholics who are earnestly seeking to follow the Lord will invariably come to recognize the purpose and wisdom of Church teachings and discipline, or the natural law of God, or at least be willing to accept it in faith and trust, even if they do not yet fully understand it or agree with it.[14]

Private dissenters differ from public dissenters, in part because the former cause less trouble. There is room for both. The Second Vatican Council's *Declaration on Religious Freedom* exhorts everyone to follow his conscience faithfully; moreover, no one "is to be forced to act in a manner contrary to his conscience. Nor, on the other hand, is he to be restrained from acting in accordance with his conscience, especially in matters religious" (n. 3). The Church itself allows someone to follow even an erroneous conscience.

Catholics referring derogatorily to others as merely "cultural Catholics" make implicit judgments about disloyalty. Even devout Catholics may have an occasional difference with the Church. By no means does the Church say that the faithful may believe whatever they like. A Catholic whose beliefs differ from institutional teachings is charged with responsibility for bringing his beliefs in line with Church teachings. The important point to be taken here is that dissent fits in Catholic culture. Vatican II offers renewed and explicit support for the freedom of conscience.[15] The Council of Trent arguably made this freedom clear in the sixteenth century. I say "arguably" since Trent endorsed compulsion by the State in religion and the Inquisition was taking place at the same time.

The criticism cultural Catholics level against the institutional Church is an attempt to work through differences, as opposed to a war cry. Cultural Catholics worry that the institutional Church is described in such an outmoded way that future generations will have no choice but to turn away from the description or "mission statement," as a modern corporation or non-profit agency would say. In their own quiet way, cultural Catholics seem to be waiting for the Church to evolve; in the meantime, they are trying to avoid appearing hypocritical.

Private dissenters may or may not attend Mass every week. Someone who attends Mass faithfully while disagreeing on the teaching on ordaining women or using the birth-control pill qualifies as a private dissenter, just as someone who stays away from Mass but says the Rosary whenever he rides his bicycle does. Their dissent does not threaten the public image of the Church in the way that public dissenters do.

"Lapsed" Catholics

The entire category of "lapsed Catholic," familiar though it may be, cries out for explanation. If you fail to show up for work for a certain period of time, you will likely be fired. If you fail to show much interest in practicing your Catholic faith, however, you will not be cut off from the Church. You just sort of wither on the vine, without falling off. In his sociological study of religious teens in the United States, Christian Smith explicitly faults Catholic parents for the crisis in the American Church.[16]

One of the most suitable criteria for gauging whether or how lapsed a Catholic might be is the obligation of Catholics to attend Mass every Sunday. The obligation to attend Mass every Sunday is based on Scripture (Acts 2:46–47; Heb 10:25) and on many early Christian writings that consider worship together on the Lord's day as an essential part of Christian life. Very few Catholic children know this; Catholic education may not work as well as it ideally should. The lapsed may not understand why and where they went wrong, so they are not knowingly neglecting their faith.

Lapsed Catholics who might have formerly been active don't necessarily go out with a bang. Instead of a formal protest, their departure more closely resembles ripe fruit falling from the vine. Falling fruit doesn't make noise; suddenly a survey will reveal the fact of the fall. Lapsed Catholics may still see the world in a distinctly Catholic way— what Father Andrew Greeley has described as the Catholic sacramental imagination.[17] And lapsed Catholics may not be simply lazy, for Father Greeley has concluded elsewhere that many American Catholics (especially those who practice their faith but reject much of the Church's teaching) now see God not as a stern judge but as a loving friend or parent who appreciates any participation in the Church at all.[18] No account of lapsed Catholics could do justice to them without some mention of their psychological disposition: Poll after poll seems to show that lapsed or occasional Catholics do not see themselves as damned or hopelessly lost.[19]

Germaine Greer and Sinead O'Connor may well have felt they had justifiable objections to the Catholic Church; both women still cared about the Church enough to criticize it. Indifferent Catholics, on the other hand, really couldn't care less. They may never have felt much of a tie to the Church in the first place, much as the faithful of any religion may report that they never felt religious. Lapsed Catholics don't care enough about their faith to come back, nor do they care enough about another church to switch to it. More than any other reason, inertia may explain why lapsed Catholics neither learned much about their faith nor abandoned it. Learning and leaving would require more effort than either would be worth.

The English novelist David Lodge furnishes us with a useful example of the post-Vatican II lapsed Catholic. Writing about a fictional British novelist, Lodge describes Helen's inner confusion as follows:

> It's perhaps time I admitted to myself that I'm totally muddled and inconsistent about religion. I'm deeply grateful that I had a Catholic education even though I suffered unnecessary agonies of guilt, frustration and boredom on account of it in childhood and adolescence; and in retrospect I feel only nostalgic affection for the nuns who taught me even though most of them were more or less deranged by superstition and sexual repression, which they did their best to instill in me. I ceased to be a practicing Catholic in my second term at Oxford, at the same time that I lost my virginity. The events were connected—I could not with sincerity confess as a sin something I had found so liberating, or promise not to do it again. Intellectual rejection of the rest of Catholic doctrine quickly followed, whether as a consequence or a rational-ization of this moral decision would be hard to say. Some years later, by dint of a certain amount of fudging and dissembling, I was married in a Catholic church, to avoid giving needless pain to my parents but also because when all's said and done I wouldn't have felt properly married in a registry office. When I had chil-dren of my own I had them baptized, again ostensibly to please Mummy and Daddy, but secretly because I should have felt uneasy myself otherwise.[20]

Its psychological aptness justifies quoting the lengthy passage here. Lodge understands well the predicament of the lapsed Catholic who is not exactly coward and certainly not stupid. Sin, and particularly sexual transgression, has a lot to do with that predicament.

Laziness or indifference will not necessarily prevent the lapsed Catholic from seeking a Church baptism, wedding or funeral. Like the proverbial "Christmas and Easter Catholic," the lapsed may still feel, or want to feel, some inkling of belief in God. For a variety of ethnic or familial reasons, the lapsed Catholic may still self-identify as a Roman Catholic (as in France, for example). Sometimes the lapsed Catholic will struggle to explain even to himself why he behaves as he does. The American author John Grogan dwelt on his residual Catholicism in his memoir *The Longest Trip Home*.[21] After rebelling against a strict Catholic upbringing, Grogan decided on a full Catholic wedding and, when his children were born, he had them baptized in a Catholic Church. The actress Susan Sarandon, a cultural Catholic, made a similar decision:

> My kids are baptized, because why not give them that? I was living in Rome with my daughter, and I wasn't married to her father. So I thought, "Well, let's have a baptism—it gives the family something." But it wasn't because I was taking away the original sin from her. I really don't believe that.[22]

It could be that such nostalgia or wishy-washiness fails to honor properly a magnificent tradition, but my point here is to defend the lapsed, not damn them.

Anyone attempting to understand why disgruntled Catholics don't simply leave the Church must keep in mind the psychic pay-off of this religion, the transcendental assurance that everything happens for a reason and that you are loved. The English writer John Lanchester, a non-Catholic, came to understand as much in the course of writing a biography of his recently deceased mother, a devout Catholic who had never mentioned the fact that she had spent some fifteen years as a cloistered nun before his birth. Toward the end of his sleuthing through the remarkable details of his mother's double life, he wrote:

> . . . I understood for the first time the difference between the Church as an institution that tried to be nice to people, and the Church as a body to which people belonged because they had a living, vivid, strongly felt and daily belief in the supernatural.[23]

Lapsed Catholics still tend to believe in God: this may be the most significant difference between cultural Catholics and cultural Jews. It would be a gross mistake to wave off "lapsed" Catholics as cowards who have not yet found the mettle to declare their atheism. Occasional

Catholics and lazy Catholics and *á la carte* Catholics alike have at one time questioned the next step for them: Where do you go when you don't believe everything the Church says, but you still believe much of it? Perhaps to the Episcopal Church.

The American comedian Woody Allen famously said, "Eighty percent of success is showing up." On some level, lapsed Catholics live out this insight. Simply showing up for central rituals will be enough to keep them in the Catholic fold. I believe their desire, inchoate as it may be, must count for something: It speaks to the power and energy of cultural Catholicism.

It is the desire to be some kind of Catholic that keeps someone in the American Catholic family. I say "American" because "global" would add too many complications. Cultural Catholics comprise a group of people who are not apostates; they are "slackers" in the Church's view, but not their own. Cultural Catholics often believe that they are faithful. Their complaints about the Church do not amount to reasons for leaving the Church.

The twentieth-century philosopher Ludwig Wittgenstein, himself a cultural Catholic, observed that certain terms "have no one thing in common which makes us use the same word for all . . . they are related to one another in many different ways."[24] "Roman Catholic" is one of those terms. We use it to mean a family of emotional relationships, not all of which need to be present in all cases of "Roman Catholicism."

Catholic Culture vs Cultural Catholicism

What makes the distinctions I offer here tricky is an overlap between Catholic culture and what I am calling "cultural Catholicism." Catholic culture has little, if anything, to do with politics or dissent as we think of them in the early twenty-first century. Catholic culture results from communities of more or less like-minded believers.

Catholic culture does not spring directly from the Gospels, which were written from forty to seventy years after the death of Jesus. The authors of the four Gospels drew from an oral tradition in which we can responsibly anchor the beginning of Catholic culture. Catholics do not view the Gospels as an exhaustive or perfect account of Jesus' life. Catholics do not quit the faith in the face of conflicting details in the Gospels (for example, disagreement between Matthew and Luke on the date of Jesus' birth). Indeed, belief in the divinity of Jesus was not even defined until the Council of Nicaea in 325.

Catholic culture springs in part from scripture and in part from a tradition of interpreting not only Scriptures but also deeply difficult questions regarding the moral life. Art, music, public debates, nostalgia for Catholic pasts in different areas and eras, and, a tradition of interpreting the Gospels have produced Catholic culture.

Catholic culture might be said to consist of the worldview or ethos of Roman Catholics, as opposed to their theology. Processions, holidays, ways of eating and other distinctive social practices, then, would be part of "Catholic culture." Voting patterns and social taboos may feed into that culture, but they would not dominate or define it. Given the global reach of the Catholic Church, we would expect "Catholic culture" to differ from Europe to Africa to North America to Asia. The future of Catholic culture in the United States may well hinge on Latino immigrants, and the Catholic culture they bring to our shores differs from what they find, to be sure. It may not be long before lily-white Catholic girls across America join in the quinceañera craze. Once criticized by some American Catholics as an exercise in excess, this elaborate coming-of-age ritual for Hispanic girls on their fifteenth birthday emphasizes their Catholic faith and sexual responsibility.

What I am calling cultural Catholicism resembles the term "cafeteria Catholicism." Cultural Catholics pick and choose which rules they want to obey, much in the way decried by Cardinal Ratzinger in 1984. Cultural Catholics might embrace Catholic culture but disregard Catholic theology. Since 1984, Catholics have been subjects of many polls. I have not proposed another poll, as it would be hardly necessary. Although the causes are varied and complex, it is a rigid expectation of compliance and conformity—typical of the pre-Vatican II era—that is driving many Catholics to become "cultural Catholics." The relationship between "Catholic culture" and "cultural Catholicism" has been a moving target, for until recently Catholic culture implicitly stood on a conviction that the ultimate goal of Catholic art, labor, and generation was a friendship with God. As that belief recedes further into the background, the boundary between the two spheres will be harder to make out. This is not to say that cultural Catholics eschew obedience to God, only that some do, while others do not.

Who Cares?

The Roman Catholic hierarchy in the United States and in Rome should care about cultural Catholics. Cultural Catholics in the United

States grow more numerous and enjoy some social power. The frankness of imperfect Catholics can be remarkable.

One's point of view on Catholic rule-following practically determines how you construct the category of cultural Catholicism, as well as whom you place there. The most observant Catholics are the most likely to call others "cultural Catholic." What difference does it make to anyone whether one is a devout Catholic or a cultural Catholic? Non-Catholics may object that Catholics should at least aim to be faithful to their own ecclesiastical or cultural ideals. Devout or traditional Catholics ("traditional Catholics" are those who press for a return to the Latin Mass, among other conservative reforms) may reject cultural Catholics as an embarrassment, as a discredit to the Church. Senator John Kerry found this out the hard way during the Presidential election of 2004, for example. Senator Joe Biden was more fortunate in 2008; the media only rarely ran stories of Catholics calling Biden an impostor.

Catholic identity naturally matters to the many people seeking rootedness in an institution or tradition, an orientation. They surface in every faith community. One simply wants to know if one is getting it right. The cut-off point between a good Catholic and a non-Catholic may be every bit as vivid in the mind of a lapsed Catholic as it is in the mind of a devout Catholic, for the lapsed may fear they are closer to the tipping point.

Beyond that, one's credentials as a proper Catholic may come under scrutiny at key moments: baptisms, weddings, burials, and the Eucharist itself. Dissent may be held against a Catholic who wanted to update her or his Church: Rainbow Sash wearers protesting the Church's stance on gay marriage or Catholics for a free choice may feel disapproval on the way to taking Communion. Excommunication isn't often formal anymore; more likely, it happens unofficially, from one's fellow Catholics. Faith is confusing for many North American Catholics to understand, because while they may hear about stories of ecclesiastical strictness, they see more and more moral laxity around them. The strict stories risk scaring away the tepid Catholics, and so more and more parishes may tone down the messages about rules.

Lastly, it is certainly true that the Church has withstood similar challenges in the past. The eighteenth-century Enlightenment resisted authority and rejected tradition, for example. And early twentieth-century Catholics had already pressed for "updating," long before Vatican II.[25] Cultural Catholics do not aim for separation, though, but for enrichment and acceptance. Unlike Catholics in Africa and Asia, where the Church grows rapidly, most cultural Catholics in North America have enjoyed years of education and understand that some tension with received ideas is healthy.

As constituents of a voluntary community that is losing adherents, cultural Catholics should be a desired commodity. How far is Rome willing to go in order to woo them back? Could Catholic institutions be scrambling to be as inclusive as possible? Certainly some Jewish institutions have done so. With only 40–45 per cent of American Jews affiliated with a synagogue at any given moment, Jewish congregations are under enormous pressures to institute "inclusive" policies to demonstrate just how welcoming they are.[26] Pastorally, priests and nuns often present a sympathetic, accommodating face to cultural Catholics striving to conform to Church expectations. What cultural Catholics hear locally may not always clearly dovetail with what the Vatican is promulgating.

Because cultural Catholics may appear to threaten the power or stability of the Church hierarchy, conservative Catholics may take a dim view of them. Virtually any family or social group gives rise to internal squabbling, but disagreements can turn vicious. The African-American community, for example, loathes their race traitors, who have craved white approval and supposedly betrayed the black struggle.[27] "Sellout" blacks allegedly gave up too much in the 1960s and 1970s in order to advance personally. Understanding these divisive accusations of selling out is crucial to understanding black culture, just as understanding the rift between observant and cultural Catholics is a necessary step toward understanding American Catholicism in the early twenty-first century. According to some pious Catholics, cultural Catholics have surrendered too much to seductive secular forces.

Drawing Lines around the Catholic Community

Even (or perhaps especially) after the taxonomy offered in this chapter, it may seem unclear where Catholicism ends and Protestantism begins. Doesn't every Catholic fit into one of the subgroups described above? Don't even the most traditional of Catholics sometimes gripe? They almost certainly do complain, but their attitude toward that dissent distinguishes them from cultural Catholics. Remember that I focus on the United States in this book; it would be impossible to stretch a description of "cultural Catholic" to fit every nation, each of which will likely include sub-cultures. Remember, the Catholic Church is a global enterprise. Even when examining traditional Catholics, those distinctive elements of American culture—democracy and self-definition—must be reckoned with. One day, the gap between what Rome says and what cultural Catholics do may become so wide as to be implausible, but we haven't reached that point yet.

Whereas many Christians say that the Bible alone contains all of Christian truth (the principle of *sola scriptura* or "scripture alone"), cultural Catholics may be happy to accept that proper interpretation of scriptures requires the teaching authority of the Church. Cultural Catholics want the guidance of their tradition, but they want that tradition to respond to changes in the secular world which they as spiritual people accept and endorse. More traditional Catholics may believe that the Church would be purer and stronger without cultural Catholics, but it seems that a pluralistic, diverse membership better suits a global Church with outposts nearly everywhere.

Peter Steinfels's book *A People Adrift: The Crisis of the Roman Catholic Church in America* (2005) offers a sense of the vastness of the institutional dimensions of cultural Catholicism.[28] In higher education, health care, social services and independent journalism, a whole range of useful work is being done by institutions founded under Catholic auspices which are now unaffiliated. Many of these social forces had always been Catholic but independent; today, they may still be Catholic, but they are often led and operated by non-Catholics and Catholics who dissent from official doctrines. With the declining number of priests, nuns and brothers, lay Catholics increasingly oversee Catholic institutions.

Cultural Catholicism is not a movement, but rather a glass through which we can only see darkly. That so many North American and Western European Catholics are struggling with central aspects of their faith underscores broad dissatisfaction with the Church. That dissatisfaction arises from a passionate, loyal sense of belonging that is as hard to resist as the call of eternal salvation. Cultural Catholics do not form a natural kind. Beyond that, cultural Catholicism means more than dissent—it comes through processions, rituals and devotion to the Virgin Mary. I turn now to these ways of expressing devotion to Catholic tradition.

Chapter 2

European Origins

An attempt to isolate Catholic culture should begin a tacit division within the faith between the required and the optional. As Catholics increasingly turn away from the required, the menu of optional practices assumes greater importance. The fact that Catholics may forego the required does not necessarily mean they will forego everything related to the practice of their faith. How cultural Catholics funnel and direct their religious impulses interests me, and now I turn to processions as a largely forgotten but useful example of the purely optional that, unlike saying the rosary or reading Scriptures, requires a community. The Church is not actively cut out, as a priest is usually involved, lending the practice legitimacy.

This chapter details a practice which represents the culture rather than the doctrine of Catholicism. An overview of the European origins of the religious procession will help us understand how Catholics in previous centuries performed their faith, professed it publicly. Few Anglo-American Catholics take part in processions in the twenty-first century; for Hispanic Catholics, who make up roughly thirty per cent of the Catholic community in the United States, processions remain popular. If the largely conservative Latino community were to come into ascendancy within American Catholicism, we could expect a resurgence of processions.

Baptisms, weddings, and funerals represent a required (or at least expected) element of a good Catholic's life, and I will turn to them after finishing here. Processions provide us with a good example of a practice which is neither required nor necessarily expected of a good Catholic, yet a practice that says something important about a Catholic—that he is willing to "go public" with his religious commitment, in the streets no less. A cultural Catholic who approaches the Eucharist in a church full of neighbors or peers, people who may insist he should not be taking communion, may feel a kind of anxiety which I consider important; that anxiety might find a parallel in the fear a Catholic feels in the streets, the fear of being called a hypocrite.

Church authorities did not require processions in previous centuries; much of the laity just wanted to participate in them. The ceremonial parade at the beginning and end of a high Mass evoked the grand spectacle of a parade, but I explore here processions through public streets. Although I don't aim to prove as much, it should not seem far-fetched to posit an internal connection, however unreflective, between the march to the Eucharist and the procession through streets. I don't provide any empirical evidence for the decline in public processions, as such evidence is hardly necessary. Nor do I mean to imply that Catholics ever had a monopoly on processions.[1]

The Performance of Belief

Parades may be solemn or raucous, but they tend to move along a preconceived path to a particular destination. Festivals, a close relative of processions, tend to take place in a bordered area; they also tend toward the raucous. By no means did Catholics invent processions and festivals: Some of the ancient festivals no doubt absorbed and transformed pagan rites (for example, Lupercalia). What's important about processions is that they tend to be highly localized, to focus on pinpointed characters or events, some of which resist exportation. Part of what makes the parades and festivals interesting is that the laity could take them or leave them (just as most devotion to saints remains optional, as is belief in many of the so-called miracles underpinning these festivals and sainthood in general). Participation in a procession provided an opportunity to perform one's faith and publicize one's commitment to the Church: Spontaneous expressions of grief or gratitude in a Church were less staged or scripted than a procession, but not necessarily more compelling.

Various generalizations about those who marched in processions suggest themselves. Even if the lack of autobiographical evidence makes it difficult to prove any of these generalizations, we must try to see processions as instances of genuine devotion in the lives of ordinary Catholics. It is precisely because they were optional that these events merit analysis: One stood less to gain from social conformity to a practice the ignoring of which carried no obvious penalties. I will move quickly through a series of examples of processions of adoration in Italy (Corpus Christi, San Gennaro, Santa Rosa) to examples of processions of gratitude (Venice). In the subsequent discussion of the festival of Carnival, we can see principally legalism at work: respect for the social custom of fasting, sacrificing, and praying through Lent led to a last-minute blow-out, a final grasp at fun before rules preempted it, for forty days.

We lack first-hand accounts from previous centuries of what it felt like for ordinary Catholics to join in these parades and festivities, yet we can safely attribute to these faceless people a sense of joy and pride in the public affirmation of their faith. Superstition and fear may well have mingled with these other, more positive, emotions. Fundamentally, the Church aimed to establish Christian piety for life; as generations passed, the lay aristocracies of Western Europe, and even their monarchs, came to see an advantage to themselves in Catholic processions and festivals. The processions may have amounted to more than a colorful interruption of a dreary routine by stirring respect and responding to deep emotional needs in the laity. After all, the Church did not require participation, as I have said, and the Church provided other ways (for example, Masses and almsgiving) to express piety. By processing together in public, Catholics were (and are) rehearsing or modeling the kind of piety expected of them and the social solidarity they aspire to (I am skeptical of the possibility that mirroring is the more appropriate metaphor here, as the various processions take place only once a year).

Any attempt to sum up several centuries of ritual practice in European Catholicism is bound to be reductive and to involve suspect selectivity. In the next chapter I will focus on baptisms, weddings, and funerals because of the enduring popularity of these rituals, especially among cultural Catholics. In this chapter I choose parades and processions because of the public nature of what might otherwise be considered quite private devotions: The bursting into or spilling over onto the social realm highlights the enduring tension in Catholic culture between local or personal piety and universal or social skepticism. When contemporary observers refer to a decline in participation in parish life, they tend to focus on Mass attendance, monetary contributions at Mass, charitable activity, and the frequency of confessions. A gaping lacuna in this category, processions should also be counted as a valuable example of what the French scholar Danièle Hervieu-Léger has called "lived religion."[2]

Awesome Processions

Processions of adoration express fear and awe of God.[3] By processing outside in addition to inside of church, worshippers acknowledge that God's dominion surpasses Church grounds and spills into
streets, towns, and daily lives. At its best, a procession of awe ele-
vates an individual, eliciting confidence about the future, as well
as a silent energy surge. Although such processions occur in a vast
number of Catholic enclaves and countries, I will focus on Italy,
which makes for a particularly vivid example. Unlike Italy, long an
almost entirely Catholic country, America lacks a widespread
network of processions. Let's take a look now at some of the oldest of
what I call awe processions in order to gain a clear sense of the
"optional list" and of what fruit Catholic piety has borne. Anyone
who laments the lack of Catholic enthusiasm might naturally call for
the creation or revival of rites which would produce greater cultural
communion.

The Feast of Corpus Christi celebrates the real presence of Christ
in the Eucharist. Sometimes referred to as the Solemnity of the Body
and Blood of Christ, Corpus Christi originated in Liege in 1246, based
on revelations of the nun Juliana of Mont-Cornillon (1192–1258).
Enthusiastic acceptance in Europe led to universal promulgation by
Pope Urban IV in 1264.

From its inception, the feast celebrated both the body and blood of
Christ (much as Holy Thursday did by highlighting the redemptive
effects of the Eucharist). A prominent feature of the feast since the
fourteenth century has been a Eucharistic procession. The procession
takes place immediately after the Mass in which the host to be carried
has been consecrated, or after a lengthy period of public adoration.
The procession may take place on or near the feast day itself.[4]

The procession seems to have responded to a rather widespread
crisis of belief, not entirely unlike the post-Vatican II era. In 1208
Julianna reported a vision through which she understood that Jesus
lamented the absence of a particular feast focused on his sacramental
presence on the altar. Her vision launched a campaign on the part of
the Beguines (an order of women who had devoted themselves to God)
for a feast centered on the real presence of Christ in the Blessed Sacrament. Julianna's fervor met with reluctance on the part of some clergy.

A separate and roughly concurrent event deepened the sense of need
for a celebration devoted to the Eucharist. In 1263 the German priest

Peter of Prague set out for a pilgrimage to Rome and stopped at Bolsena along the way. As the story goes, this pious priest had found it difficult to believe in the real presence of Christ in the consecrated host. While celebrating Mass above the tomb of St. Christina (located in the church named for this martyr), he had barely spoken the words of consecration when blood started to seep from the host and trickle over his hands, onto the altar and what is called the corporal, a small tablecloth of sorts.

Confused, the priest at first attempted to hide the blood. Then he interrupted the Mass and asked to be taken to the neighboring city of Orvieto, the city where Pope Urban IV was then residing. The pope listened to the priest and then ordered an immediate investigation. After gathering the facts, he ordered the bishop of the diocese to bring to Orvieto the host and the linen cloth bearing the blood stains. With archbishops, cardinals, and other Church dignitaries in attendance, the pope met the formal procession and, amid great pomp, directed that the relics be placed in the cathedral. Today, visitors to the cathedral of Orvieto can still view the linen cloth bearing the spots of blood.

It is said that the miracle prompted Pope Urban IV to seek assistance from Thomas Aquinas. St. Thomas then composed the theological justification for a feast (the "Proper for a Mass and an Office honoring the Holy Eucharist as the Body of Christ"). One year after the miracle, in August of 1264, Urban IV instituted the Feast of Corpus Christi by means of a papal bull which relied on St. Thomas's document. Thomas Aquinas was later canonized in 1328.

Although its official promulgators (including Pope Urban IV) do not mention a Eucharistic procession or exposition connected with the feast, the procession to which Eucharistic fervor eventually led came to be a hallmark of the feast for many local churches and contributed to the popularity of the feast through the fourteenth century.[5] Rome later adopted the practice. In addition to expressing popular devotion, the Eucharistic procession took on great social and commercial significance as well. Corpus Christi is not a holy day of obligation in the United States, although it is one in several European countries.

On what basis can we assert that the procession expresses awe? The Corpus Christi parade in Orvieto follows a tapestry depicting the miracle of Bolsena. After visiting the cathedral of Orvieto, many pilgrims and tourists journey to St. Christina's Church in Bolsena to see for themselves the place where the miracle occurred. From the north aisle of the church, one can enter the Chapel of the Miracle, where the stains on the paved floor are said to have been made by the blood from the miraculous host. The altar of the miracle is now situated in the grotto of St. Christina, in which rests a reclining statue of the saint. The procession revolves around contemplation of God's power. A miracle by definition defies the laws of physics. By culture and theology, Catholics believe in miracles and see God's hand in them. Miracles and reflection on them elevate Catholics psychologically; further, such reflection binds individuals to others who also believe.

In August of 1964, on the 700th anniversary of the institution of the feast of Corpus Christi, Pope Paul VI celebrated Mass at the altar where the holy corporal is kept in the cathedral of Orvieto. (Paul VI had journeyed to Orvieto by helicopter and thus became the first pope in history to use such a means of transportation, another miracle of sorts.) Twelve years later, the same pontiff visited Bolsena and spoke from there via television to the 41st International Eucharistic Congress, then concluding its activities in Philadelphia. During his address Pope Paul VI spoke of the Eucharist as being ". . . a mystery great and inexhaustible."

Do all Catholics have to believe in Bolsena? The so-called "miracle of Bolsena" is not officially supported by the Roman Catholic Church, though it is considered a private revelation for the doubting priest. The historical evidence is hearsay, and its tradition is not altogether consistent. Beyond that, scholars have noted that similar legends of the "blood-stained corporal" surfaced before the fourteenth century and coincided with the great Eucharistic polemics, which spanned from the ninth to the twelfth centuries. Pope Urban IV makes no mention of the miracle in the bull by which he established the feast of Corpus Christi, although the legend of the miracle is set in his lifetime and is claimed by its proponents to have compelled him to establish the feast. Urban's position is not exactly clear, which is perhaps what he had intended.

And yet the Feast of Corpus Christi remains one of the major religious events for the city of Orvieto. In this enthusiasm and pride, the residents of Orvieto resemble those of Naples, further to the south in Italy. The miracle of the liquefaction of the blood of San Gennaro (or St. Januarius) in Naples involves an elaborate procession; like the miracle at Bolsena, a San Gennaro procession expresses awe—as well as elevation in the face of a miracle.

The blood of the saint is contained in a vessel kept in the cathedral of Naples. Twice a year, the blood turns liquid again, through the intervention of the saint, to attest to the faithful that he still watches over the city. It is difficult to predict whether the blood will liquefy on time, but hard times are said to follow those occasions on which the miracle fails to happen at all. Three times a year—on 19 September (his feast day); on the Saturday preceding the first Sunday in May, which commemorates the transference of his relics to Naples; and on 16 December—believers focus on his dried blood, contained in two sealed vials. On these days, devout Neapolitans offer up prayers in his memory. Seeing dried blood become liquid (or hearing reports that it has) excites Neapolitans, who not only find in the miracle a renewal of their Catholic faith but also cause for pride in their ancient city (because that is where the miracle regularly takes place).

Conceptually, the procession in Naples resembles the procession in Orvieto. One focuses on the blood of Christ, the other on the blood of a man who adored Christ. Both processions inspire awe in the faithful. It would be difficult to pinpoint which comes first: the faith of the excited onlookers or the supposed fact of the miracle taking place. Skeptics might protest that if the supposed miracle really did take place, its occurrence would convert the world to Catholicism. It seems safe to conclude, however modestly, that those who join processions in either Orvieto or Naples *want* to believe in miracles.

I have considered only two examples here; certainly, there are many others. Processions sometimes combine athleticism and reverence for local saints. Although an event such as Gubbio's may not at first seem to focus on God, it still qualifies as an awe procession, because each of the three saints honored therein gained renown through almost heroic devotion to God. (Catholics are permitted to revere, although not adore, saints.)

The *Blue Guide to Umbria*, a well-known travel guide, no doubt motivates curious tourists to witness Gubbio's *Festa dei Ceri*.[6] Although the guide is not written for pilgrims, some tourists who happen to be Catholic may come to feel like pilgrims while observing this event, which may have pagan origins. The procession is held every year on 15 May, the vigil of the feast day of St. Ubaldo (d. 1160), the town's patron saint and bishop. The whole town participates in the celebrations and many tourists annually assemble to watch. After an early Mass, three statues of St. Ubaldo, St. George, and St. Anthony are taken in procession through the streets. Afterward, another procession forms. The three confraternities of builders (St. Ubaldo), peasants (St. Anthony), and artisans (St. George) then erect the three extremely heavy wooden *ceri* (floats in the form of giant candlesticks), four meters high, crowned by the three statues of saints. The *ceri* are then each carried through the crowded, cheering streets.

Another procession later traverses the entire town before returning to Piazza Grande. The clergy and bishop participate in this procession. From here the mayor waves a white flag from the central window of Palazzo Pretorio to start the race which is the culmination of the day's festivities: The *ceri* are swiftly carried along several streets to Porta Del Monte, where they rest temporarily. The race then resumes and follows the steep path all the way up the hillside to the Basilica of St. Ubaldo. Each of the three confraternities relies on ten official bearers (who have to be replaced about every ten meters because of the great weight). The race is a demonstration of strength and endurance, and the first *cera* to arrive at St. Ubaldo attempts to shut the church door in the face of the following two teams. The *ceri* are then left in the church while the three statues of the saints are brought down again in a triumphant candlelight procession to the church which had hosted the early Mass. In Gubbio we see that religious awe admits of, does not exclude, the thrill of a street race.

So many other processions suggest themselves as illustrations of how Catholics can be bound together in the streets that I cannot expect the reader to find useful more than just three or four further examples, briefly stated. The Basilica of Santa Rosa in Viterbo, Italy contains the body of St. Rose, who died in 1252. Since then, Viterbo has honored the Saint with a magnificent festival on the night of 3 September. On this night, the so-called *Macchina di Santa Rosa*, a huge lighted tower over a hundred feet tall and 11,000 pounds, is taken along the medieval streets of the city. The event initiates a series of cultural and other popular events which continue throughout the month.[7]

Although not commonplace, some processions (including Corpus Christi parades) do take place in the United States. At the church of Our Lady, Queen of the Americas in Washington, DC, for example, parishioners mount an elaborate parade every All Souls' Day. The Italian parish of Holy Rosary in Cleveland has a long tradition of a procession that grew to nearly a week of celebration built around the Feast of the Assumption in August. St. Rocco Parish, also located in Cleveland, can trace its origin to the desire of the Italian community living there to celebrate their patron's feast day in America, rather than sending money to help underwrite the celebration in their home village in Italy. The parish has also long mounted a Good Friday procession.

Ethnic assimilation in the twentieth century eroded some interest in processions; as foreigners became Americans, children of foreigners lost interest in certain traditions.

Processions of awe generated paintings, carvings, and other art to focus Catholic solidarity outside of churches. The Victoria and Albert Museum in London includes a remarkably intact wood carving of Christ seated upon an ass, from the early sixteenth century. Catholic Germans would annually organize a procession on Palm Sunday, marching behind the large wood carving of Christ (and thus symbolically joining the joyous crowds that followed Christ on his ancient ride).

Regardless of geographic location, the more conservative the American parish, the more likely it is to sponsor a procession of the Blessed Sacrament through city streets (the very conservative Society of St. Pius X, for example, is fond of this practice). In the face of a parish unaccustomed to marching in processions, it is not clear that the faithful would take to the practice. Some, but not all, Catholics would welcome the chance to take their faith to the streets. Processions are not the only means of indicating one's faith publicly: One sees in many cities and in many college campuses people going about their business with ashes smeared over their foreheads on Ash Wednesday. Most of these people are Catholic.

Many European Catholics brought their religious customs with them to the United States, where those customs withered. It is difficult to think of ways in which twenty-first century Catholics find community in the streets, exhibit their distinctiveness to non-Catholic neighbors (abortion protests staged silently along busy streets are perhaps an exception). A thorough account of these customs would require a book in itself. For my purposes, it is enough to note not only the popularity of awe processions but also a common formula. The most compelling explanation here must be that American Catholics do not want or need such occasions for building solidarity. Before leaving off with this possibility for performing one's faith publicly, let's probe further what function processions have served.

Gratitude Processions

Even a secular parade such as, for example, the Macy's Thanksgiving Day Parade in New York City, can involve gratitude on some fundamental level. In this section I want to focus on communal attempts in ritual form to express thanks specifically to God, even if a particular saint mediates the act of giving thanks (saints, after all, derive their glory from heroic submission to God).

When we receive a gift or favor from someone else, we often feel gratitude. Depending on the magnitude of the gift, we may indicate our gratitude in dramatic ways. When the person to whom we are grateful is God, we may enter into a contract of sorts. We see this, for example, in the well-known novel of Manzoni, *The Betrothed* (1847). A young girl is prevented from marrying her lover because she is kidnapped; fearing for her life, she promises lifelong chastity to the Virgin Mary in exchange for deliverance from the kidnappers. (When the young girl ultimately finds herself free, she demonstrates the argumentative skill of a corporate lawyer to justify invalidating the contract.) Through expressing gratitude, we strive to shape the attitude of the giver toward us. We want to make sure the giver understands we appreciate the gift; we may also fear that the giver will withdraw the gift if we fail to show sufficient appreciation.

We'll see that Europeans on various occasions promised to honor God through successive generations; that's to say that people who had not been born yet would come under the contract and would continue to give thanks for a gift that had been bestowed long before. Gratitude processions and Passion plays are among the most interesting examples in this category (which might also include erecting a monument and ensuring that it would remain there in perpetuity, or pledging financial support in perpetuity to a convent).

Two separate processions over gondolas in Venice illustrate nicely the procession of gratitude, which will later be shown to have an obvious tie to the performance of some Passion plays in Europe. The Franciscan church of the Redentore was built in thanksgiving for the deliverance of Venice from the plague in 1575–77, which left some 46,000 dead (25–30 per cent of the population). The doge (a rough equivalent of an American senator or a British MP) vowed to visit the church annually across a remarkable bridge of boats which united the Zattere with the Giudecca. The feast of the Redentore (the third Sunday in July) remains one of the most popular Venetian festivals and the bridge of boats is still usually constructed for the occasion. Its vigil is celebrated with aquatic concerts and elaborate fireworks. A similar festival is held at the Venetian church of Della Salute. The *Festa Della Salute* (21 November) is also usually celebrated by a bridge of boats across the Grand Canal at the Dogana and also commemorates deliverance from a plague. Unlike, say, Memorial Day or Veterans' Day (civil holidays in the United States), thanks for deliverance goes directly to God.

Long before Elisabeth Kübler-Ross set out the stages of dying in her influential book *On Death and Dying* (1969), Westerners already understood the business of making a contract with God. It seems only natural for a religious believer to promise God something in return for a gift (be it personal survival or that of a loved one, or happiness in a marriage, or success in a business venture). The example of Manzoni's *The Betrothed*, only one among many, suggests how natural it might have seemed to a Catholic individual or community on the apparent verge of extinction to make a promise to honor God in a particular way in order to try to thank him properly.

Catholics throughout the world have gathered to consecrate a particular building, city, or nation to the Virgin Mary (this ritual entails giving away something as vast as, say, a city by promising it to the Virgin, akin to the honor of "giving the keys to the city" to a mere mortal). By consecrating a place to the Virgin, Catholics simultaneously demonstrate their respect for her, their gratitude for perceived assistance, and their desire to follow Christ's wishes, to elevate his mother. In Tennessee Williams' play *The Rose Tattoo* (1951), a Sicilian widow living in Louisiana refuses to allow a young sailor to date her fifteen-year-old daughter until he kneels before a statue of the Virgin Mary in the family living room and vows not to have sex with the young girl. A promise to Mary or God is only made in a context in which the seriousness of the oath is implicit.

Fidelity to God can be understood in two principal ways, one general and the other specific. Ancient Israelites, for example, saw themselves as explicitly entering a covenant with God. At the dawn of monotheism, the attachments that used to lead to a pantheon of pagan gods became focused on a single deity. Note that the Israelites saw their pact as a distinctly corporate—as opposed to individual—one. Salvation would come through the community; each Israelite combined to form a whole that was greater than the sum of its parts.

In contrast to this general model is a more specific one: a solitary person makes a highly qualified promise to God. "If you give me X, I will give you Y." This kind of promise is probably more familiar to Western readers in the context of the devil. Goethe's story of *Faust* springs naturally to mind, as do various sayings involving the devil (for example, we sometimes say that a youthful-looking adult or a lucky person generally has "made a deal with the devil"). In Christopher Marlowe's *Doctor Faustus*, the title character promises his soul to an agent of the devil in exchange for twenty-four intervening years during which Faustus may be a "spirit in form and substance," may have the devil's agent as his servant, and may obtain true answers to any questions that Faustus asks that agent. When portrayed as the sale of one's soul for knowledge, this sort of Faustian bargain has found resonance as a metaphor in the age of nuclear weaponry and genetic engineering; when portrayed more generically as a relatively ignorant individual striking a bargain with a powerful adversary, the metaphor appears in discussions of plea bargains and employment in corporate law firms.

Deals or contracts with God must happen more frequently than business ventures, and yet we rarely hear of them. Let's take a closer look now; we'll see that such spiritual contracts harbor important cultural ramifications.

Contracts with God

Contracts with God not only bind a living community such as Venice closer together, contracts also work to unite the living with the dead. As we'll see in the next chapter, Luther largely did away with elaborate funeral rituals and, in so doing, left his followers with the frustration of feeling even more distant from the dead. Contracts with God blend readily with that hallmark of Catholic culture, mediation. Just as priests and saints mediate an individual's relation to God, so does a festival of the sort to be found at Redentore. Catholics believe that salvation will come through the community, and at Redentore we can see this belief in action.

A sales contract usually involves mutual understanding between two parties: a buyer promises to provide a sum of money or certain services or goods in exchange for a seller's promise to deliver some item of value. A court of law can usually enforce these contracts, but obviously not one between a human being and God. Presumably God takes these contracts as irrevocable, much in the way that a harmed plaintiff hopes a court of law will. Lawyers frequently argue over validity, breach, and remedy, yet God brooks no lawyer. We tend to think of God in black-and-white terms, for better or for worse, and we believe there is no finagling God, much less fooling him.

How can an examination of contracts with God help us understand Catholic culture? The deepest kind of contract involves no signature, no affidavit. It is written on the heart. Whereas contracts with the devil tend to involve the promise of one's own soul for some temporal benefit, the religious believer instead promises some temporal good or pleasure for a special intention (for example, avoiding physical harm or relief from disease or deliverance from an enemy).

A contract with God, and the good that issues from it, can lend an aura of enhanced sacredness to an already emotionally charged event. Gratitude combines with mystery to suffuse the believer with a sense of wonder. God doesn't need anything from mere mortals, and yet the Hebrew and Christian Scriptures offer up numerous instances in which God *does* seem to crave a loving relationship with humans.

Certainly, a procession can express both gratitude and awe. The elaborate Good Friday procession of the Umbrian town of Betona (Italy), while worshipful, collectively expresses gratitude at Christ's sacrifice for mankind. What's interesting about the Venetian practice of annually building a walking bridge out of boats across a large lagoon is the promise that motivates the practice. Even if religious belief in God were eventually to fade, it is possible that Venetians would still devote the same day each year to festivities. Old habits die hard, particularly when they are fun. A religious festival without God, though, would revolve around something other than gratitude for having been delivered from a plague. The danger of debauchery or even paganism lurks here.

The Feast of the Snake Holders of Cocullo

Some Catholic processions press on the division between adoration and gratitude. The procession at Cocullo, in southern Italy, might seem more superstitious than anything, despite the curious coincidence between a deeply Catholic event and the distinctly rural Protestant practice of snake handling in the United States.[8]

The feast of the snake holders of Cocullo has evolved from pagan origins. Local historians do not deny that the ancient people of Marsica worshipped reptiles to honor the goddess Angizia (in Latin, *angius* means serpent) that had taught them the use of poison and antidote. Through the related practices of medicine and magic, she achieved the status of a protective goddess. In time, with the advent of Christianity, the Marsican people replaced Angizia with St. Domenico Abate.

The feast of the snake holders, honoring St. Domenico, takes place the first Thursday of every May. The people of Cocullo begin gathering serpents in early spring, when the heat wakes the serpents from their hibernation and brings them into public view. Those who gather the snakes are sometimes reputed to know magic. The animals are stored in earthenware vases or cloth sacks full of dried leaves; the snakes are not released until the feast day of St. Domenico. On that day, all the serpents are placed not only on the statue of the saint but also on the bodies of the snake holders. The real stars of the show are the serpents, and people travel from all parts of the province of Abruzzo to see them.

The procession of Cocullo represents a rather extreme example of religious processions, as the serpents may seem to be the object of awe, not the figure of St. Domenico. Beyond that, non-Catholics (and even some Catholics) may object that any public displays of affection for saints amount to little more than evidence of ongoing fascination with magic. Continuing a tradition of religious processions or Passion plays may come down to superstition. Skeptics will naturally attribute some, if not all, of the motive for participating in such "extracurricular" Catholic devotion to superstition. I myself resist this explanation, even as I acknowledge the difficulty of defeating it.

In the following chapters I will explore cultural Catholicism as a matter of veering off of the required or orthodox course. Superstition plays off of a similar deviation, with the important exception that the "optional" menu in Catholicism is not denounced. We might think of superstition as beliefs and practices which presuppose a misunderstanding of cause and effect. Superstitious people may attribute responsibility for something to an agent considered imaginary or irrational by modern science. Keith Thomas has noticed the inclination of the medieval church to define superstition in such a way as to guarantee ecclesiastical authorities final say. This advantage would have proven crucially useful, given the resemblance of some theology to superstition. The Church did essentially claim to be magical, after all. As Thomas argued,

> Although theologians drew a firm line between religion and super-stition, their concept of "superstition" always had a certain elasticity about it. It was "superstitious" to use consecrated objects for purposes other than those for which they were intended. It was "superstitious" to attempt to achieve effects, other than those which might have natural causes, by any operation which had not been authorized by the Church. But in these, as in other definitions, the last say would always lay with the Church.[9]

It was certainly not superstitious to believe that a priest could transform ordinary bread into the body of Christ. Although it is possible that religious participants and spectators at Cocullo believe that St. Domenico can subdue and control all the serpents in the procession, it seems far-fetched to classify the procession as one of awe. For to do so might involve the unappealing notion of designating a day each year in which you force a saint onto center stage and command him to demonstrate that his powers still work.

A Sacred Procession Turned Secular

So far I've given a few brief illustrations of how Catholics can live their faith partially through the "optional menu." Now let's turn to potential problems with the category of optional. Note that priests do not take part in the examples presented next.

It is doubtful that all contemporary marchers in Europe or anywhere proceed in the proper spirit, that is, of gratitude for their forebears having been delivered from a plague, or reverence for the ancestors who made a pledge that the procession would be continued. We can find a clear example of slippage from the original intention in the St. Patrick's Day Parade in New York and Boston. St. Patrick is believed to have driven the snakes from Ireland. Once a pagan himself, St. Patrick is one of Christianity's better known figures. These parades might easily be mistaken as a gratitude procession, given St. Patrick's legendary achievements, but the events have lost their religious underpinning.

The modern secular holiday is based on the original Christian saint's feast day, also thought to be the date of the saint's death. In 1737, Irish immigrants to the United States began observing the holiday publicly in Boston; they held the first St. Patrick's Day Parade in New York City in 1766. Today, the tradition continues to unite people in wearing green, eating Irish food, and attending parades. St. Patrick's Day crowds may display shamrocks and leprechauns; the throngs may also pinch observers who fail to wear green.[10] A procession, whether explicitly religious or not, foments opposition and deepens an "us-them" mentality.

Roman Catholicism condemns gay sex, and even the secularized version of the St. Patrick's Day Parade shuns gays and lesbians (suggesting perhaps another vestige of the original religious model). In the 1990s, the Irish Lesbian and Gay Organization protested its exclusion from the parade. Courts mainly sided with the parade committee. In a case involving the Boston St. Patrick's Day Parade, the US Supreme

Court ruled unanimously in 1995 that a parade committee has a constitutional right to exclude marchers whose message it rejects, including those who seek to identify themselves as gay, lesbian, or bisexual Irish-Americans. In this important case, we see that identity is at stake in an event that is all about heritage and ethnic distinction (and maybe a little about Catholicism, given that legitimate churches are named after this saint).

The St. Patrick's Day Parade in both Boston and New York serves as a useful counterexample to the procession over the gondolas in Venice, as entertaining and fun as those gondola leapings might be. The explicit aim of the St. Patrick's Day Parade in Boston and New York today is to "celebrate being Irish." Although many Irish people are devout Catholics, not all are. And so the parade doesn't have any intrinsic link to Catholicism. The parade is a celebration of ethnic or nation origin, much in the way that a Fourth of July day parade might be in the United States or a Bastille Day Parade in France might be. As to the American example, it is worth noting that two days before the first Fourth of July, John Adams envisioned a celebratory parade, "a great anniversary festival" which he hoped would be "celebrated by succeeding generations." Writing to his wife Abigail, Adams speculated, "It ought to be solemnized with pomp and parade, with shows, games, sports, guns, bells, bonfires, and illuminations, from one end of the continent to the other, from this time forward forevermore."[11]

Part of John Adams' pride came down to having triumphed over a powerful and unjust enemy, over having won the struggle to liberate the American colonies from British rule. We do not find Catholics parading through the streets, calling themselves "Catholic Survivors," and rejoicing over having extinguished their Catholic identity. The Fourth of July parade or the St. Patrick's Day Parade helps us understand better what the Catholic procession of gratitude is *not*. In addition to a celebration of being Irish, the St. Patrick's Day Parade also involves the simple joy of being in a parade. Anyone who has witnessed in New York City both the St. Patrick's Day and the Halloween parade may quickly recognize a family resemblance.[12]

Some anthropologists have distinguished between specifically religious instances of social celebration and secular ones, calling the former *ritual* and the latter *festivity*.[13] A ritual claims a salubrious spiritual effect, whereas a festival ushers in a play day, an opportunity to forget religious and familial commitments or aspirations and to erupt in a carefree, laughing, perhaps naughty, state of mind. The St. Patrick's

Day Parade in New York City and Boston would appear to qualify as a festivity, properly speaking, as would Mardi Gras. Although most of the people in the parade may be Catholic, Catholics do not bond as Catholics in the event. They may perhaps bond together as cultural Catholics or Catholics who feel ambivalent about their church involvement.

Part of what makes a raucous parade interesting is the built-in plan for an ending. Far from an addiction, which might go on indefinitely, a parade, no matter how raucous, will end—and so will the loud partying and drinking which may go with it. Speaking in tongues offers a similar opportunity for the thrill of stepping outside of routine. Although I am happy to hold on to a distinction between non-religious festivities and religious rituals, I want here to note that both may turn on this signal moment of stepping outside of the familiar, and both may rely on a built-in end. Wayne A. Meeks argues that glossalalia or speaking in tongues was a more or less controlled and ritual element of early Christian worship, erupting "at predictable times, accompanied by distinctive bodily movements," perhaps triggered by other ritual events, and serving "to both increase the prestige of the gifted and heighten the solidarity of the group."[14] Although Catholics as a group (as opposed to some Protestants) rarely go in for speaking in tongues, it is instructive to note the possibility of finding a non-routine thrill in individual religious experience. Processions of both gratitude and awe—like the standard parade generally—capture and cultivate this same sort of thrill. Secular parades have a starting and an ending point: In between the two, people may misbehave in all sorts of ways. Part of the fun involved joining the crowd.[15]

Whether it was frivolity for frivolity's sake, or frivolity as a means through which to highlight the imminent sacrifices of Lent, a Mardi Gras reveler caroused in a context steeped in religious significance. Individual flouting of this context, while possible, conflicts with the very inversions (high/low, rich/poor, sacred/profane) Carnevale celebrated.[16] Not everything a Catholic does should be considered Catholic, and the enduring popularity of Mardi Gras points up the extent to which Catholic culture absorbs and is absorbed by secular values.[17]

Collective Effervescence

I have examined here only a few examples of Catholic processions. It would take a separate book to due full justice to the variety of

Catholic processions. Even papal installations could be taken as an example of a parade of awe or adoration. Americans have shown widespread fondness for graduation processions, with public displays of pomp and circumstance marking the end of high school or college, but there is nothing intrinsically religious about such processions. Catholic processions at least profess to honor God (again, even if through honoring a saint who lived heroically to glorify God). Catholic processions aim to deepen and solidify the invisible bonds of a Catholic community, of a distinctive fellowship between like believers.[18] These long-gone Catholics were not inventing something new but merely putting into practice a tenet that had already been there, a central aspect of their religious culture: a transcendental commitment to continue in the faith. Note how the contract with God implicates children in the same way as Jews did when they once cried, "May his blood be upon us and upon our children" (Matthew 27:25).

We see such processions in popular films such as *Divorce, Italian Style* (1960), *The Godfather* (Part I, 1973), *Antonia's Line* (1995), *Kika* (1995), and *The Talented Mr. Ripley* (2000); Catholic life was to a certain extent patterned around paying festive tribute to a local saint. It will never be fully clear whether the motives of paraders were sincere or tactical: Each case would have to be evaluated on its own merits, and in any event, a mind-reader or perhaps an expert psychoanalyst would be required. What must have been true was the power of this spectacle to onlookers, who understood a little better the social engine which such a procession served to fuel.

I classify such processions as instances of what Durkheim referred to as *collective effervescence*: the ritually induced passion or ecstasy that cements social bonds and, he proposed, forms the ultimate basis of religion.[19] Catholic processions may not immediately seem to resemble the spectacle of savages drumming and dancing with wild abandon before a blazing fire, but the goal of the separate processions is largely the same. As I have indicated, it would have been quite unusual for anyone in a Catholic procession to enter a trance: no one loses control of his body, no one speaks in tongues, no one has a vision.[20] But marchers were allowed to feel a religious and social joy that the Church had not required.

It is also worth noting that marchers in both gratitude and awe processions freely acknowledge their inferiority to God. Far from a Promethean struggle against a greater power, far from an intellectual revolt against a seemingly irrational power forever mysterious to human beings, marchers accept their lower status and perhaps even revel in it. In this aspect of processions, we can understand some of what might make skeptical onlookers uncomfortable. Generally speaking, we want to be strong, not weak. And generally speaking, we feel sad at the sight of weak people giving up a struggle to overcome weakness and emerge strong (hence why we may feel elevated at, say, athletic competitions for the disabled or mentally retarded).

Parades look plainly rational if you agree with La Rochefoucauld that the principal reason people express gratitude is out of hope to receive further favors. For the streets tell the truth. Parades were the optional element in religious experience; it should not seem far-fetched to claim that ordinary Catholics felt much more pressure to attend Mass (missing it was a serious sin, after all) than to march in processions. Processions were entirely optional and, although relatively fun, only one option on a menu of fun things to do. People *really* wanted more favors, and people *really* believed that saints could help bring the favors about.

Gratitude resembles both sexual desire and love, for in gratitude, we think enthusiastically (perhaps longingly) about another. Romantic love requires a kind of specific knowledge of another that gratitude does not. We may not know much about the person or group who helped our family, nation, or religious group centuries ago, but we may still feel gratitude gushing up within us when we hear the story of how that person or group once benefited us.

That said, an important part of what makes the Catholic processions mentioned here interesting is that gratitude tends to be a short-term state.[21] Contemporary Catholics who join these processions can hardly be said to feel the gratitude that those delivered from the plague did, centuries ago. Either contemporary Catholics take the vow of their forebears seriously, or contemporary Catholics join the processions because it brings them pleasure. Most likely, it is a combination of the two motives that captures the driving force behind the decision to take part in these processions.

Festivals

Let's circle back now to the distinction between proper rituals and "mere" festivals I mentioned earlier. More raucous and less overtly reverential than, say, the Corpus Christi or San Gennaro processions are Mardi Gras festivals (or "Carnevale," as it is also known).

Of course Catholic culture has given rise to other festivals, but Mardi Gras is the best known of them all.

Mardi Gras came to America in 1699 with the French explorer Iberville. Mardi Gras had been celebrated in Paris since the Middle Ages, where it was a major holiday. During the late 1700s, pre-Lenten masked balls and festivals were common in New Orleans, while it was under French rule. When New Orleans came under Spanish rule, the custom was banned. In 1803 New Orleans came under the US flag and, twenty years later, the governor permitted masked balls. In 1827 street masking was again legalized; the first documented parade occurred in 1837. Mardi Gras gained a negative reputation because of violent behavior attributed to maskers during the 1840s and 1850s. The situation deteriorated to the extent that public cries for ending the parade seemed destined to prevail.

In 1857 six New Orleaneans saved Mardi Gras by forming the Comus organization. These six men were former members of the Cow-bellians, an organization which had put on New Year's Eve parades in Mobile since 1831. The Comus organization supposedly enhanced Mardi Gras and demonstrated that it could be a safe and aesthetically pleasing event. Comus organized the parade around floats and a grand ball, held after the parade. The celebration of Mardi Gras was inter-rupted by the Civil War, but in 1866 Comus returned. In 1950 the Duke and Duchess of Windsor visited New Orleans during Mardi Gras. They legitimized and glamorized the New Orleans Mardi Gras tradition by publicly bowing to kings of Rex and Comus at the Comus ball.

It isn't difficult to understand why Martin Luther objected to Mardi Gras blow-outs, for such fun no doubt often led to debauchery and undermined Lent, which entailed various sacrifices. To Luther Mardi Gras seemed to make a mockery of Lent; the festival seemed to turn on obeying the letter, rather than the spirit, of the law. Nonetheless, Catholic culture has given rise to these popular celebrations known throughout the West. Whether in Cologne, Germany; Rio de Janiero, Brazil; Venice, Italy; or New Orleans, non-Catholics and Catholics alike can pretend to be preparing for the austerity of Lent, even as they party it up with little or no thought to the solemnity of Lent.

Passion Plays

Processions dovetail with other activities of traditional Catholicism, such as prayers and Masses on behalf of the dead, the invocation of saints, the veneration of images and relics, and the performance of Passion plays. Long before Mel Gibson's blockbuster film *The Passion of the Christ* (2004), Roman Catholics had been rehearsing and performing theatrical reenactments of the death of Jesus. These plays conceptually qualify as a religious procession of gratitude and an effective way to tie the periphery of believers to the center. Although performing in or viewing a Passion play was optional, the experience was no doubt often powerful.

In various European locales, communities would perform a Passion play to thank God for deliverance from a plague. The earliest Passion plays in Latin that we know of date from the twelfth century. The earliest of the German and Latin-German Passion plays appeared a century later. The late fourteenth-century *Second Shepherd's Play* (based on Luke 2:8–18) was widely performed in England (we know the author only as the Wakefield Master). The most famous of these thanks-for-deliverance-from-plague plays still takes place in Oberammergau, Germany once a decade. According to James Shapiro, "The genre of the Passion Play has never strayed far from its liturgical roots, though for the past six hundred years it has led an ambivalent existence, seeking the protection and blessing of the Church, fearing suppression or control by it."[22] The problem with the traditional Passion play is that it cast the Jews in the role of the bad guys. The contract with God underlying the Oberammergau play required fine tuning in the late twentieth century. The point of examining anti-Semitism here is to make the point that items from the optional menu can evolve just as surely as they can also disappear. Mel Gibson learned this in front of the American public (especially American journalists).

The Second Vatican Council (1962–65) denounced anti-Semitism, insisted that Roman Catholics show respect for the Jewish faith, and stated clearly the error of accusing Jews of the death of Christ. Instead, Christians were to think that all people jointly shared responsibility for that death. Some three decades before Vatican II, Hitler had traveled to Bavaria to witness a performance of the Oberammergau play. He voiced enthusiasm for the production, which depicted Jews as bent on killing Christ. The reforms of Vatican II compelled the Oberammergau directors to update their production; the writers managed this with considerable difficulty. If humans were the bad guys and not just the Jews, a stage production of Jesus' death would lose much of its punch. And yet the production has survived. Despite the lack of an obvious and odious villain (as compared to the pre-Vatican II script), the once-a-decade performances draw consistently larger crowds than ever. It would be a mistake to ascribe purely religious motives to the crowds which throng to the performances: the desire to observe or experience an old tradition could explain some of the appeal.

Mel Gibson was surely aware of the widespread appeal of the Oberammergau play. In any event, he has cited his own gratitude to Christ and admiration for his sacrifice as a reason for developing a cinematic version (not the only one, to be certain) of the final days of Jesus.[23] The Anti-Defamation League (ADL) expressed early concern about Mel Gibson's *The Passion of the Christ*, months before the film's release, and the *New York Times Magazine* featured an article about the film in February 2003. After reviewing an early version of the script, an ADL representative watched a rough cut in Houston later that year. In January 2004, some members of the ADL viewed a version of the film at a pastors' convention in Orlando, Florida. Mr. Gibson had declined various ADL requests for permission to view the film.

Abraham Foxman, head of the ADL, told the *New York Times* he feared an anti-Semitic backlash, especially because the film was scheduled for release on Ash Wednesday that year. According to Foxman, *The Passion of the Christ* offered an unambiguous portrayal of Jews as being responsible for the death of Jesus. He said the Gibson film consistently reinforced the notion that the Jewish authorities and the Jewish mob are the ones ultimately responsible for the Crucifixion. In a sense, Foxman contested the contract with God underlying the Passion play tradition.

The ADL feared that Christians only familiar with the Gospel narratives might conclude that everything in the film derives directly from the New Testament. The ADL insisted that much of the film amounted to Mr. Gibson's artistic vision, pointing out that some of the film had been inspired by extra-Biblical sources. The ADL feared that those already disposed unfavorably toward Jews would use this film to fan the flames of hatred. The ADL never called Gibson himself an anti-Semite. The ADL claimed that Gibson's images of Romans (especially Pontius Pilate) demonstrated compassion toward Jesus, whereas Jews were depicted as blood-thirsty. According to the ADL, the Jewish high priest, Caiaphas, was shown as bullying Pilate, and the hundreds and hundreds of amassed Jews as demanding Jesus' death.

Just as we cannot know for certain the content of a procession marcher's thought, nor could American critics discern Gibson's motivation. In any event, Gibson's great success in *The Passion of the Christ* figured not only as simple drama but also a close cousin of a gratitude procession. Despite a well-known alcohol problem, Gibson showed himself willing to go public with a very personal avowal of faith. In his place, many other people might have feared being called a hypocrite. Of course, Gibson might have shared that fear, but he went through with the project. Although he would seem to qualify as a traditional Catholic, he perhaps learned what it feels like to walk in a cultural Catholic's shoes. Cultural Catholics in the twenty-first century may experience a similar anxiety when attending Mass or especially when marching to the altar for communion. Catholic onlookers may view Gibson (or a cultural Catholic generally) unworthy of communion (before a serious confession and a genuine renouncing of one's sinful ways), which means Gibson might naturally tremble while waiting for communion in front of people who might be silently reproaching him as an anti-Semite.

Cultural Borrowing

The accumulation of examples of performing one's faith—in a procession or in a play—leads to the question of how a contemporary Catholic may settle upon new ways to act Catholic, to devise new items for the optional menu. One particularly compelling example of such creativity might be the new "eco-nuns" or "green sisters" who see themselves as serving God through protecting the environment.[24] Although these women have taken religious vows, lay Catholics could follow them in the sense of viewing care for the environment as a way of performing Catholic identity.

Cultural Catholics tend to see most of Catholic doctrine as optional—thus making doctrine equivalent to private revelation. Do all Catholics have to believe in the sanctity (or point) of processions? The short answer is no. It is easier to opt out of a procession or a Passion play than it is to opt out of an apparition of the Blessed Virgin Mary. Even belief in Fatima, much more important than any of the processions I've mentioned in this chapter, is optional. The choice to believe given by the Church may deepen a cultural Catholic's sense of entitlement to demure (the freedom of conscience may be a good analogy here).

According to Catholic doctrine, the essentials of the faith are contained in the Old and New Testaments.[25] Belief in any private revelations is optional. Apparitions, Rome insists, cannot furnish new truths of faith; they can only help Catholics understand the existing tenets of their faith better. Indeed, church authorities have been very wary about visions. Although many thousands have flocked to the appearances of Mary in Medjugorje in the former Yugoslavia, (and in dozens of other places), the Holy See has resisted acknowledging the events as legitimate. The Vatican seems more likely to validate new devotions than apparitions. Pope Pius XII encouraged Father Harold Colgan, an American parish priest who founded the Blue Army of Our Lady in the United States in the mid-twentieth century. Colgan had fallen very ill and prayed to Our Lady of Fatima; he promised her that if she cured him, he would spend his life spreading devotion to her (which in fact he did). Colgan never claimed to have had a vision of Mary. This is not to suggest that the Church hierarchy resists miracles (and an apparition of Mary is a miracle of sorts); canonization relies on miracles performed by saints.

A parade can transform and uplift a community. We can never know for certain whether a religious procession can effect lasting change in an individual's behavior. Given that confession often fails to achieve this goal, it is likely that religious processions might as well. What is noteworthy is the determination to go back next year, to keep trying. The authority of tradition holds considerable explanatory power here. Until the late twentieth century, the gullibility of the laity may have also explained much. In the twenty-first century, the laity no longer seems quite so gullible. It is all the more remarkable, then, that part of the laity continues to evince a hunger for processions. These processions provide us with an outstanding example of the "optional" element of Catholicism—the element on which cultural Catholicism turns. Certainly there are other options (for example, a pilgrimage to Assisi or volunteering in a soup kitchen or joining the social justice committee in a local parish).

Both processions of awe and of gratitude rely on a robust appreciation for the supernatural. Apparitions of the Virgin Mary begin and end in the supernatural, and one can hardly fail to see the sheer weight of popular piety with regard to appearances of the Virgin Mary at Fatima, at Lourdes, and at Guadalupe in Mexico. Popes Pius XII, John XXIII, Paul VI, and John Paul II all voiced their acceptance of the supernatural origin of the Fatima events. And although some liberal Catholics consider visions of Mary a superstitious residuum of the credulous folk culture of medieval times, many of the world's one billion adherents of the faith hold such apparitions dear.

What is Catholic about any characteristically Catholic institution? Do the roots of Catholic cultural practice lie outside the religion? How far is traditional Catholic culture always by definition borrowed? Such questions defy easy answers. We may not know the genealogy of various Catholic rituals, but we do know that somewhat similar rituals predated the Catholic ceremonies. The originality lies in the blending, the Catholic character in the acquired—perhaps recycled—nuance. Various scholars have noted in both Europe and North America a sort of ritual melting pot, in which traditional distinctions have gradually broken down and both sacred and profane elements have seeped together into some quasi-hieratic ceremonial, a combination of religious ritual and popular entertainment.

What is the significance and the intent of these ceremonies? Some of the contemporary enthusiasm for a celebration of the Eucharist (particularly outside an overwhelmingly Catholic country such as Italy) may involve the joy of being different. As Protestants of course deny the real presence in the Eucharist, Catholics may feel a special pull to this feast, which clearly sets them apart from Protestant Christianity. Pride strikes me as a much more compelling explanation here than escapism (to a purer past, when idealized forebears overcame contemporary skepticism about processions).

Nostalgia can surely play a role here as well, provided that an adult's religious impulses, such as they are, continue to include reminiscences of a childhood into which processions figured (I will have more to say about this psychological motive in the chapter on family romances). Young Catholics casting about for an identity may feel drawn to old traditions, among which processions figure. And any interested Catholic seeking a richer sense of community or a clearer sense of what makes Catholics distinctive will find in processions (especially ones devoted to Corpus Christi or the Virgin Mary) a ready outlet in processions.

Beyond that, Catholic processions in either Italy or the United States may illustrate the imaginative adoption of Catholic ideals and forms. The recovery of a culture's past does not simply precede imaginative revival, for the curiosity about Catholic ideals and customs can itself be a romantic impulse. This chapter chiefly addressed the imaginative Catholicism of the processions, though it began with a look at the examples provided by the fact of plagues from which communities had been delivered. Curiosity toward what had gradually dimmed from memory or been demoted as an embarrassing example of earlier superstition may signal what Freud termed "a return of the repressed."

A devaluation of ritual overtook nearly every branch of Protestantism in the centuries following the Reformation and left its mark on

Judaism as well. In *Natural Symbols*, the anthropologist Mary Douglas attacked this anti-ritual attitude, which became a standard element in the Enlightenment critique of religion. A ritual such as a procession can awaken Catholic piety much in the way that wearing a medal blessed by a priest or keeping statues of saints in the home can. Catholic culture can help anchor cultural Catholics in the institutional church.

Until the advent of (largely evangelical and Protestant) "megachurches," piety could easily remove a person from the larger social body (unless you found yourself in a convent or monastery). Drinking and feasting after a solemn procession can reintegrate pious souls into the society of workaday people after their moments on the borderline of divinity.

Participating in a procession amounts to a public display of faith. No matter the century, there were bound to be scoffers in any community. The processions described in this chapter are overwhelmingly a Catholic show, of Catholics to Catholics. Of course, some have stronger faith and some weaker. The procession serves to put those of weaker faith on guard: They need to work harder. In an America full of non-Catholics, a procession provides an optional opportunity to testify to one's inclusion in the Catholic community. The march to take the Eucharist, brief and relatively private as it is, may evoke an anxiety about public identification with the Church about which previous generations of Catholics were largely silent.

Although it seems unlikely that the optional category could soon supersede the required category, still it bears noting the appeal of the optional. When it comes to finding optional ways to express and experience their faith, Catholics are bounded only by their own imagination and creativity.

Chapter 3

Baptisms, Weddings, and Funerals

This chapter will explore a few of the most vital links cultural Catholics maintain to the Church: the sacraments. This is another way of suggesting we examine the rules cultural Catholics *do* choose to obey, except that the seven sacraments are not exactly required. Not everyone gets married, for example, and very few people take Holy Orders. The three sacraments discussed in this chapter do not include the Eucharist, in part because it is available daily and therefore structures life less obviously, and in part because cultural Catholics frequently neglect it (because they skip Mass).

Cultural Catholics may keep their distance from much of the institutional Church, but they cling to three central rituals: baptisms, weddings, and funerals. What is it about these three events that keeps them coming back? These rites provide a visible basis for common identification and communication. Beyond that, participation in these rites may continue hope for delegitimating the existing power relations between the church hierarchy and the laity.

In this chapter I will briefly examine the history of these three rites of passage and then speculate on their respective futures. Weddings appear the most vulnerable to erosion, largely because of distaff dissatisfaction with the idea of serving a husband and because of rising rates of (civil) remarriage after divorce. Continuing support for artificial birth control and creeping support for gay marriage may also play important roles. It would be too simplistic to maintain that beginning-of-life and end-of-life anxiety compels cultural Catholics to rush back to their mother church, given how broadly cultural Catholics tend to approve of IVF (a violation of church teaching) and of euthanasia (another infraction).

I see the participation of cultural Catholics in these defining rituals as principally *creating the experience of solidarity in the absence of*

consensus.[1] Cultural Catholics understand that their church is fractured along various lines (clergy/laity, male/female, affluent/poor, het-
erosexual/homosexual) and hope for a unity about which they remain
sadly skeptical. Cultural Catholics hope for a better day, yet understand the enormity of the challenges before them. In particular, the
disagreement among traditional and cultural Catholics creates the
need for a ritual of solidarity. In my chapter on family romance, I will
turn to the psychological theory that cultural Catholics use these three
rituals to honor their parents, who had taught the central importance
of these rites of passage in the first place.

Before closing the chapter, I'll account for the Mass, because each of
these three defining events may occur within the setting of a Mass
(cultural Catholics regularly defy the ecclesiastical rule to attend
Mass every Sabbath). In 2007, Pope Benedict XVI eased the way for a
widespread return to the Latin Mass. Upon assuming the papacy
two years earlier, he had announced that he wanted to thwart the
rampant secularization of Western culture. Wider availability of the
Latin Mass may well appeal to conservative Catholics but will do
little to motivate cultural Catholics, many of whom associate the
"traditional" Mass with the subjugation of women and a certain deni-
gration of non-Catholics. Most Catholics born after 1960 are
strangers to the Tridentine Mass, and promoting it could backfire in
the struggle against the secular.

Baptism

This section will include mention of people who want a Catholic baptism but can't get it and people who don't want it but get it anyway
("secret baptisms"). It turns out that once you are baptized, you can
never undo the process (because, according to Catholic theology, the
sacrament leaves an indelible mark on the soul).[2] Novelist Milan
Kundera mused in *The Unbearable Lightness of Being* (1984) that
communist teenagers might envy other European teenagers who can
torment parents by renouncing a baptism; since Communist teenagers
were never baptized, they didn't have that arrow in their quiver.[3]

Without imputing too much expertise in theology to cultural Catholics, I want to suggest the possibility that ambivalent members sense
the usefulness—and perhaps the urgency, given their relative lack of
participation in the Church—of the sacrament of baptism. Cultural
Catholics do not want to sever *all* ties to the Church, and cultural

Catholics may well fear the possibility of eternal damnation. Baptism presents itself as a good idea, as a safeguard of sorts (much in the way captured by Pascal's famous wager). This manner of thinking is by no means outrageous, as Jesus himself said that the one "who believes and is baptized will be saved" (Mark 16:16). Cultural Catholics sometimes seem to be following the minimum requirements to obtain a graduation of sorts, unlike more demonstrably devout Catholics, who, by analogy, hope to graduate with honors. Beyond that, ambivalent Catholic parents may feel a strong sense of responsibility to provide for the hypothetical, future spiritual needs of their children.

Cultural Catholics generally know what Augustine argued about baptism, even if they can't identify him as the theologian who instructed that baptism was a *sine qua non* to heaven. Without that ticket, entry to paradise would be refused. Augustine did not believe that he *invented* this requirement; he rather discerned it from Scriptures. Where does the practice of baptism come from? 2 Kings 5:14 relates the story of Naaman, commander of the army of the king of Aram, who immersed himself seven times in the Jordan. The Fathers of the Church would later interpret this gesture to be quasi-sacramental and then articulate its role in eternal salvation. Even the Fathers realized, however, that they were innovating a tradition, not inventing it.

Ancient Jews sought moral correction through the ritual purification bath.[4] The Torah instructed that Jews became impure after touching a corpse (Numbers 19:19) or after being cured of leprosy (Leviticus 14:8–0). Once purified through immersion, one was fit for worship again. It is not difficult to see the similarity to Christian baptism, which washes away the stain of Original Sin. Beyond that, Jews had already worked out a concept of baptism, which was required of gentile converts to Judaism. Shortly before New Testament times, such converts were initiated with rituals of circumcision, baptism, and sacrifice. These rituals made them legally pure and officially incorporated foreigners as full-fledged Israelites.

What exactly did John the Baptist accomplish through his well-known work? The Gospels classify his work (Mark 1:4; Luke 3:3; Matthew 3:11) a baptism of repentance for the forgiveness of sins. John asked for a confession of sins and a manifest conversion; he sought moral purity. John expected his baptism to be superseded; it was provisional, as Matthew 3:11 indicates. John expected someone to surpass him, one who would baptize with the Holy Spirit and with fire. This messianic baptism would inaugurate a new world.

According to Christian theology, Jesus did not need baptism (because he was born without Original Sin). Acts points out that the baptism of John, in contrast to that of Jesus, did not confer the Spirit (1:5; 11:15–16; 19:1–6). Jesus's submission to John's baptism did not indicate his sinfulness but rather his union with sinful humanity (John 1:32–34). The synoptic accounts (Matthew 3:13–17; Mark 1:9–11; Luke 3:21–22) see this as the inauguration of the messianic mission of Jesus. The voice of the Father and the appearance of the Spirit as a dove mark the proclamation of the sonship of Jesus as his investiture with the Spirit, which fulfills the prophecies (Isaiah 11:2; 42:1; 61:1). In a similar way, each newly baptized Christian becomes a child of God through the gift of the Holy Spirit.

After his resurrection, Jesus instructed his followers to preach the gospel to all nations (Matthew 28:19–20) and to exhort them to observe all that he had commanded, which may have seemed a directive to baptize everyone. Mark 16:15–16, while more reserved than Matthew, stresses that baptism requires faith (which would seem to make the idea of a forced baptism nonsensical). Both passages contain the commission to baptize. While the explicit formula in Matthew might come from the liturgy of the Church, the commandment to baptize and the central meaning of baptism come from Jesus.

Although the New Testament does not provide the exact rite of baptism, it does seem that baptism in the early Church entailed immersion. Paul's reference in Romans 6:4 to being "buried" with Christ implies immersion. The account of the Ethiopian eunuch also refers to immersion in water (Acts 8:36–38). The Catholic manner of administration of the sacrament today is optional: full immersion or sprinkling water on the head. Either way, Catholics are to understand baptism not simply as purification but the sacrament of being joined to Christ.

So how do Catholics justify infant baptism? Catholics resort not only to their tradition but also to Scriptures for support. Catholics recognize that even though Scriptures do not explicitly instruct them to baptize infants, neither do Scriptures forbid the practice. Catholics interpret key passages in a way they understand to be something like an exhortation to baptize small children. For example, Peter once urged an audience not only to get themselves baptized but also their children: "For the promise is to you and to your children and to all who are far off, every one whom the Lord our God calls to him" (Acts 2:39). Scholars of the ancient Greek language also point out that the New Testament references the baptism of "whole households" (1 Cor 1:16;

Acts 10:48a; 16:15, 31, 33; 18:8) which in the normal Greek usage would include children. Perhaps the most persuasive scriptural passage in favor of the practice appears in Jesus' teaching on the children who were brought to him for blessing:

> And they were bringing children to him, that he might touch them; and the disciples rebuked them. But when Jesus saw it he was indignant, and said to them, "Let the children come to me, do not hinder them; for to such belongs the kingdom of God. Truly, I say to you, whosoever does not receive the kingdom of God like a child shall not enter it." And he took them in his arms and blessed them, laying his hands upon them. (Mark 10:13–6)

The fact that Jesus did not refuse to bless children and taught that the kingdom of heaven belongs to them influenced the Catholic Church in its decision to baptize infants and children.

Gone are the early days of mass conversions, which frequently entailed the baptism of many people at once. In the twenty-first century, baptism tends to be a more personalized sacrament for Catholic families—often a Catholic couple's child is one of only three or four being baptized at a Mass. It is worth noting that converts to Catholicism do not have to undergo a second baptism upon entering the Church of Rome. Protestant baptisms "count" in the eyes of Catholics—the exception here applies to Mormons. Because Mormons believe in a pantheon of gods, the Catholic church does not regard Mormons as properly baptized Christians. A Mormon convert to Catholicism would have to be baptized; in the eyes of the Church, this would be the Mormon's first baptism.

The ordinary minister of baptism is a bishop, priest, or deacon. If a person is in imminent danger of death and no ordinary minister is available, any member of the faithful or anyone with the right intention may, and sometimes must, administer the sacrament. The ministers, whether ordinary or extraordinary, must use water either by immersion or pouring while repeating the Trinitarian invocation: "I baptize you in the name of the Father, and of the Son, and of the Holy Spirit."

In past centuries, many Catholic parents suffered terribly over the death of an infant who perished before baptism.[5] It was long believed that the souls of such infants went to a place called limbo. The Roman Catholic Church officially abolished limbo early in the twenty-first century. Although the Church talks significantly less about Purgatory than it did in previous centuries, the official teaching of the Church still supports Purgatory, a halfway house of sorts for baptized Catholics who, at death, are not ready for heaven and not deserving of hell.

Secret Baptisms

In previous centuries, well-meaning but unlettered Catholics would sometimes take matters into their own hands and baptize non-Christian children, particularly Jewish children. The most famous of all such cases occurred in the late nineteenth century and centered on an Italian boy named Edgardo Mortara.[6] In this example we can see the utter seriousness with which even (or especially) ordinary Catholics took the sacrament. It is not difficult to imagine how strained friendships between Catholics and non-Catholics would have been, given the Catholic belief that non-Catholics were essentially damned ("Error has no rights").

Although St. Thomas Aquinas had explicitly forbidden secret baptisms (whereby a Christian takes it upon him or herself to baptize a non-Christian infant apart from and without the consent of the child's parents), still they happened on occasion. In the event that a Christian did perform this unacceptable practice, the newly baptized child had to be cared for properly, that is, given a Christian upbringing. It was the Church's moral responsibility to provide for the education necessary for a Christian child's salvation.

We do not know how many Jewish families cried over the secret baptism of one or more of their children. We can reasonably conclude, though, that many Jewish parents understood the danger implicit in employing Christians in the home, or even living among Christians generally. A brief account of a baptism nightmare will make this danger clear enough.

In the nineteenth century, the Christian maid employed by a Jewish couple in Rome became quite attached to the little boy in her care. Out of fear for his eternal soul, she secretly baptized the child, named Edgardo Mortara. Prompted later by a guilty conscience, she confessed to a priest what she had done. That priest felt the urgency of breaking the seal of the confessional (priests are normally forbidden from revealing what they have heard in confession) and informed his superior of the problem. That superior in turn escalated the issue, until church authorities knocked on the door of Edgardo's house and informed the Jewish parents that they would either have to convert to

Roman Catholicism or surrender their little boy. Because the parents refused to do either, the church authorities removed the little boy from his home.

Deeply distraught, the Mortaras pleaded for the release of their son, who was being held in a nearby monastery. Media attention spread news of the incident. Jewish families from around Europe (including very wealthy families such as the Rothschilds, whose bank helped finance the Vatican's annual operations) quickly sent letters and petitions to the Vatican, urging the release of the little boy. Finally, the pope himself, weary of the international cacophony, adopted the little boy and moved him to the Vatican, where Pius IX (d. 1878) raised Edgardo as his own son. Edgardo eventually became a priest, and, over a century later, Mortara family descendents still criticized the Vatican over the incident.[7]

A new problem has arisen in the Church, and it highlights a group that might qualify as a new category of outcasts. The Cardinal of Montreal proclaimed in July 2005 that he would deny baptism in certain instances. This story contrasts sharply with Edgardo Mortara's, although both stories point to the instinct of Catholics to baptize children.

A Canadian cardinal who had been considered a possible successor to Pope John Paul declared that the children of married same-sex couples could not be baptized in the Catholic Church.[8] (The Ontario Court of Appeal required that same-sex marriage be legalized under the Canadian Charter in June 2003. Canada legalized same-sex marriage in 2005. Quebec had already legalized it, and the cardinal was from Quebec City.) Testifying at a Senate committee hearing into the same-sex marriage bill (Bill C-38), Marc Cardinal Ouellet said that the Conference of Catholic Bishops had decided against the request in the event that both parents wanted to sign the certificate of baptism. The position seemed a sort of retaliation, as it emerged after Independent Senator Marcel Prud'homme, a Catholic, took issue with testimony from the cardinal at Senate committee hearings into the same-sex marriage bill.

"If I take the example of the ceremony of baptism, according to our canon law, we cannot accept the signatures of two fathers or two mothers as parents of an infant," Cardinal Ouellet told the committee. "With a law that makes these unions official, situations of this sort will multiply and this threatens to disturb not just the use of our territory, but also our archives and other aspects of the life of our communities." Ouellet presented same-sex marriage as anti-Catholic and suggested that it threatens religious freedom. He told the committee that priests no longer felt comfortable preaching Catholic morality for fear of being branded homophobes. "There's a climate taking shape where we don't dare say what we think anymore or we don't dare teach," he said. "Even in the pulpit we feel threatened in teaching the church's sexual morality. . . . That's also part of religious freedom." It is significant that Ouellet opposed what some church leaders had recommended— excommunicating or refusing communion to proponents of same-sex marriage, abortion or any other violation of church doctrine. Despite Ouellet's remarks, the committee approved the legislation.

Prud'homme, a Catholic, maintained that the church should not be free to refuse baptism under any circumstance. "It's a question of rules, but I consider a baby a gift of God," he said in an interview. Prud'homme would seem to qualify as a cultural Catholic by virtue of his signal disagreement. Even within the ranks of Canadian clergy, though, dissent could be heard. Msgr. Francis Coyle, pastor of St. Patrick's Basilica, and Rev. John Walsh, pastor of St. John Brebeuf Parish in LaSalle, both said they considered a basic Catholic principle that the church never refuse baptism to a child. What's more, Walsh disclosed he had already baptized children of same-sex couples—and had even allowed the register to list a mother and "parent" rather than mother and child.

Same-sex couples can upset or challenge Catholic tradition by rearing children, that is clear. What happens, for instance, when such children enter Catholic school? Catholic schools have played such an instrumental role in Catholic culture that it would be difficult to overstate their importance. One Catholic school in particular did not exactly oppose baptism, but rather entrance to the children of same-sex households. The following story may be only the first of many, much as Cardinal Ouellet predicted. This example raises further concern over shutting out certain persons from Catholic baptism or the privileges it may be said to offer.

In 2005, Orange County (California) parishioners and parents upset over the attendance at a Catholic school of two boys adopted by homosexual parents asked the diocese of Orange to clarify its position on homosexual marriage and domestic partnership.[9] The parents/ parishioners group had demanded that the pastor of St. John the Baptist parish in Costa Mesa, Norbertine Father Martin Benzoni, remove the children from the parish school's kindergarten and require prospective parents at the school to sign a "parental moral covenant" before their children would be admitted to the school. Father Martin said he would not dismiss the children, since they "have been baptized Catholic and the adults who are responsible for them have an obligation to raise them in the Catholic Faith." He also clarified that his parish does "not approve of homosexual unions nor of the law that permits adoptions by homosexuals."

But this explanation did satisfy the parishioners' group. Michael Sundstedt, a lawyer representing the group, asked the diocese both to clarify its own position on homosexual unions and send to St. John the Baptist parish papal writings condemning same-sex unions and adoption of children by same-sex couples. "This parish has virtually no idea what the church's teachings are on these issues," Sundstedt told the *Los Angeles Times*. Like Edgardo, these two boys suffered because of the political implications of their parents' identity.

The nun who served as principal of the school subsequently lost her job, and some parishioners told the media they suspected the change came in response to the nun's insistence on welcoming the two little boys in question. Sister Vianney—who had worked at the school for forty-three years—felt it would be discriminatory to enforce a policy proposed by St. John the Baptist pastor Father Martin Benzoni. The policy, set to go into effect in that fall, would not have allowed a same-sex couple with children enrolled at the school to be on school grounds together at the same time. Such a couple could not have attended teacher conferences, back-to-school night, or other functions that families regularly attend at the school. Parishioners were later told that Vianney's employment change was not retaliation for her decision to oppose Father Benzoni's ruling. After a prayer vigil in support of Sister Vianney, parish priests allowed her to continue as principal of the school.

Protestant Criticism of Infant Baptism

I have tried to indicate that baptism remains important today in Catholic culture. I have also indicated certain efforts to limit baptism. These efforts are noteworthy, given that Catholics long believed that an unbaptized child would be refused entry to heaven and, furthermore, that baptism required the kind of nurturing and guidance traditionally found in a Catholic education. Local bishops and cardinals have used their power to define an identity for gay and lesbian Catholics. In a struggle for symbolic inclusion, perhaps equality, some gay and lesbian Catholics have pressed for the baptism of their children into a church that insists on setting the entrance criteria. Whether they expressly intend to or not, such gay and lesbian Catholics challenge and delegitimate the existing power relations between the hierarchy and the laity. Before leaving off with a brief history of baptism, it is important to note that non-Catholics have questioned the validity of infant baptism, the norm for Catholics.

Even in the most cursory glances at the history of baptism, we see challenges to the practice. Luther, likely the most influential of the Protestant reformers, embraced baptism. It was rather the Anabaptists, whom Luther thwarted openly, who opposed baptism as it stood. Opposition arose not to the practice itself, but rather to the idea of administering baptism to infants.

Luther denied that baptism caused a magical transformation in a person, apart from engendering or increasing faith. "For if the sacrament give me grace merely because I accept it, truly it comes out of my own word, and I do not obtain this grace through faith, nor do I apprehend the promise in the sacrament but only the sign instituted and taught by God."[10] He favored full immersion because it most closely resembled the death, burial, and resurrection of Christ. This was the medieval practice, as any baptismal font from the Middle Ages will indicate. As for those who said—as the Anabaptists soon would— that infants cannot believe God's promises, Luther explained that he believed in infant baptism in the same way that he believed children were helped by the praying and believing church.

A few years later the lure of biblical literalism attracted large numbers of Anabaptists, who rejected infant baptism. With the full approval of Ulrich Zwingli, the town authorities in Zurich had them drowned, even though the theology of the Anabaptists amounted to a radicalization of Zwingli's own thinking. Drowning seemed fit punishment for those who demanded that adults who had been baptized as children be baptized again when they were old enough to profess their faith. Luther was exasperated with the Anabaptists, whose cradle was in Zurich and whose branches included the Swiss Brethren, the Moravian communities, the Melchiorites, and the Mennonites. Nonetheless, Luther did not think they should be killed. In early 1528 he published an open letter *On Anabaptism to Two Pastors*, whose names are not known. In it he argued the case passionately for infant baptism.

His tolerance for the Anabaptists would soon dry up. By 1529, he believed that those who spoke out peacefully against infant baptism should be exiled. By 1530, he had become convinced that the Anabaptist preaching against infant baptism inevitably led to sedition, and he saw their teaching as blasphemy against the Word of God. Although it was cruel to punish them with the sword, he said, it was more cruel to let them condemn the ministry of the Word and suppress sound doctrine and destroy the political order.

Calvin too faulted Anabaptists. He claimed they had failed to recognize that baptism unleashes the forgiveness of sins. Further, Anabaptists worried about the moral state of the minister who baptized a person; Anabaptists rejected the baptism of the unworthy minister. Calvin found this thinking foolish, for the baptism relies only on the Trinity, in whose name it is administered. Calvin undermined the argument Anabaptists constructed from Acts 19, in which we learn that Paul rebaptized those who had once been baptized by John. Calvin held that the followers of John were not, in fact, rebaptized. Calvin paid comparatively little attention to infant baptism; Calvin defended Luther's position, which emphasized the possibility of child faith. Calvin reasoned that just as in ancient times believers had to circumcise infants, so too should believers now baptize infants.

In this brief outline of baptism's history, we see a cultural difference between Catholics and Protestants. A Catholic couple that decided to wait until a child could ask to be baptized at the age of, say, ten or twelve would likely be considered irresponsible by priests and even by cultural Catholics. It could be that cultural Catholics worry that their children would never ask to be baptized or would never assume a Catholic identity at all if they as parents could not eventually use the fact of a baptism as evidence for their child being Catholic. Cultural Catholics, ambivalent about having drifted from their own tradition, may see some good in stamping a religious identity on their children before it's too late. Even though it can't be proven that lapsed Catholics feel a more urgent need to baptize children than lapsed Lutherans or Episcopalians, polls and parish records indicate that baptism remains a priority for Catholics who seldom attend Mass.

Weddings

The French philosopher La Rochefoucauld (d. 1680) once wrote that the vast majority of people would never fall in love if someone didn't first explain to them the concept of falling in love. We might debate whether love (as opposed to lust) is a natural concept, but for our purposes here it is enough to note that marriage did not become a sacrament in Roman Catholicism until quite late, relatively speaking—

that is, the thirteenth century. In ancient Rome, and through the first twelve centuries of the Church, marriage was principally an economic arrangement. Only later was the word *sacramentum* canonized in the Vulgate version of Ephesians 5:32, for the hidden truth which likened the union of husband and wife to the union of Christ and the Church. A new tradition was born then. Increasing opposition to that tradition seems to be emerging in the twenty-first century.

St. Thomas Aquinas (1225–1274) bridged Aristotle's thought with Augustine's by attempting to show how reason and revelation enhanced each other. He began to look at marriage as both a civil and a sacramental institution. He departed from the Augustinian tendency to distrust all pleasure. Aquinas viewed pleasure as natural insofar as it was governed by reason. Aquinas was more optimistic than Augustine, but Aquinas used reason to accept the "procreative rule" for sexuality.[11] This use of reason eventually led to natural law theory, which has strongly influenced Catholic moral theology. In contrast to Protestantism generally, the Catholic tradition has insisted that its moral teaching is based primarily on natural law and not primarily on faith or Scripture. The natural law is understood to be human reason reflecting on human nature. The natural law supposedly explains and justifies the indissolubility of marriage (as well as, among other things, the sinfulness of homosexuality).

Catholic thinking about marriage evolved from at least two distinct views about the difference sex makes. Sex amounted to a deal-breaker, to the extent that some Christians refused to consider a couple married until the man and wife had had sex. Peter Coleman has described the medieval division as follows:

> The situation of the two empires was different. The Western Empire succumbed to the invasions and immigrations of a succession of Germanic and Frankish tribes, and this led to an ambiguous arrangement, because Alaric and some of his successors had already been converted to Christianity, albeit as Arians, before marching south. Clovis, king of the Franks, and eventual ruler of the vast Merovingian empire from the Pyrenees to Bavaria, whose wife Clothilde was a Catholic Christian, was himself baptized at Rheims c. 500. An informal accommodation of the marriage customs was the result, the immigrants observing Germanic rules, the Roman Christians keeping to their own system. The Germanic view of what made a legal marriage was different from the Roman and they did not adopt the patristic preference for virginity and celibacy. Instead

of mere consent between the partners, they looked for evidence that the woman had been transferred into a new kinship unit. Whereas the Roman Christian tradition accepted as valid a marriage in which the partners remained continent, in the Germanic tradition an unconsummated marriage was void. Obviously there was some sense in both views. Only in the eighth century, in the time of Boniface, Charlemagne and Pope Leo I, was a serious attempt at harmonization made and the matter was still being debated in the twelfth century.[12]

Still, many Catholics can sense a certain ambivalence toward sex in their faith. Sex is technically considered good in marriage, although avoidance of sex was long considered even better. For non-Catholic Christians, non-consummation of marriage amounts to a legal justification for divorce. Ian McEwan's novel about the 1962 marriage of a young British couple, *On Chesil Beach* (2007), plays on this law in a particularly moving way.

Throughout the Middle Ages, the Christian churches continued to teach the precepts hammered out in the Patristic age with very little modification, and the legacy of Augustine remained dominant. Until the Reformation, the view that celibacy was the more perfect way and marriage in some ways a second best was attested by the monastic life. In the Western church, especially after the twelfth century, it was also attested by the rule that clergy should not marry.

The medieval church vigorously debated the theological arguments for the sacramentality of marriage; the Catholic theologian Edward Schillebeeckx (b. 1914) sums up these arguments as follows:

The difference between the patristic view of the indissolubility of marriage and the view which came into prominence in the twelfth and thirteenth centuries may be briefly summarized as follows. According to the church Fathers, marriage as a *sacramentum* in the older sense of a "life commitment" or an "oath of fidelity" was something that *might not* be dissolved, since it involved a personal commission to live married life in such a way that the bond of marriage was not broken. The indissolubility of marriage was a task which had to be realized personally. According to the later, scholastic concept of the *sacramentum*, on the other hand—a concept developed in the twelfth and thirteenth centuries especially from the ontological participation in the covenant between Christ and his church—marriage was seen as something that *could* not be dissolved. There was in marriage an objective bond which—once made—was exempt from any action or interference on the part of man. These two visions— the patristic view of marriage as a moral obligation and the scholastic view of marriage as an ontological bond—are not mutually exclusive, but rather mutually implicit. Both the patristic and scholastic doctrines are firmly based on scripture.[13]

An abundance of scholarly literature details the relation between the inheritance of estates and kingdoms and the history of family and marriage in the Middle Ages.[14] In the late twentieth century, the availability of "no-fault" divorce underscored the extent to which marriage had remained an economic arrangement.[15] In the twenty-first century, when women enjoy unprecedented freedom and professional opportunity, divorce suggests itself as an increasingly rational means of terminating an unsatisfactory marriage.[16] Marriage was far from passé in the new century, though, as gay and lesbian couples pressed for the right to enter into it. Although perhaps more an economic and legal desideratum for same-sex couples, marriage simply had to remain a sacred institution, according to the Vatican.

Before moving on, it may be useful to note that marriage had been a sacred institution for Jews during the first twelve centuries of Christianity, when marriages did not take place in a church. The four-post canopy *chuppah* held over the bride and groom anchors the Jewish wedding ceremony. Rife with symbolism, it faces the holy city of Jerusalem, with all four sides open, to represent the hospitality of the biblical Abraham. Some groups, notably the Hasidim, place the *chuppah* outdoors at night in full view of the stars in order to remind the couple of God's promise to Abraham: to make Abraham's descendants as numerous as the stars of the heavens. It is one of various fertility reminders in the ceremony. Catholic weddings likewise reflect concern with fertility. Like Jewish weddings, Catholic ones involve an important belief in the superiority of the husband over his wife. For both Jews and Catholics after the thirteenth century, marriage was a holy act, blessed by God and performed in the sight of a community which took great pains in safeguarding the rights of the new wife.

Divorce

Next I will move to the topics of divorce and annulment—both of which further unpack the topic of Catholic marriage. Although it is widely believed that divorce is forbidden in Roman Catholicism, that is no longer in fact the case. Divorced people may not remarry in the church, as long as their divorced spouse remains alive (at which time the remaining spouse becomes a widow). Divorced Catholics who remarry before the death of the former spouse may not take communion.

In the example of divorce, we can see some Catholic distinctiveness. Although divorce is allowed now, Catholics used to forbid it. Taking its cues from the Vatican, Italian civil law forbade divorce well into the twentieth century (Napoleon briefly legalized civil marriage and divorce in Italy during his short reign at the very end of the eighteenth century; civil marriage was reintroduced in 1865). Released in 1960 to popular acclaim, *Divorce Italian Style* played off of the absence of a divorce law in Italy. The film's narrative follows various schemes hatched by a Sicilian baron to murder his wife of many years so that he can marry a nubile sixteen-year-old. Fefe, the baron, knows Italian civil law upholds the indissolubility of marriage, but he also knows that if he can contrive to have his faithful wife commit adultery and make his subsequent murder of her appear a crime of passion, the criminal law will show mercy and he will soon be free to marry again. Fefe succeeds in luring his wife into adultery. He kills her, subsequently serves three years in prison, and then marries his very young wife (who subsequently cheats on him).

Marriage presented numerous challenges, not the least of which was divorce. Unwanted pregnancy was certainly one of these problems, and, for centuries, abandoned children strengthened Catholic monasteries and convents.[17] Although contraception and abortion may have played large roles in twentieth-century Catholic dissent, I will not devote much space to them here. These roles were already quite well known by the early twenty-first century. I will instead press on with the investigation of marriage disruption.

For centuries, critics have targeted the Catholic idea of marriage. Catholic teachings on human sexuality and marriage played a role in the sixteenth-century Protestant Reformation. Anglicanism began when England's Henry VIII (1491–1547) led the Church of England out of the Roman communion, placing it under his own leadership. Though the direct issue leading to the separation hinged on papal authority, Henry's desire to divorce and remarry played a part in his decision to split from Rome. Unable to divorce and remarry, Catholics dissolving a marriage today may hope for an annulment. It is by no means the case that only traditional or especially devout Catholics file for annulments.

Annulments

Annulments may confuse and confound non-Catholics. Sometimes referred to derivisely as "a Catholic divorce," annulments declare that a marriage was never valid in the first place, which means that a proper divorce is unnecessary.[18] In 2004, presidential candidate John Kerry renewed popular interest in this topic. After an annulment years earlier, Senator Kerry had married the Catholic philanthropist (and widow) Teresa Heinz.

Canon law, the law of the church, codifies the mission of the Church and certain building blocks within the Catholic communion (for example, procedures in the adjudication of conflicts). Canon law is a natural source to consult for guidelines on marriage and, especially, annulments.

Canon 1095 sets out the following categories of people incapable of contracting marriage:

1. those who lack the sufficient use of reason;
2. those who suffer from a grave defect of discretion of judgment concerning the essential matrimonial rights and duties mutually to be handed over and accepted;
3. those who are not able to assume the essential obligations of marriage for causes of a psychic nature.[19]

Note the importance of children. According to Canon 1096, "For matrimonial consent to exist, the contracting parties must be at least not ignorant that marriage is a permanent partnership between a man and a woman ordered to the procreation of offspring by means of some sexual cooperation." Obviously, gay marriage does not qualify (although barren heterosexual couples who adopt children do qualify). Catholics see child-rearing as the goal of marriage.

Gay marriage roiled Catholic leaders in the early twenty-first century. Spain, an overwhelmingly Catholic country, legalized gay marriage in 2005. And Canada, whose Catholics comprise over a third of the entire population, followed suit in 2005, much to the consternation of Catholic leaders, who had strongly urged Catholic voters to reject such measures. Massachusetts, an American state with one of the highest percentages of Roman Catholics, led the way to a gradual mindshift in the United States. Gay Catholics may marry and divorce one another in parts of the world, but annulments will remain out of the question.

Funerals

Civic or secular funerals may seem paltry in comparison to any sort of ecclesiastical burial. Cultural Catholics and their families, recognizing as much, find another incentive to maintain an affiliation to the Church of Rome. As meaningful as a Catholic funeral may be to a family, it is worth noting the relative lack of ritual when compared to Judaism.

Philippe Ariès has argued persuasively that Western attitudes toward death and dying have shifted significantly since the late Middle Ages.[20] Catholic culture differs from Protestant culture most particularly here. Craig Koslofsky has usefully highlighted the process by which Luther effectively overhauled the social response to death in Germany. After Luther, burials often took place at night, in private. What had been a quite public affair became a family matter. Here we can see a marked contrast with Roman Catholic funerals, especially the funeral of a cardinal, bishop, or public figure. And despite Luther's heated opposition to Purgatory, Catholics continue to believe in it.[21]

According to Edward Muir, "In effect the Protest Reformation attempted to eliminate the obligations of the living toward the dead, but in so doing it made the dead more dangerous and more marginal to the living."[22] The ceremonies attendant on death became more of a burden than a benefit for the living, and so the living followed Luther in his effort to eliminate the need for funeral rituals. On the one hand, the living no longer felt obligated to pay for funeral Masses for the deceased: This represented a financial relief. On the other hand, the living no longer felt that they could help the deceased or intercede on their behalf. This left the living feeling more separated from the dead.

Although it would be an overstatement to say that contemporary Roman Catholics, who can and do still pay for Masses for the dead, feel obligated to remember the dead, the contemporary Mass invites, indeed exhorts, the faithful to remember and pray for the departed. In regard to remembering the dead, Roman Catholics would seem to resemble Jews more than Lutherans. Particularly on All Saints' Day (1 November) and All Souls' Day (2 November), the dead seem to have a legitimate expectation that the living will mind them, remember them, pray for them. (Not all efforts to remember the dead need be called or considered religious; the *Washington Post*, for example, features a regular page on which the living mark the anniversary of the death of a loved one and a number of American towns display memorial plaques listing the names of townsmen who died in one war or another.) Catholic relations with the dead do not rise to the level of Chinese ancestor worship; rather, Catholic piety aims to create and sustain an imaginative solidarity with the deceased faithful.

Roman Catholics believe in the resurrection not only of souls but also of bodies. In part for this reason, cremation was long forbidden to Catholics. Pope John XXIII changed that tradition and officially allowed cremation in 1963. And it used to be that people who had committed suicide were subsequently refused church burials; the Church relaxed this rule in the late twentieth century, due no doubt to some extent to a deeper clinical understanding of mental illness.

Catholics differ from Jews with regard to funerals; Catholics work with fewer rules governing the actual burial. Whereas Jews rush to bury the body within two days, Catholics do not. Samuel Heilman has written:

> While most Jews who die these days are prepared for their last rites by professional undertakers, Jewish tradition considers these final concerns with the body as a matter of profound religious and community obligation—something that should not be transferred to those who share neither faith nor fellowship with the dead. This preparation called *tahara* (purification) for burial, which traditional Judaism considers the only appropriate disposal of the body, becomes the responsibility of the women and men of the *Chevra Kaddisha*, literally the "holy fellowship." These are Jews who, although not immediate relatives of the deceased, come from the same (broadly defined) community as the dead for the bereaved. In creating the *Chevra*, Jewish tradition has tried to ensure that each Jew's body and the spirit that departs it will receive their final touch from the hands of those for whom the disposition of his or her earthly remains has religious and spiritual meaning. . . .[23]

Roman Catholics do not follow the Jewish practice of sitting shiva either; Catholic mourning tends to take its own, independent forms. It is the tradition of Kaddish that Catholics might possibly be said to follow; Catholic prayers for the dead, however, are not expected to reach as far into previous family generations as Jewish prayers for the dead often do.

Funerals take different forms in different lands (for example, in an Irish wake you can find the departed dressed formally and seated in a living room chair), but the funerals tend to invite, rather than discourage, broad participation. The 2005 funeral of Pope John Paul II was a gigantic media spectacle—and a public performance of a Catholic sacrament as well.

We have already considered officially withholding the sacrament of baptism, a more unusual phenomenon than the withholding of a Catholic burial. Cultural Catholics may routinely arrange for or request a Catholic funeral. The Church will usually, although not always, honor such requests. (Even Jacqueline Kennedy Onassis received a Catholic burial, despite having been denounced by Pope Paul VI as "a public sinner" for having married a divorced man, Aristotle Onassis.) Let's now take a look at the criteria under which the Church justifies denying someone a Catholic burial.

Denial of Church Funerals

With regard to those who may not be given Christian burial, Canon Law expressly forbids ecclesiastical funerals to three classes of Catholics:

1. Notorious apostates, heretics and schismatics (CIC c. 751 gives definitions for apostasy, heresy, and schism). The offense must be publicly known. One who ceased the practice of Catholic religion without formally abandoning the Church does not fall under this heading, and should not be denied Catholic funeral rites.

2. Those who have commanded that their body be cremated for reasons contrary to Christian faith. Officially forbidden for centuries, cremation is now permissible, so long as "it does not demonstrate a denial of faith in the resurrection of the body." The Eastern Code permits cremation "provided it does not obscure the preference of the Church for the burial of bodies and that scandal is avoided." In the Order of Christian Funerals approved for use in the United States, guidelines have been provided for funeral liturgies involving the cremated remains of the deceased.

3. Other manifest sinners who cannot be granted ecclesiastical funerals without public scandal. The term manifest indicates that the person must be publicly known to have lived in a state of grave sin. For example, some who might qualify are those involved in the drug trade and those who have admitted to murder. It is also required that having an ecclesiastical funeral

would provide public scandals among the Christian faithful. Only when both conditions are verified would Catholic funeral rites be prohibited. Persons who have divorced and remarried do not come under this heading. Nor are persons who have committed suicide included under this heading. According to most medical authorities, a person who commits suicide is considered deprived at least temporarily of the full possession of his faculties.[24]

The Church acknowledges doubtful cases and handles them liberally. If the deceased has given any sign of repentance, he is not to be denied a Catholic funeral. Such a sign of repentance might be summoning a priest or making an act of perfect contrition. These signs show that the deceased in some way preserved an attachment to the Church. The dramatic climax of Evelyn Waugh's *Brideshead Revisited* centers on the patriarch's deathbed. Despite entreaties to make the sign of the cross, and thus express his allegiance to the Catholic Church and also his desire for forgiveness, he consistently refuses. Then, just a moment before his expires, he wordlessly struggles to bless himself. The burial of the renowned philosopher Ludwig Wittgenstein (d. 1956) took place under similarly dramatic circumstances.

Despite discussion among priests and bishops to deny communion to cultural Catholics such as John and Teresa Kerry (because of the Kerrys' reluctance to fight *Roe v. Wade*), canon law would seem to prohibit denying a traditional Catholic burial to a cultural Catholic.

Mass

In different form, the Tridentine Mass dates to the sixteenth century.[25] We don't know much about the shape of earlier Masses.[26] The highly scripted ritual of a traditional or vernacular Mass can not only soothe individuals (think of the enjoyment brought on by repetition of music or poetry) but create communities. Durkheim reasoned: "It is by uttering the same cry, pronouncing the same word, or performing the same gesture in regard to some object that they can become and feel themselves to be in unison."[27]

A plan by Benedict XVI to authorize the widespread return of the Latin Mass, despite concerns that parts of it are anti-Semitic, provoked a backlash among senior clergy in Britain and, according to some, threatened to divide the Catholic Church worldwide. The sixteenth-century Tridentine Mass—which includes references to "perfidious" Jews—was abandoned in 1969 and replaced with liturgy in local languages, to make worship more accessible to the bulk of churchgoers. Since 1984, the Vatican allowed limited use of the Latin Mass, on the condition that Catholics request permission from local bishops, who did not always consent. But the Pope announced in 2007 that he was prepared to release a long-awaited document liberalizing the use of the Mass, which some clergy feared would also limit the Church's dialogue with Jews and Muslims. On 7 July 2007, Benedict XVI issued the four-page apostolic letter to the world's bishops entitled "Summorum Pontificum."

Cardinal Cormac Murphy-O'Connor, the leader of the Roman Catholic Church in England and Wales, had written to the pope to say that no liturgical changes were needed. There had been months of debate about the impending statement within the higher echelons of the Church. Cardinals, bishops, and Jewish leaders expressed concern over the text of the "old" Mass, which has passages, recited every Good Friday, which say Jews live in "blindness" and "darkness," and pray "the Lord our God may take the veil from their hearts and that they also may acknowledge our Lord Jesus Christ."

Nonetheless, the pope sent the document to all bishops, accompanied by a personal letter from him. The pope declared that the Mass celebrated according to the 1962 Roman Missal (the "Tridentine rite") should be made available to every parish that wanted it. At the same time, the new Roman Missal, introduced in 1970, would remain the ordinary mode of Catholic worship.

Some had feared that the papal ruling might be the precursor of further changes to the reforms approved by the Second Vatican Council, which called for the Mass to be said in local languages, for the priest to face the congregation, and for the use of lay readers. Latin could still be used to recite the Mass, but the "new" Mass was to be used, not the "old" Mass. After 2007, to celebrate the old Latin Mass, a priest no longer had to obtain permission from the local bishop. Cardinal Tarcisio Bertone, the Vatican secretary of state, said bishops would still have a "central role"—but echoed the Vatican's new enthusiasm for the old Mass by calling it a "great treasure" of the Church.

Pope Benedict's move was widely seen as an attempt to reach out to an ultra-traditionalist and schismatic group, the Society of St. Pius X, and bring it back into the Vatican fold. The late Archbishop Marcel Lefebvre founded the society in 1969 in Switzerland, in opposition to the Second Vatican Council's reforms. Pope John Paul II excommunicated Lefebvre in 1988, but then, shortly before John Paul's death, invited Lefebvre back. The Society of St. Pius X rejected the old Mass and several teachings of Vatican II.

The liturgical shift portended wider implications for church life. Proponents of the old Mass tend to oppose the laity's increased role in parish life, collaboration with other Christians, and dialogue with Jews and Muslims.[28] Although the 1962 Roman Missal no longer included references to "perfidious Jews," it did request prayers to convert Jews and include a reference to "the blindness of that people."

The emotional and liturgical climax of the Mass is communion, the distribution of the Eucharist to Catholics in good standing. We have already examined the possibility of being barred from baptism; now let's turn to keeping Catholics out of communion. Support (such as it was) for *Roe v. Wade* prompted several American bishops to bar John and Teresa Kerry from communion in their respective dioceses in 2003. Sex underlay this problem, and sex has raised a similar problem for a different group—those who support gay rights (of course, divorced Catholics are to abstain from the Eucharist as well). Wearers of the rainbow sash, the symbol for a group of homosexual Catholics which protests Church teachings on homosexuality, were not to receive communion, said the head of the Holy See's Congregation for Divine Worship and the Sacraments. In February 2005, Cardinal Francis Arinze declared, "Rainbow Sash wearers are showing their opposition to church teaching on a major issue of natural law and so disqualify themselves from being given holy Communion." The cardinal, however, refused to elaborate on his statement.

Subsequently, members of Rainbow Sash announced that they would present themselves, wearing rainbow sashes, for communion on Pentecost Sunday in cathedrals and churches throughout America to proclaim their active sexuality. While Cardinal Francis George, the archbishop of Chicago, said he would refuse communion to Rainbow Sash wearers, Cardinal Roger Mahony of Los Angeles notified Rainbow Sash that his cathedral would welcome sash wearers and give them communion.

Both the structure of Mass and permission to partake in its Eucharistic climax came under debate in the early twenty-first century. Cultural Catholics largely espoused liberal positions on both matters. The second, eligibility for the Eucharist, threatened many Catholics personally, and I'll turn to the subject of Eucharist anxiety in the next chapter.

Emotional Needs

Although Greek, Russian, and other Orthodox Christians share the same range of seven sacraments, still it remains that these sacraments begin to explain the distinctiveness of Catholic identity. For this reason, the sacraments suggest themselves for scrutiny in a study of what binds cultural Catholics to an institution with which they are sometimes fundamentally at odds.

These rites have persisted even in the face of social or governmental efforts to suppress them. Shortly after the French revolution, for example, the French state expropriated baptism, marriage, and funerals. The political anthropologist David Kertzer, drawing on the work of various scholars, has observed, "The new rulers substituted the Declaration of Rights for the Bible as the sacrament to which allegiance should be sworn; revolutionary hymns replaced those of the church; and festivals marking the great events of the revolution replaced local saints' day processions."[29] Nearly a century and a half later, the Nazis tried to do the same thing. "Quite a bit of effort . . . went into trying to wrest marriage and funeral rites from the churches, but with limited success."[30] Some of this resistance no doubt has to do with what Kertzer has called "the lasting importance of childhood rites."[31] (I will explore this idea in detail in Chapter 7.) Part of this has to do with the intuitive and enduring need of communities to mark rites of passage in ritualistic ways. Potentially stronger than any governmental force is apathy or inertia; when people just don't care any more about these rituals, the Church will have a much graver problem than it does with protesters.

Catholic experience of these rituals has evolved. Catholics baptizing their children no longer have to bestow a saint's name upon the infant, for example. Catholics gained this freedom in the twentieth century. Catholics marrying in the twenty-first century enjoy more freedom to alter their vows (in a less patriarchal direction). Funerals have become more liberal as well, as suicides can now be buried on Church property, and the faithful may elect cremation.

Cultural Catholics distinguish themselves from traditional Catholic Christians more by validating certain outward signs of behavior than by professing coherent beliefs or by reciting scripture. The sacraments unite both cultural and traditional Catholics.

With regard to baptisms, weddings, and funerals, it's not exactly the case that cultural Catholics jump in line without being directed to do so (as in, for example, processions). Without question, Catholics are expected to participate in the sacraments of baptism and extreme unction (or the "blessing of the sick," as it came be called after Vatican II). And yet Catholics are supposed to do plenty of other things; why do cultural Catholics cling to these distinctive rites of passage? For one thing, the secular equivalent of filing for a birth certificate, getting married before a Justice of the Peace, and a civil burial, lack the pomp and depth of the religious rituals. Note that these rites require mediation—a priest performs these three rites, so these rites cannot be analogized to cults of the saints. Various scholars have noted that lay Catholics have often acted independently of the Vatican when it comes to revering saints. In a study of martyrdom and its psychological effects on the living, for example, one scholar has written, "In the late sixteenth and early seventeenth centuries, rather than waiting for papal approval, Catholics assumed the saintly status of the recent martyrs from whom they sought heavenly aid."[32] And various scholars have noted that lay Catholics have harnessed sacraments to satisfy their own deep emotional needs: In the seventeenth century, the Inquisitor of the Holy Office of Udine noted that some women, with the approval of the local parish priest, would take a stillborn child from its mother, pretend to resuscitate the tiny corpse for a few moments through recourse to the Virgin Mary, and then quickly baptize the infant before it expired again.[33] "Emotional needs" must be the best reason why cultural Catholics will keep the Church in business generally and keep asking for the three rituals outlined here specifically.

Chapter 4

A Brief Sketch of Catholic Dissent in the United States

Breaking from the Catholic Church in the early sixteenth century, Martin Luther championed the authority of the Scriptures over the Vatican—*sola scriptura*, as the movement came to be called. Catholics have never been a *sola scriptura* people. Mediation broadly characterizes Catholic culture: Individuals don't so much contact God directly as appeal to him through a priest (for example, going to confession), a saint (for example, praying for a miracle), or the community of believers (for example, gaining salvation collectively). Like Jews, Catholics read Scriptures through the interpretive lens supplied by many centuries of previous leaders within their own tradition. The essential point to be taken here is that Catholics believe, at least in principal, in the importance of sticking together generally and in falling in line behind their leader (if only ideally). Even if Jesus never mentioned the words "pope" or "priest," Catholics maintained a tradition of honoring both popes and priests.

The Vatican is God's gatekeeper in Catholic thinking; while working through the Vatican is neither a necessary nor a sufficient condition for God's attention, Rome is a force to be reckoned with. Even though Catholics may increasingly disagree with the Vatican, Catholics still instinctively think of it when puzzling over the Bible or in deciding which side to take in moral debates. Again, Catholics resemble Jews, who rely on a long tradition of reading Scriptures in a particular way or thinking through ethical dilemmas in the context of what previous rabbis have concluded.

It would be ridiculous to try to speak for all Catholics in the United States, much less to nail down pat summaries of Catholic culture in specific contexts. That said, we can discern certain patterns of Catholic belief which indicate, however broadly, cultural tendencies. What

Catholics think of immigration, for example, or capitalism, or racism, or the equality of the sexes, makes sense to the extent that ordinary Catholics take some of their basic life-orienting cues from the Vatican. The extraordinary outpouring of emotion upon the occasion of Pope John Paul II's death, and perhaps more importantly, the media attention focused on the event, speak to the instinctive tendency of even occasional Catholics to think of the pontiff as a beacon.

Like Jews, Catholics in nineteenth-century America found themselves often despised or distrusted by Protestants, who were in the majority. Nonetheless, American Catholics worked in concert to establish a recognizable way of life on these shores, even though Catholic culture could vary considerably from, say, Germany to Italy—two of the home countries from which many immigrants arrived on the East Coast. (California missions, built by Franciscans, spread Catholic faith and a significantly similar Catholic culture through the early American West.) The experience of being different from Protestants strengthened a sense of solidarity among Catholics, even if old ethnic bonds remained vibrant. Adoration of the Eucharist, public recitation of the rosary, and public processions could unite otherwise (ethnically) disparate Catholic cultures. Generally speaking, Catholics obeyed their nearby authorities (nuns in parochial schools, priests in the local parish, and bishops who presided over a diocese). Catholics felt pride in their religious identity and often cared what non-Catholics thought of them.

By the twenty-first century, the bloom was off the rose. It was considerably more difficult for Americans to romanticize their faith (think of the popular 1940s film *The Bells of Saint Mary's*) than it had been even in the 1960s. Old ethnic identities (Poles, Irish, Italians, Germans, for example) had also faded to a significant extent. American Catholic culture moved from obedience to dissent (although perhaps neither has ever been unqualified). In this chapter I approach the history of Catholic dissent topically, focusing on reasons why some Catholics might take pride in expressing defiance of the Church. I also focus on the twentieth century, which means I leave out a good deal of interesting history.

Through a top-down approach, the Catholic hierarchy continues to try to shape the instincts and attitudes of lay Catholics throughout the world. Topics under consideration may vary from age to age and place to place. According to the Catholic historian Jay Dolan, three issues in particular dominated the public outreach of American bishops in the 1980s and 1990s: the threat of nuclear war; the national economy and how it affected the dignity of each person; and abortion.[1] The top-down strategy still operates, but the bottom-up force has gathered considerable steam. Particularly when it comes to sex, ordinary Catholics often disagree with the voice at the top. Other thinkers have noticed that American Catholics have become quite secular, but a more illuminating observation would be that Catholics have become more like Jews who take pride in their nonobservance. "Secular" *tout court* suggests an indifference or a distance which fails to capture the extent to which cultural Catholics may define themselves in terms of the Holy See.

I will now introduce examples which serve as both central sources of twenty-first-century dissent and burning reasons why cultural Catholics may take pride in disagreeing with the Vatican. These examples, taken together, will provide a brief sketch of recent Catholic dissent and a glimpse of the arteries of cultural Catholicism.

Americanism

At the end of the nineteenth century, Pope Leo XIII saw fit to denounce a new sin, which he named "Americanism." He deemed America a relativistic culture in which a variety of wrongdoings found moral justification. So it was that America came to emblematize the fear of modernity. American Catholics at the dawn of the twentieth century may have felt shame that the Vatican named an ominous, emerging trend after them, but twenty-first-century Catholics might, in retrospect, take pride in the chastisement.

It was a group of Irish priests, interestingly enough, who generated in America the problem to which Leo XIII reacted. The great potato famine in Ireland (1845–1849) led to a mass exodus of Irish people to America. The Irish in quick order enjoyed a plurality of bishops, because of the size of the Irish community in the United States. These bishops, who had chafed under British rule in Ireland, championed the view that freedom of religion was a nobler idea than simple religious tolerance.

Leo XIII (d. 1903) feared that some Catholic leaders had gone too far in the attempt to assimilate into secular American culture. Archbishop John Ireland of St. Paul had opposed the move of other bishops to pull Catholic children out of public schools. Ireland embraced American social culture, built of course upon religious tolerance, and blessed the idea of Catholic children attending non-Catholic schools.

Ireland supported the participation of Cardinal Gibbons in an 1892
event in Chicago which had featured Christians, Hindus, and Muslims
working together publicly in an affirmation of "basic religious truths."
Although Gibbons had obtained permission from Leo XIII himself to
take part in the Chicago Parliament of Religions, Leo apparently had a
change of heart later—perhaps because of the shock of Catholics and
Protestants sharing in public worship. The idea of Catholics respecting
other religions or worshipping with non-Catholics was regarded as the
sin of "indifferentism." Leo's aversion to Cardinal Gibbons' outreach
spawned the denunciation of "Americanism" in the 1899 letter *Testem
Benevolentiae*. Leo averred that supernatural virtues, such as faith,
hope, and charity, outranked natural virtues, such as a desire to get
along well with foreigners.

Eamon Duffy has remarked that, "The continuing eagerness of
'progressive' Catholics to participate fully in American life and to inte-
grate Catholic values as fully as possible into the 'American way' led
many to fear a dilution of Catholic truth."[2] In the example of these
so-called "progressive Catholics" we can find the seeds of what I am
calling in this book "cultural Catholicism." Two distinct camps were
divided over the question of the extent to which to adapt Catholic
teachings to the American way of life. The divisions between these two
camps would only grow, especially in the last three decades of the
twentieth century.

At the end of the nineteenth century, women and homosexuals had
not even appeared on the moral radar screen. The anti-Semitic Pope
Pius X had not even begun his reign yet. The idea of ordaining women
priests, campaigning for gay marriage, or apologizing to Jews for an
abuse of power would have seemed preposterous. But the same controversial impetus to adapt an old faith to a new culture was there;
the same resolve to respect rather than dismiss or distrust what was
going on outside a church or local parish was already in evidence in
the actions of Cardinal Gibbons (or in the influence of John Carroll
[d. 1815], who had championed religious liberty as the first American
bishop).

But why single out America? Other countries had suddenly become
modern, such as England. And other countries, such as Germany, also
contained Protestant/Catholic religious divisions. America stood out
as unique because it had been conceived of as a nation devoted to
religious freedom, as opposed to religious tolerance (which character-
ized the German states). Already in the late nineteenth century, Roman
Catholics constituted the largest faith community in the United States

(which is not to say that there were or are more Catholics than Protestants in America). And so America offered itself as a convenient hook on which to hang the sin of openness to new moral ideas. Although it is true that the Church had not fared well in previous trips down such a road (think of the French Enlightenment, with its hostility toward clergy, or the *Kulturkampfen* in Germany, which produced similarly negative social conditions for the Church), still it remains that America was singled out for prominence in the realm of non-observance of orthodoxy. Anxiety and even anger over worshipping publicly with non-Catholics is not over; it surfaced in the aftermath of 9/11, when various Americans thought it would be a good idea to put officials from various faith communities together on a stage or a football field, to bring healing to a fractured nation.[3] The problem underlying "Americanism" has not yet receded into the past.

What bears emphasizing here is the importance of what a Catholic cares about. Feeling indifference to the religion of the next-door neighbors or the children at your own child's school could lead to a dangerous escalation. Maybe someday you would show indifference to the religion of your children or the spouses your children take. Maybe someday you would show indifference to the sexual orientation of your co-workers or dinner hosts: whether they were attached to someone of the same sex or the opposite sex might matter nothing to you, just so long as your friends were happy. Further, you might someday feel indifference to the gender of the local parish priest—whether the priest were a man or a woman would hardly concern you, so long as the priest got the job done. And so on. The duties of Catholicism extended to the emotional life, and Catholics could be judged by what they cared about and fought for.

It should not seem far-fetched to assert that the invasion of personal conscience by an institution might somehow shape marriage choices. In Chapter 7 of this book, I will press on Freud's theory of the family romance to suggest that part of the reason people remain Catholic is because of a sense of loyalty to and (not necessarily sexual) attraction toward one's parents. If your parents really cared about Catholic self-identification, you might as well. Or at least you might feel as though you *should* care—this ambivalence is also worthy of acknowledgment and exploration.

Note well the genesis here in what I consider a crucial moment in the arc of cultural Catholicism: It was the Vatican that opposed an American decision, and not the other way around. In the rest of this chapter, we'll see for the most part a different dynamic: The Vatican will take a position and then American theologians, religious, or lay people will dissent. Let's not forget the larger picture, though. Americans are doing their own thing, and the Vatican is, in its way, reacting. Upon beginning his papacy, Benedict XVI stated that one of his goals was to fill the empty churches of Europe. Although he did not mention America then, many cultural Catholics in America would have felt some sort of reproach upon reading the statement.

The account of Americanism I offer here was more than religious indifferentism, although I have focused on that indifferentism. Americanism involved the belief that natural virtues counted morally for as much as supernatural, that ordinary believers (not just bishops) could receive the Holy Spirit, and that the active life is superior to the contemplative life. The Vatican condemned these views as heretical. Although I do not mean to argue that cultural Catholicism began in America or is unique to it, the sin of "Americanism" makes it a little easier to understand why America seemed fertile ground for such a mindset to grow. Cultural Catholics do not, for the most part, link themselves together in a network. They may recognize one another when they meet, but they don't necessarily feel a need to organize. They understand each other when speaking not only about failing to qualify as a devout Catholic but also satisfaction in not fitting that category.

Lastly, Leo XIII should not take all the blame here. In 1864 Pius IX issued his infamous *Syllabus of Errors*, which, among other things, denounced the freedom of conscience and new ideas generally. My focus on the twentieth century explains the neglect of Pius IX; in no way do I mean to imply, though, that reasons cultural Catholics list to distance themselves from the Vatican are limited to the twentieth century (think, for example, of the trial of Galileo). It's just that more and more Catholics wanted to emphasize respect for other religions in the late twentieth century. Many Catholics didn't want their culture or their theology to be so insistent on its own superiority. This shift manifested itself in various ways. In the 1960s, for example, Pope Paul VI gave to Mary the title Mother of the Church, despite the fact that the Second Vatican Council had dragged its feet in this matter, fearing further separation from the rest of redeemed humanity. Paul VI also delayed the Decree on Religious Liberty (the Council had taken a stance not too far from the one Leo XIII had decried a century earlier). That is to say that new reasons for Catholic dissent seem to keep popping up, long after Pope Leo XIII.

Although no one has yet said it, American Catholics who criticize the Vatican may feel themselves part of a self-fulfilling prophecy. Dissenters predict doom and gloom for their Church and then congratulate themselves when they read press reports about the Church being in crisis. And dissenters may well take the position that history has vindicated them. As Mass attendance declines and Catholic pride diminishes, cultural Catholics may feel that they have the numbers on their side. At the very least, cultural Catholics in the late twentieth century were not simply moral relativists or lazy, but rather well-meaning Americans who wanted to get along with everyone.

Sex

Americanism has nothing to do with natural law, a distinctively Catholic idea, but sex does. Much of Catholic dissent in the twenty-first century springs from suspicion that the "natural law" is not really very natural after all. It would be all too easy to dismiss the sexual protests of cultural Catholics as self-indulgent, but such rebellions may actually stand on a compelling rationality which deserves respect. In any event, the sheer volume of dissenters in the sexual arena should prompt serious reflection on what disgruntled American Catholics say. Thomas Fox, the editor of the *National Catholic Reporter*, wrote in 1995: "Most reflective, discerning, and open-minded Catholics . . . cannot accept Catholic sexual morality as pronounced in strict absolutes. Many end up walking away."[4] The point of my book is to focus on those who sort of walk away and sort of don't, which is to say that Thomas Fox and I may be talking about different groups. Cultural Catholics as a group lack a clear boundary.

Let's take a brief look at specific poles of opposition to the central authority of the Vatican in matters of sexual morality.

Birth Control

One of the interesting conclusions to be drawn from the birth control controversy is just how very important sex is to people. While this insight might seem utterly obvious, it is important to remember that religions which demand much of their members tend to flourish. It is one thing for a religion to make people give up caffeine, alcohol, pork, shellfish and much more, but apparently another thing to demand married couples to sacrifice some sexual activity. In the final analysis, it may be that Catholicism lost churchgoers not because of *Humanae Vitae*'s rejection of birth control but because the Church did not enforce the doctrine.

The 1968 encyclical *Humanae Vitae* unleashed a social crisis, according to various Church historians. It had been widely expected that "the birth control encyclical" would overturn a previous encyclical (*Casti Connubii*, from 1933) and allow Roman Catholics to use the birth control pill, which had just been invented in the United States a few years earlier. When Pope Paul VI dramatically took matters into his own hands and rejected the favorable vote of bishops he had appointed to study the matter (the vote of the bishops had not been unanimous), Catholics in Western Europe and North America voiced their disappointment in newspapers and magazines. This marks the first time American Catholics felt comfortable criticizing the Vatican publicly; the dissent was not limited to the laity but also included some priests and nuns.

In *Humanae Vitae*, the Church reaffirmed the moral legitimacy of what is called "the rhythm method." The Church considers this form of birth control natural. As *Casti Connubii* had stated:

> Nor are those considered as acting against nature who in the married state use their right in the proper manner, although on account of natural reasons either of time or of certain defects, new life cannot be brought forth. For in matrimony as well as in the use of matrimonial rights there are also secondary ends, such as mutual aid, the cultivating of mutual love, and the quieting of concupiscence, which husband and wife are not forbidden to consider as long as they are subordinated to the primary end and so long as the intrinsic nature of that act is preserved.[5]

In contrast to a distant, authoritative edict, the Church here adopted a "personalist" approach to human sexuality, which represented something new. In *Humanae Vitae*, the Church pressed further the "personalist" approach, voicing concerns about the dignity of women in a new world in which sexual relations threatened to become even further divorced from traditional marriage. Women could find themselves used by men who saw them simply as sex objects, and the Church wanted to avoid this misery.

Perhaps in part to understand better recent changes in the secular world, Pope Paul VI had appointed an advisory commission of theologians, scientists, doctors, and married couples. The commission, operating in confidentiality, urged the Vatican to allow birth control in certain circumstances. Although Paul could have changed church tradition on this matter, he chose not to. As is now quite well known, Paul's move created a firestorm of dissent; a number of priests were forced to leave the priesthood because of vocal opposition to *Humanae Vitae*, which was, after all, the pope's teaching.

The theologian Charles Curran of Catholic University published a public denunciation of *Humanae Vitae*, one signed by six hundred Catholic intellectuals from around the United States.[6] Father Curran argued that the individual conscience should prevail in this quite intimate issue. Two months later, the "Winnipeg Statement" of the Canadian Conference of Catholic Bishops took the position that those Catholics who disagreed with the encyclical should not be pushed out of the Church. Once again, dissent was given a home in Catholic culture, it seemed.

At a time when Americans were increasingly rejoicing in a new-found sexual freedom, the Vatican warned against negative consequences. Of course, the Vatican never even considered the possibility that an unmarried couple could morally use contraceptives. What the Vatican condemned was the use of *artificial* contraception (again, the natural "rhythm method" incurred no moral disapproval) in the context of a marriage. The number of Americans who had sex before marrying increased steadily throughout the 1960s and 1970s, in part because of the availability of a fairly reliable contraceptive pill and in part because of a rapidly changing social culture in which young adults could enjoy pre-marital sex without the penalty of social ostracism.

American Catholics increasingly felt torn between their faith and their secular culture. By the late 1990s, various polls showed that over ninety per cent of Americans who self-identified as Roman Catholic morally approved of the use of birth control not only within a marriage but also as a thoughtful component of pre-marital relationships.

Increasingly, the appeal to nature in order to condemn artificial birth control fails to persuade many cultural Catholics. It is one thing to obey a rule just for the sake of obeying it (and thus feeling more tied into the Church, more obedient to the pope), but it is another thing entirely to make yourself agree with the logic of the rule. The Vatican's logic would seem to rest on what philosophers call the naturalistic fallacy: Because a penis in a vagina *can* create a baby, then a penis in a vagina *should* create a baby (or should at least be given full opportunity to do so). Humans intervene in nature in any number of ways, though, and don't feel immoral about, say, stopping tidal waves or interrupting bodily cancers. That heterosexual intercourse can lead to a baby doesn't strike everyone as sufficient reason why it should always.

Beyond that, animals defecate and copulate in public: This "natural" behavior can land humans in prison. And so it is not true that the natural world always serves as a reliable model for human sexual morality. Lastly, we now know that some animals demonstrate homosexual attraction (for example, foxes, hyenas, and mice). What seems natural to Church authorities may obscure a political agenda—an agenda which can change over time. In the twenty-first century, many cultural Catholics take pride in siding with gay and lesbian causes and, less controversially, in approving of artificial birth control for both married and unmarried partners.

John Paul II and Benedict XVI never wavered in support of *Humanae Vitae*, but relatively few pastors or priests enforced it on the parish level. It cannot easily be said that John Paul and Benedict deserve blame here, for permissiveness works not only to eliminate rules but also, sometimes, to erode personal and group identity.

Abortion

Early Christian moralists argued over whether abortion amounted to homicide because they could not agree on when human life began. Augustine condemned both birth control and abortion because both interfered with the natural relation between sexual intercourse and procreation. It is worth noting that Augustine did not consider early abortions homicide. He wrote in *On Exodus*:

> The great question about the soul is not hastily decided by unargued and rash judgment; the law does not prove that the act [abortion] pertains to homicide, for there cannot yet be said to be a live soul in a body that lacks sensation when it is not formed in flesh, and so not yet endowed with sense.[7]

Some seven centuries later, the second lynchpin of the Catholic moral tradition, Thomas Aquinas, confirmed Augustine's authority. Until the fetus is "ensouled" or "animated," it is not a person, and the question of homicide does not apply. Aquinas was convinced that the fetus did not receive a soul until sometime after conception. For centuries, a certain unofficial view circulated: Males received souls forty days after conception and females at eighty days. Cultural Catholics and others might predictably object to this position as one which unfairly privileges males over females. Beyond that, cultural Catholics could find in Augustine and Aquinas allies in the moral defense of embryonic stem cell research, which ignited broad controversy in the first decade of the twenty-first century (I'll have more to say about this later in the chapter). The Vatican condemned such research and perhaps left the impression of unanimity. Well-informed Catholics, while not in a position to invoke the authority of Augustine or Aquinas here, may note the historic discord with interest and subsequently feel something less than full confidence that the Church is right this time.

Skipping ahead several centuries: Pope Pius IX published *Apostolicace sedis* in 1869 and required excommunication for abortions performed at any stage of pregnancy. Just a few years later, in 1875, scientists would determine that fetal life begins at the moment a sperm pierces an egg. This scientific finding seemed to provide stronger support for Pius IX's position, which of course could never be proven scientifically. There was just something convenient about the equation of ensoulment with conception. And why not err on the safe side? In time, certain exceptions to this abortion rule would be granted. Abortion was prohibited in two cases: ectopic pregnancy (when the egg became ominously anchored in the fallopian tube) and a cancerous uterus. These two exceptions came into force in 1924, at the behest of the Belgian Jesuit Arthur Vermeersch. Abortions were not permitted in the case of rape, despite controversy on this question.

So far in this section, we've seen internal disagreement about the universal Catholic position, if you will, over the criminality of abortion. Eventually, of course, that disagreement ended and the official Catholic position emerged. The United States criminal law returned American Catholics to a much earlier historical debate over whether abortion amounts to murder (of a fetus). In 1973, the US Supreme Court handed down its monumental decision in the case of *Roe v. Wade*. This decision legalized abortion under certain circumstances. The Vatican denounced the ruling. American Catholics would subsequently be reminded repeatedly that abortion is anathema.

In the 7 October 1984 issue of the *New York Times*, an advertisement sponsored by Catholics for a Free Choice (www.catholicsforchoice.org) called for open dialogue among American Catholics on the issue of abortion. The Vatican commanded the twenty-four signers to retract publicly their statements or face dismissal from their congregations. The Vatican made clear its distaste for public dissent.

Pope John Paul II issued the encyclical *Evangelium Vitae* in 1995; it condemned abortion and capital punishment as lying together on a spectrum of moral atrocities. The encyclical amounted to an urgent plea to reverse the "culture of death" overtaking the world, specifically by opposing abortion and euthanasia (John Paul also mentioned the immorality of using embryos in medical experiments, a practice which would later feed the public debate over the morality of stem cell research). John Paul lamented "a profound crisis of culture" which had misled many and caused otherwise good people to lose their moral bearings.

Abortion debates generate animosity and division between American Catholics. Of course, some Catholics publicly support *Roe v. Wade*. Particularly with regard to Catholic politicians, Americans have heard individual Catholics declare private abhorrence of the act but public resolve to allow women to make the choice for themselves, individually. It is no secret that the Vatican dislikes this *via media* of Catholic politicians such as Geraldine Ferraro, John Kerry, and Rudy Giuliani.

Beginning in the early 1970s, most conservative Roman Catholics voted Republican, in large part because of the Republican Party's opposition to abortion. In the early twenty-first century, however, more and more conservative Catholics began to rethink the allegiance to the Republican Party, largely because of angry public debates over immigration reform. Republicans wanted to crack down on illegal border crossings and penalize illegal immigrants. Some Republican Catholics came to see themselves in these desperate immigrants; only a few generations earlier, hundreds of thousands of poor and unlettered Catholics had migrated to the United States in the hope of greater economic opportunities. For this and other reasons, the two-party political system frustrated some Catholics. Aside from the abortion issue, the Republican Party did not seem very Catholic to many Catholics who supported their Church's "preferential option for the poor."

Polls conducted by the *National Catholic Reporter*/Gallup revealed that between May 1987 and November 1993, the number of Roman Catholics supporting a woman's right to choose an abortion increased substantially. For women, the percentage shot to 56, from 34; for men, the percentage jumped from 45 to 55. In May 2007 the annual "Gallup Values and Belief" survey revealed that Americans were evenly divided along "pro-life" and "pro-choice" lines, although a majority supported restrictions on abortion in most or all cases. Forty-nine per cent of Americans considered themselves "pro-choice" and forty-five per cent called themselves "pro-life." At that point, the relatively even split had held constant for nearly ten years. In the 1990s, then, American Catholics became largely indistinguishable from non-Catholic Americans with regard to support for abortion.

Early in the twenty-first century, Roman Catholics came to constitute a majority on the US Supreme Court. Intense public scrutiny surrounded the nominations of John Roberts and Samuel Alito, conservative Catholics who might project their private revulsion to abortion onto the Court. Catholic support for conservative justices was splintered at best, but various polls have suggested that abortion can pull together Catholics of various ideological stripes. Cultural Catholics tend to see the question as pertaining essentially to justice and social equality. Even cultural Catholics, though, will generally not dissent from the core of official teaching on abortion. Where Catholics are divided is over secondary matters: Does opposing abortion necessarily mean making it illegal? How much emphasis should abortion be given on the menu of all the Church's social concerns? Should pro-choice politicians be denied communion?

Divorce

I discussed divorce at some length in Chapter 3, "Baptisms, Weddings, and Funerals." For now, it is enough to note the long-standing Catholic opposition to divorce.[8] Harvard professor Mary Ann Glendon has explained the great increase in divorces in the United States and Western Europe in terms of no-fault divorce laws, which became popular in the 1970s. "Between 1969 and 1985 divorce law in nearly every Western country was profoundly altered. Among the most dramatic changes was the introduction of civil divorce in the predominantly Catholic countries of Italy and Spain, and its extension to Catholic marriages in Portugal."[9] Here again, we see Catholic culture forced to fight against quite significant changes in the surrounding secular culture.

The point of introducing divorce here only to dismiss it is to nod once again to a distinctive aspect of Catholic culture: annulments. Many non-Catholic Americans puzzle over the Catholic institution of annulments. It would be wrong-headed to assert that cultural Catholics oppose annulments; it is enough to note that cultural Catholics may sometimes find themselves struggling to explain or justify this Catholic practice. John Paul II had decided shortly before his death to re-examine annulments with an eye to reducing the number of them granted from Rome.

Twenty-first century debates over gay marriage would only bring out the extent to which many Catholics had gown uncomfortable with the traditional view of marriage—in which a woman pledges subservience to her husband—and the corresponding moral unsuitability of remarrying before one's former spouse had died. No one likes divorce, and cultural Catholics are no exception here; if they are less inclined to denounce it publicly, it may be because they see a strong resemblance to annulment.

Women

The Church has frequently been disparaged as patriarchal and unfair to women generally. Most cultural Catholics want to overturn Church policy barring women from ordination.

On the occasion of Pope John Paul II's first visit to the United States, a nun confronted him about the role of women in Catholic culture. Sister Theresa Kane, the superior of the Sisters of Mercy, had been appointed to greet the pope in a public ceremony. To the shock of onlookers, Kane boldly challenged the new pope as to why "half of humankind" had been denied a chance to be "included in all the ministries of the Church."[10] It is no exaggeration to say that since Kane, many American Catholics have taken pride in supporting the ordination of women as priests.

I will diverge briefly from the focus on America to relate a similar incident, one which occurred in Canada. On 7 March 2000 at the Montreal Church of Marie Reine du Monde, a band of women screamed obscenities at worshippers, spray-painted anti-Christian slogans on the high altar, ripped hymn books, turned over flowerpots, affixed tampons and sanitary napkins—some soiled—to pictures and walls, and threw condoms, panties and bras around the church. These Canadian women blamed the Catholic Church for abusing its power and maintaining a social order that subjugated women to men. Canadian women could not achieve social equality with Canadian men, the argument went, until women enjoyed full reproductive freedom (that is, until the Catholic Church stopped condemning birth control and abortion), as well as the right to ordination as a priest.

In such invasions of the sacred space that is a Catholic church, cultural Catholics may well feel inclined to side with hierarchy. Catholics in the United States have largely been sensitized to widespread employment and workplace discrimination against women, which makes it somewhat more difficult to side with the Holy See here. Sympathy for the anger many women feel toward the Church could also make cultural Catholics take pride in breaking ranks with the Vatican over the ordination issue.

John Fialka has argued that Catholic women in America have done the bulk of the work for keeping thousands of individual churches and schools running, but that Catholic women have received little credit for their remarkable efforts. "They were America's first feminists, battling for the rights and opinions of women in a workplace where bishops sometimes regarded nuns as their subjects or, worse, part of their 'turf'."[11] A sense of fairness drives much of the cultural Catholic support for ordaining women.

Particularly with regard to women's rights, the twenty-first century differs significantly from the nineteenth. The question remains as to how far the Church has evolved from the stance Pope Leo XIII articulated in a highly influential encyclical on the working world, *Rerum Novarum* (1891). Leo wrote, "Women [, again,] are not suited for certain occupations; a woman is by nature fitted for home-work, and it is that which is best adapted at once to preserve her modesty and to promote the good bringing up of children and the well-being of the family" (no. 42). Contemporary Catholics may wonder about the trajectory of this belief. Although John Paul tried hard to finesse the issue in his 1988 Apostolic Letter *Mulieris Dignitatem* (*On the Dignity of Women*), he never considered allowing the ordination of women. In 1994, John Paul declared the question closed in his letter *Ordinatio Sacerdotalis*, stating: "Wherefore, in order that all doubt may be removed regarding a matter of great importance . . . I declare that the Church has no authority whatsoever to confer priestly ordination on women and that this judgment is to be definitively held by all the Church's faithful."

In 1995, the congregation for the Doctrine of the Faith issued a clarification, explaining that *Ordinatio Sacerdotalis*, though

> itself not infallible, witnesses to the infallibility of the teaching of a doctrine already possessed by the Church. . . . This doctrine belongs to the deposit of the faith of the Church. It should be emphasized that the definitive and infallible nature of this teaching of the Church did not arise with the publication of the Letter *Ordinatio Sacerdotalis*.

Instead, the link to infallibility was "founded on the written Word of God, and from the beginning constantly preserved and applied in the tradition of the Church, it has been set forth infallibly by the ordinary and universal magisterium," and for these reasons it "requires definitive assent." Of course, many American Catholics do not assent.

The reasons cited for limiting the priesthood to men (because Jesus' disciples were all male and because he was himself male) fail to persuade many cultural Catholics, who often take pride in the work of their wives and daughters and who may believe that women would bring something invaluable to the ministry. Employment discrimination on the basis of gender is formally prohibited by American law, moreover, and Catholics in the United States know that. Telling a woman who wants to serve as a priest that her gender disqualifies her can expose the competing loyalties of an American Catholic as few other issues might.

Gay Marriage

Even though the Catholic Church adamantly opposes gay marriage, the Church has, since 1975, consistently urged compassion toward gays and lesbians (who are simply born that way, according to God's mysterious will). One of the more surprising social developments of the late twentieth century was gay marriage. This issue mushroomed into another emotional conflict between the Church and many (although certainly not all) cultural Catholics. Siding with the Church on this issue made an American seem more conservative and, perhaps, less sensitive to the plight of a downtrodden minority.

In the 1990s, many Catholic Americans gradually felt the influence of foreign change. In May of 1989, the Danish Parliament voted to enact the Registered Partnership Act, which accorded almost all the same rights and duties of marriage to registered same-sex partners. Within the next few years, Norway, Sweden, Finland, and Iceland would follow suit. The sticking points in these national debates, in which religion played a prominent role, were the questions of adopting children, whether to call the union a "marriage," and whether the ceremony could take place in a Christian church. The majority of Scandinavians came to see the question as one of social equality, of basic human goodness—not of faithfulness to biblical injunctions. The framing of the question would ultimately make a critical difference.

In 1993 the Hawaii Supreme Court put same-sex marriage on America's national agenda. Roman Catholics contributed prominently to fighting gay marriage; conservatives such as Robert Bork (a Yale law professor), Rick Santorum (a Pennsylvania senator from 1995 to 2007), and Antonin Scalia (a Supreme Court justice) marshaled natural law arguments to oppose new ballot measures. Meanwhile, more and more Americans began to see the issue as one of civil rights and equal protection under the law. Cultural Catholics began to conclude that it was up to them to decide how to apply their Catholic faith to the vote. Although the Hawaii vote ultimately denied marriage to gay and lesbian couples, the matter was far from resolved. In fact, Hawaii was only the beginning. Voters in Massachusetts, Connecticut, and New Jersey—states with particularly large Catholic populations—expressed sympathy with the gay marriage movement through polls and statewide votes.

Early in the twenty-first century, the topic of gay marriage polarized Americans. Catholic leaders feared another defeat in the United States, given that predominantly Catholic countries such as Belgium and Spain had legalized gay marriage. Several American states legalized either gay marriage or its counterpart, civil union. Many thoughtful Catholics either cringed at the new gay-friendly atmosphere or worried that opposing the change today would make them seem like bigots tomorrow. Caught in the middle was the institutional Church, which had gone on record as vigorously opposed to embracing legal recognition for same-sex couples.

Various polls conducted in the first decade of the twenty-first century showed that the number of Americans who supported same-sex marriage continued to grow. This growth extended into the Catholic community as well. In the traditionally conservative state of Virginia, for example, a *Washington Post* poll published shortly before the 2006 vote revealed that a majority of Roman Catholics in the state favored gay marriage.[12] It was then that the bishops of Richmond and Arlington began a massive letter-writing campaign in which they contacted as many parish-registered Catholics as possible in order to remind individuals of their church's stance on the issue.

Individual Roman Catholics may themselves play a role in the eventual acceptance of same-sex marriage in the United States. Each of the Scandinavian governments recognized partnerships only after public opinion polls demonstrated support for such domestic arrangements.[13] Although the Roman Catholic Church is not likely to follow suit, still it remains that Roman Catholics following their conscience may, by virtue of their vast number, eventually persuade many American states to legalize same-sex marriage: This idea would require polling data. It is worth noting again the traditional Catholic strongholds in the first states that supported gay marriage and civil unions, namely Massachusetts, Connecticut, and New Jersey. Cultural Catholics may someday make traditional Catholics proud—for having moved the Church in a direction which may seem obviously right decades from now. This is not to imply that *all* cultural Catholics supported or will support gay marriage.

It should also be made clear that Catholic opposition to gay marriage supposedly does not intend harm to gay people; the point of this opposition is to resist a redefinition of marriage. When California voters approved the controversial Proposition 8 (hereafter "Prop 8"), defining marriage as a union of a man and a woman, in 2008, Cardinal Roger M. Mahony of Los Angeles made a conciliatory message to homosexual Catholics in his archdiocese. He stated that "Prop 8" did not in any way diminish the importance or dignity of gay people and should not under any circumstances be taken as an attempt to harm the gay community. Many of the 48 per cent of Californians who opposed the ballot measure in November 2008 questioned how "Prop 8" could avoid harming the gay community, and some lamented the Catholic Church's vigorous public support for the state constitutional amendment. Although Cardinal Mahony claimed to be committed to eliminating discrimination against gay people, gay activists, and those who sympathized with them concluded that the Catholic Church was part of the problem—particularly since the Vatican had recently opposed a United Nations homosexuality declaration (December 2008) aimed at decriminalizing homosexuality. In 2008, over seventy countries prohibited homosexuality activity and several nations went so far as to stipulate the death penalty for those caught in such activity.

Capital Punishment

While the vast majority of American Catholics support capital punishment, Pope John Paul II made clear the Church's near total opposition to the death penalty. In the already referenced encyclical *Evangelium Vitae* (*The Gospel of Life*), issued 25 March 1995 after four years of consultations with the world's Roman Catholic bishops, John Paul II wrote that execution is only appropriate in cases of absolute necessity, in other words, when it would not be possible otherwise to defend society. The pontiff took the bold step of stating that steady improvement in the penal system made such cases very rare. Until this encyclical, the death penalty had been viewed as sometimes permissible as a means of protecting society. The universal catechism (that is, rulebook) for Catholics had affirmed the right of the state to punish criminals with appropriate penalties "not excluding in cases of extreme gravity, the death penalty."

The encyclical addressed various threats to human life, as we'll see later in this chapter, when I refer back to the same encyclical in a discussion of embryonic stem cell research. Specifically addressing capital punishment, John Paul declared that the moral question should be viewed in the context of a system of penal justice ever more in line with human dignity and thus, in the end, with God's plan for man and society. The primary purpose of the punishment which society inflicts is "to redress the disorder caused by the offence." Public authority must redress the violation of personal and social rights by imposing on the offender an adequate punishment for the crime, as a condition for the offender to regain the exercise of his or her freedom. In this way authority also fulfills the purpose of defending public order and ensuring safety, while at the same time offering the offender an incentive to change his or her behavior permanently (see especially paragraph 56).

John Paul asserted that, for these purposes to be achieved, the *nature and extent of the punishment* had to be carefully evaluated and decided upon. In any event, that punishment ought not to go to the extreme of execution except in cases of absolute necessity. Here as well we find Catholic dissent. Supreme Court Justice Antonin Scalia, to take a prominent example, publicly broke from the official teaching of the Church. Recent rulings by the US Supreme Court on the death penalty had focused attention on the high court's attitude toward capital punishment—a practice still upheld by thirty-eight US states at the time. In a 6–3 decision on 20 June 2002, the Court ruled that executing the mentally retarded is a violation of the Constitution's Eighth Amendment ban on "cruel and unusual punishment." National opinion had shifted, and the judges indicated that they were responding to that cultural shift.

The decision angered three dissenting justices—Chief Justice William Rehnquist and Justices Antonin Scalia and Clarence Thomas, all known for their especially conservative views—who denounced the Court's majority for caving in to international and domestic public opinion opposing execution of the mentally retarded. In his dissenting opinion, Scalia argued that such individuals should not escape execution because "deservedness of the most severe retribution [the death penalty], depends not merely (if at all) upon the mental capacity of the criminal . . . but also upon the depravity of the crime." In other words, this supremely well-educated Catholic not only supported the death penalty but also stood ready to see it inflicted on mentally retarded criminals.

Reporting on the 20 June 2002 ruling, the British *Guardian* newspaper drew attention to remarks Scalia had made earlier that year, remarks the paper felt cast further light on the deeply reactionary outlook underpinning his support for the death penalty. Scalia had spoken in January at the University of Chicago at the Pew Forum on Religion and Public Life, appearing on a panel with former Democratic Senator Paul Simon and Beth Wilkinson, lead prosecutor in the United States government's case against Timothy McVeigh (the "Oklahoma City bomber"). According to the *Guardian*, again, a foreign newspaper, Scalia's comments had been virtually blacked out in the American press.

Scalia cited the New Testament to claim that government "derives its moral authority from God . . . to execute wrath, including even wrath by the sword, which is unmistakably a reference to the death penalty." He then made the following remarkable declaration:

> Indeed, it seems to me that the more Christian a country is, the less likely it is to regard the death penalty as immoral. Abolition has taken its firmest hold in post-Christian Europe and has least support in the church-going United States. I attribute that to the fact that for the believing Christian, death is no big deal.[14]

Scalia went on to attribute any Christian opposition to the death penalty—including that of the pope—to the "handiwork of Napoleon, Hegel and Freud."

Three years later, Justice Scalia criticized the Supreme Court's 2005 decision to strike down the juvenile death penalty, calling it the latest example of politics on the court that had made judicial nominations an increasingly bitter process. In a thirty-five-minute speech, Scalia insisted that unelected judges have no place deciding issues such as abortion and the death penalty. The court's 5–4 ruling on 1 March 2005 to outlaw the juvenile death penalty based on "evolving notions of decency" was simply a mask for the personal policy preferences of the five-member majority, he said.[15] The United States became the last country in the world officially to abolish the death penalty for offenders who were under eighteen years of age when they committed murder.

The majority had pressed on the other leg in the Eighth Amendment's standard, that this kind of killing is unusual. Scalia objected to the majority's reliance on its own notions of what is cruel or unusual as well as its reliance on the evolving trend in the rest of the world. Scalia questioned why the American people left this question up to the interpretation of nine lawyers. Citing the example of abortion, he said unelected justices too often choose to read new rights into the Constitution, at the expense of the democratic process. Scalia, a conservative Catholic, wanted to resist the influence of the secular culture in America.

Many Americans know about Catholic opposition to the death penalty from the popular 1995 film *Dead Man Walking*, starring Susan Sarandon and Sean Penn. Scalia is interesting for his combination of reverence for traditional Catholic beliefs and his conviction to support the death penalty in spite of the Vatican's general condemnation of it. Although many European countries and some American states legally prohibit the death penalty, some thoughtful Catholics in the United States have reconciled their religious beliefs to a judicial remedy they find sadly necessary.

Racism

The Catholic Church in America has overcome some internal racism. Along the way, cultural Catholics may have pushed the Church in a direction they felt convinced the Church would one day find plainly moral.

Mother Katharine Drexel of Philadelphia (d. 1955) left behind a particularly wealthy family in order to become a nun devoted to helping the poor. She worked hard to convert many African-Americans and Native Americans to Catholicism. White Catholics may have wanted such converts, but only from a distance. Both before and after Mother Drexel's saintly work, American Catholics frequently wrestled with their own racist tendencies.[16] Jo Ann Kay McNamara's history of American nuns reveals the extent to which various American convents were segregated, specifically, the extent to which Caucasian nuns did not want to share living space with African-American nuns.[17] It seems that American convents and seminaries mirrored what was going on among parishioners: segregation happened more often than not. Already in the mid-twentieth century John LaFarge, S.J. responded to a gaping racial cleft; he reached out to Catholics and urged them to try to help break down racial barriers (presumably in part because Catholics had played some role in maintaining those barriers). The Catholic Legion of Decency, working as a moral watchdog on Hollywood in the mid-twentieth century, saw to it that no interracial romance made it to the big screen. "The ultimate offense was a sexual union between a white and a black."[18] Further proof of American racism is hardly needed.

Although talk of racism in the United States often focuses on African-Americans, it cannot be denied that Latinos have suffered as well.[19] In 1972, 250 clergy and laity met in Washington, DC to discuss the role of Latinos in the American Church. Latinos coalesced around the idea that "the Church had to change from a policy of assimilation to one of pluralism." Five years later another "encuentro" took place; there, agreement formed around the idea "that Hispanic culture can no longer be ignored in teaching the Catholic faith."[20] It is important to note here that *American* Catholics were the culprit; the Vatican embraced South America and cannot properly be said to have discriminated against that continent full of (Latino) Catholics.

To return to African-Americans: In 1984 a group of ten black bishops issued a letter emphasizing the importance of articulating the contributions of African-Americans. They agreed that the Church "must preserve its multicultural identity," rather than try to mold black Catholics into an ideal white/European model.[21] These bishops were trying to save the Church from itself. The gentle spirit of their dissent and their obvious engagement with the Church make it difficult to categorize them as cultural Catholics.

Father George Stallings (b. 1948) criticized the Roman Catholic Church in America for its racist foundations. An African-American and ordained Catholic priest, he is best known as the founder of the Imani Temple African-American Catholic Congregation, an African-American-led form of Catholicism. He had been a Catholic priest, but made a public break with the Roman Catholic Church on the Phil Donahue television show in 1989 and was excommunicated the next year. He stated that he left because the Church did not serve the African-American community or recognize its talent.

The Church disagreed with Stallings. In 1989, Cardinal James Hickey (d. 2004), a lifelong advocate of racial amity, suspended Stallings. The Washington archdiocese denied the accusation of racism, said it had no objection to the use of jazz or other innovations, but said the Church could not condone "a free-standing entity" independent of Rome. Father Stallings persisted, however, and was eventually excommunicated. Critics claimed he had lived extravagantly and had been asked to seek psychiatric help. He later regained attention through association with the group *Married Priests Now!* He can perhaps be dismissed as an oddball, but it is more difficult to wave away his complaint as simply preposterous.

Of course, Mother Drexel was not the only Catholic working to help African-Americans. A PBS documentary highlights a group of nuns marching in Montgomery, Alabama in the late 1960s in support of Martin Luther King Jr.'s bid for civil rights. *Sisters of Selma: Bearing Witness for Change* makes clear that some Catholics did dissent from what might have been considered prevailing Catholic culture at the time.[22] It is important to note the obvious fact that no document from the National Conference of Catholic Bishops ever explicitly endorsed racist policies, and so the dissent of American Catholics intent on overcoming the color line is much harder to theorize.[23] With regard to racism, it could be that the issue separated them from Rome rather than united them more strongly (even though Rome may not have appointed many African or Latino cardinals in the relevant time period).

Ultimately, it strikes me as unfair for American Catholics to lambaste their Church for having been racist, given how profoundly racist the rest of America was. If anything, the Church was probably less racist than the rest of America. The only point of mentioning racism at all in this chapter is to point out yet another area in which cultural Catholics might see themselves as missionaries to their own Church, to whatever extent it has remained racist.

Evolution and Darwin

American Catholics in the early twenty-first century who knew anything about Darwin's theory of evolution tended to take pride in the modern stance of their church. Fundamentalist Protestants, on the other hand, regularly railed against the teaching of evolution in American public schools.[24] Such Protestants would also object to theme parks which featured exhibits on dinosaurs, which the park claimed had lived millions of years ago. Creationists, as they are called, insisted that the earth is only about five or six thousand years old.

Darwin's theory of evolution was already quite well known by the time Pope Pius XII issued the encyclical *Humani Generis* in 1950. After a distracting and lengthy assertion of the pope's authority, coupled with the articulation of several reservations about the progress of knowledge, Pius XII offered a ground-breaking acceptance of evolution: "The teaching authority of the Church does not forbid that, in conformity with the present stage of human sciences and sacred theology, research and discussion on the part of men experienced in both fields take place with regard to the doctrine of evolution." Note that only three years later, two researchers at Cambridge University would discover DNA and, in so doing, add inestimable credence to Darwin's hypothesis. Catholics worried about saving their Church from embarrassment of the Galileo sort must have breathed a sigh of relief in the mid-1950s that Pius XII had not condemned the theory of evolution as a falsehood.

John Paul II apologized in 1992 for what the Church had done to Galileo. Four years later, in 1996, John Paul II issued a statement about evolution which buoyed Catholic scientists around the world. Acknowledging the growing evidence for Darwin's theory, he wrote:

> Today, almost half a century after the publication of the encyclical [*Humani Generis*], new knowledge has led to the recognition of the theory of evolution as more than a hypothesis. It is indeed remarkable that this theory has been progressively accepted by researchers, following a series of discoveries in various fields of knowledge. The convergence, neither sought nor fabricated, of the results of the work that was conducted independently is in itself a significant argument in favor of this theory.[25]

John Paul saved the Church from the kind of embarrassment contemporary Catholics feel about the historical fact that their church had been completely wrong about the earth's position in the galaxy. Contemporary Catholics could take pride that the scientific world did not snicker about them the way that it did about, say, evangelical Protestants who believed that the *Book of Genesis* is a literal account of the creation of the world.

Then, in July 2005, many cultural Catholics must have felt alienated from their Church all over again. The Austrian Cardinal Schoenborn published an Op-ed piece in the *New York Times*, America's most powerful newspaper.[26] It had long been thought that the Roman Catholic Church largely endorsed the theory of evolution, but Schoenborn insisted in his brief piece that this view was somewhat misguided.

Many wondered how a largely unknown foreigner could manage to place an Op-ed piece in the *New York Times* (it turned out he had been abetted by a conservative think tank in Seattle, the Discovery Institute). And many marveled at the chutzpah of a man who dared to criticize the enormously popular John Paul II, who had only died three months earlier. While Schoenborn referred to John Paul as "our beloved," Schoenborn also dismissed the dead pontiff's "rather vague and unimportant 1996 letter about evolution."

Schoenborn, like the conservative American institute that had backed him, urged not only that schools teach Darwin's theory as just one of several competing explanations about how the earth became the way it appears today but also the attractiveness of what had come to be called "intelligent design theory." Only one year later, a controversial court case in Pennsylvania reached federal district court in that state; that court ruled that "intelligent design" was only a disguised version of creationism. Since the 1980s, it had been illegal to teach creationism in public schools, under the rationale that creationism was a form of Christianity, and the US Constitution had barred the teaching of religious beliefs in public schools. It had always been fine to study academic approaches to the study of religion, but it was illegal to teach religious ideas as truths.

In the suit *Tammy Kitzmiller, et al. v. Dover Area School District, et al.*, eleven parents of high school students sued a public school district that required the presentation of "Intelligent Design" as an alternative to evolution as an "explanation of the origin of life." In the fall of 2005, the federal district judge sided with the parents. Less than two months later, the eight school board members who had voted for the Intelligent Design requirement lost reelection. With regard to one aspect of scientific research, namely explaining how the earth came to be, 2005 was a difficult time for American Catholics, many of whom had long believed that the Vatican had allowed them to believe in the theory of evolution. Any statement from the Vatican backing "Intelligent Design Theory" is likely to alienate well-educated Catholics in the United States. The stage is set for further conflict.

Benedict XVI pointed out the principal threat posed by Darwin's theory. Shortly before ascending to the papacy, Cardinal Ratzinger had tied Darwin to natural law:

The natural law has remained (especially in the Catholic Church) the key issue in dialogues with the secular society and with other communities of faith in order to appeal to the reason we share in common and to seek the basis for a consensus about the ethical principles of law in a secular, pluralistic society. Unfortunately, this instrument has become blunt. Accordingly, I do not intend to appeal to it for support in this conversation. *The idea of the natural law presupposed a concept of nature in which nature and reason overlap, since nature itself is rational. With the victory of the theory of evolution, this view of nature has capsized: nowadays, we think that nature as such is not rational*, even if there is rational behavior in nature.[27]

Some educated Catholics will feel sadness over disagreeing with the Church on the theory of evolution and the concomitant theory of intelligent design; other Catholics will take pride in that dissent. Cultural Catholics as a group tend to struggle over sexual ethics, and cultural Catholics will find a further incentive to embrace Darwin, for doing so makes it easier to walk away from traditional Catholic teachings about birth control and masturbation.

Revulsion to Sex Abuse Scandal

No one will struggle to understand the shame and revulsion American Catholics felt during the priestly sex scandal of 2002–2003.[28] Given the ways bishops and dioceses had protected priestly pedophiles, many Catholics criticized their church publicly (especially in Boston). The pride many Catholics derived from stepping apart from their church paled in comparison to the shame, though. The Church not only lost moral prestige in the public arena but, in thousands of private cases, the confidence of Catholics who increasingly felt more legally protected in the secular world than the sacred one.

The John Jay Report, commissioned by the US Conference of Catholic Bishops in 1992, eventually found accusations against 4,392 priests in the USA, equaling about 4 per cent of all US priests between 1950 and 2002. The 2004 study revealed that 10,667 people reported that they had been abused by priests as minors between 1950 and 2002. Figures supplied by the Catholic League seem to demonstrate that abuse statistics in the Catholic Church were similar to abuse in other institutions (such as, for example, the preliminary estimate of education abuse statistics compiled by the US Department of Education). Ultimately, Roman Catholics felt scandalized not so much that abuse took place within their community (had most Catholics believed all priests were above such criminal behavior), but rather because of the duplicity of the hierarchy, which sometimes transferred known abusers from one location to another and sometimes neglected to report what was, after all, an illegal act.

Frank Keating, the governor of Oklahoma, resigned in 2003 from a separate but similar commission, in part because he claimed the Church was still hiding incriminating information about abuser-priests. Keating, a practicing Roman Catholic, told the *Los Angeles Times*: "To act like La Cosa Nostra and hide and suppress, I think, is very unhealthy."[29] He compared unnamed bishops to the Mafia. "To resist grand jury subpoenas, to suppress the names of offending clerics, to deny, to obfuscate, to explain away; that is the model of a criminal organization, not my church."[30] Here again, we see the model of a cultural Catholic: One who disagrees with authority while fiercely holding onto his Catholic identity.

The archbishop of Los Angeles, Roger Mahony, rejected Mr. Keating's comment as "irresponsible and uninformed" (Keating had specifically blamed Mahony). Keating is just one of many Catholics who took pride in differing from the Church with regard to this especially painful scandal. Realizing that Catholics might find an incentive for turning on their own bishops, Church authorities struggled quickly to contain the extraordinary crisis.

In 2003, Cardinal Mahony dedicated a chapel at the Cathedral of Our Lady of the Angels to victims of sex abuse by priests. American indignation still simmered, though. In 2005, the American Catholic group known as SNAP, or Survivor's Network of those Abused by Priests, protested outside St. Peter's Basilica as the former cardinal of Boston, Bernard Law, officiated at a memorial Mass for John Paul II. The Catholic organization blamed Cardinal Law for allowing pedophile priests to move from one assignment to another in the archdiocese of Boston, thereby continuing to target new victims.

In his first official visit to the United States as pontiff, Benedict XVI in April 2008 publicly stated his sadness for the victims of the priestly scandal. The American media generally gave Benedict high marks for this move, but much damage had already been done. In the years between 2002 and 2008, no doubt many American Catholics had felt demoralized by all the media attention paid to the scandal and what was often perceived to be the hierarchy's insufficient response to the victims.

Cultural Catholics as a group suffered through the priestly sex abuse scandal, every bit as much as traditional Catholics did. That cultural Catholics wanted to see their Church change does not mean they waited maliciously for its collapse. Had cultural Catholics not already made a home for themselves in the secular world, they may have felt even more disoriented by the scandal. This is not to suggest that they suffered as much as the children preyed upon by opportunist priests.

Embryonic Stem Cell Research

Is a cluster of living embryonic cells appropriate fodder for scientific study, or is it a human being with a soul? In steadfastly insisting on the latter, the Catholic Church has not only made some enemies publicly but also stirred up doubt among some segments of the faithful. Scientific research stands as another reason why some Catholics take pride in disagreeing with their Church.

Science thrills contemporary Americans, who have been repeatedly reminded by the Vatican of its dangers. Before turning to embryonic stem cell research, which appeared frequently in newspapers in the 1990s and 2000s, it is worth remembering official Catholic opposition to in vitro fertilization ("IVF").

By 2008, more than three million babies worldwide had been born using in vitro techniques. Approximately 27,000 procedures were performed each year in the United States. The total spent in the United States annually was estimated at around $4 billion. The Catholic Church's objections include:

- IVF separates the act of love-making from procreation, rupturing something meant to be unified, which is the same objection the Church has to birth control and to cloning. That critique applies to all kinds of IVF.
- Heterologous IVF also damages the family by separating the biological and emotional aspects of parenthood.
- Because IVF involves the creation of multiple embryos which are either discarded or frozen, it violates the right to life.
- Sperm generally comes from masturbation, compounding the moral difficulties.
- Since IVF techniques usually involve the implantation of multiple embryos to increase the odds of pregnancy, it's common for the "excess" embryos to be eliminated early in pregnancy by an injection of potassium chloride, a procedure known as fetal reduction, which the Church regards as a form of abortion.

Some reform-minded Catholic theologians, however, have reached a more positive conclusion about the morality of IVF, especially its homologous form. Usually they make two basic arguments. First, they contend that an embryo cannot be regarded as a person until it passes the point at which twinning is possible. They point to wastage: Scientists say that the natural rate of loss for embryos in the earliest stages after conception is 60 to 80 per cent. How could God bring into being so many persons, this argument runs, only to let them perish when their lives have hardly begun? Second, while IVF separates intercourse and procreation, it does so for the purpose of procreation, not contraception. They often argue that separation between intercourse and procreation is a pre-moral evil, which can be justified for a proportionate reason in this case, to conceive a child.[31]

For Catholics, the debate over the morality of stem cell research arose in a Church already hostile to a procedure which was arguably somewhat less morally fraught (that is, IVF).

A Brief Summary of Catholic Reaction to Embryonic Stem Cell Research

By the time embryonic stem cell research captured the imagination of the West early in the twenty-first century, IVF had ceased to arouse much public moral opposition. Catholic opposition to embryonic (as opposed to adult) stem cell research was another story; although a growing number of American Catholics privately supported such research, a number of prominent Catholics kept the controversy alive by denouncing the practice as the moral equivalent of abortion.

Embryonic stem cells had long been considered the holy grail of cellular biology, because they are capable of growing into any of the 220 or so types of cells found in the human body.[32] They are of research interest for two major reasons. First, studying them helps scientists understand the molecular processes that trigger degenerative cellular disorders such as Alzheimer's. Second, embryonic stem cells could provide a source of transplantable cells and tissues. Many researchers hope that embryonic stem cells may be used to treat Parkinson's disease, which affects a small and specialized mass of brain cells, or to restore function to victims of spinal cord injuries (such as the American actor Christopher Reeve).

On 10 November 1998, just four days after the US-based Geron Corporation announced that scientists had isolated stem cells from "leftover" embryos at fertility clinics for the first time, Bishop Elio Sgreccia, vice-president of the Vatican's Pontifical Academy for Life, told reporters that the procedure was morally illegitimate because it involved the destruction of embryos. Respect for human life, Sgreccia said, demands "respect for embryos and fetuses."[33] That reaction has largely defined the Catholic position ever since.

Because of their scientific and medical potential, however, a number of Catholic researchers have sought morally acceptable alternatives to acquire stem cells. Many point to adult stem cells found in umbilical cords, the placenta, amniotic fluid, adult tissues, and organs such as bone marrow, fat from liposuction, regions of the nose, and even from cadavers up to twenty hours after death. Some scientists say adult cells work just as well as embryonic cells, if not better, pointing out that to date not a single therapy has been developed from embryonic stem cells, while adult stem cells are used in scores of treatments. Other scientists, however, argue that adult cells lack the full plasticity of embryonic cells.

Catholics suffering from Parkinson's disease—and those who love them—will sometimes dissent with the Catholic Church. Even those Catholics standing on the sidelines may wince when they read press coverage of sick people crying out for a cure and condemning the Church for standing in the way of medical progress.[34] Of course the moral debate over stem cell research involves nuance and subtlety, but activists for Parkinson's and Alzheimer's research sometimes say the issue comes down to a willingness to allow needless suffering. Whether stem cell research morally amounts to abortion is still debated.

In conclusion, the two issues—IVF and embryonic stem cell research—are linked because both turn on the church's defense of human life from the moment of conception, which implies that embryos cannot be treated as a means to an end. That rules out both the destruction of embryos in research, as well as the production of "surplus embryos" through in vitro fertilization. The cost of protecting the sanctity of life is telling infertile couples that they will have to try to adopt or live childlessly and, further, telling Parkinson's families that an apparently promising research avenue is off limits.

According to a 2005 poll, twenty-seven per cent of Catholic physicians actually supported the official Catholic position on embryonic stem cell research.[35] This number seemed quite high, given how many Catholic physicians opposed the Church on forbidding the use of condoms to prevent the spread of HIV/AIDS (ninety per cent) and on using the birth control pill (eighty-seven per cent). Whether cultural Catholics will take pride in dissenting from the Church on embryonic stem cell research remains to be seen. Plenty of cultural Catholics will likely feel a duty to help people suffering from these diseases and therefore will throw their support behind science.

In summary, then, new scientific research offers hope to people suffering from Parkinson's and Alzheimer's disease. When science can unequivocally cure people of diseases such as tuberculosis and polio, virtually everyone applauds. When, however, the price of such cures involves research with human embryonic stem cells and somatic nuclear transfer, the Vatican says the prize is not worth the cost.

An Accumulation of Reasons

What we find, in summary, are numerous reasons why well-educated American Catholics might find it occasionally difficult to align themselves with the church hierarchy. The list offered in this chapter is not meant to be exhaustive.

What does this disagreement mean and how can dissenting Catholics maintain a *bona fide* tie to their Church? Father Andrew Greeley has pressed on the notion of sacramentality to set Catholics apart culturally from other religious groups. I believe mediation does a better job, not just because Russian and Eastern Orthodox Christians embrace the same sacraments as Catholics, but also because mediation subsumes the category of sacraments. Mediation is a more basic concept because Catholics cannot have performed certain sacraments without the mediation of a priest. I have suggested in this chapter that Catholics share this cultural reliance on mediation with Jews. I see Catholic dissent as leading generally to a new kind of mediation ("change from within"), not necessarily a severing of Catholic identity.

Religion, an energizing force that can build civilizations, glues together people who otherwise appear quite different. It would be ridiculous to try to speak for all Catholics in the United States, much less to nail down descriptions of Catholic culture in various contexts. That said, we can discern certain patterns of Catholic belief which indicate cultural tendencies.

Dissent from the institutional church could become a new *de facto* sacrament for cultural Catholics, who still hunger for spiritual nourishment and who may see themselves as missionaries of a sort. By their sheer numbers in the United States, cultural Catholics are serving as mediators for each other. Together, cultural Catholics are reaching for something higher. That elusive goal involves the Vatican in an as yet antagonistic way.

I have focused on dissent in which one might reasonably take some pride, from a secular point of view. I have not considered, for example, the "preferential option for the poor." Roman Catholicism has long insisted on the importance, indeed urgency, of not only taking care of the poor generally but of avoiding materialism generally. Many, if not most, American Catholics fail to give all they can to the poor, but few, if any, Catholics are proud of that gap. This is not dissent.

Because not all Catholics are well-informed, it would be preposterous to test ecclesiastical allegiance on the basis of agreement or disagreement with the issues I have sketched here. That said, it should not seem far-fetched to assert that as Catholics learn more about their Church's past mistakes and as the secular world challenges Catholic positions on various issues, more and better-informed Catholics will feel more distant from the Vatican ("the party line," if you will). Beyond that, it seems fair to expect ambivalence to spread to Africa and Asia. Enthusiasm for the Catholic Church has been exploding in relatively poor areas of the globe in the twenty-first century. It should not seem outlandish to expect that as new Catholics in Africa and Asia become well educated and more affluent, they will resemble cultural Catholics in the United States.

Some American Catholics take pride in their dissent because of a desire to save the Church from embarrassment (this is, in fact, precisely how Galileo explained his own research). Some American Catholics ruefully see their church in Eugene O'Neill's observation about Ireland: "There is no present or future," O'Neill said, "only the past happening over and over again." It is more than possible that many cultural Catholics wish their church well and would strongly prefer to see it prosper. Strategies for full health, though, differ from one faction to another. It is just as easy to see within Catholic culture a tradition of change as it is to see a tradition of changelessness. The real continuity and tradition has aimed at improving and upgrading the corresponding culture—the life which takes place outside parish boundaries.

In their own way, cultural Catholics are following Pope Leo XIII, who wrote in 1891: "Nothing is more useful than to look upon the world as it really is, and at the same time to seek elsewhere, as We have said, for the solace to its troubles" (*Rerum Novarum*, no. 18).

Chapter 5

A Pope's Apology

A papal apology in 2000 launched a new millennium and illustrated the possibility that Catholic culture might follow the Vatican, as opposed to lead it. Various devotional practices, such as regarding the heroic dead as saints or believing in the Assumption of Mary, began on the grassroots level and spread upward, eventually becoming official doctrine. It is by no means the case that Catholic culture willfully or inadvertently ignores the Vatican. A pope still wields enough influence to mold Catholic culture, although his efforts are not always immediately evident.

The remarkable *mea culpa* of 2000 may have facilitated an official response to the American sex abuse scandal, which was to unfold shortly afterwards. Word became flesh, and the spoken apology for a variety of (other, unrelated) sins eventually took physical form: It should not seem far-fetched to connect that apology (which was spoken) to an Illinois monument (which is visible) commemorating survivors of priestly sexual abuse.[1] Subsequent generations of Catholics may look back at a penitent pontiff as having shunted the Church onto a new and vital course.

John Paul II gave Catholics permission to speak publicly about harm done by the Church. Ever careful to insist that the Church never errs, John Paul publicly acknowledged that a number of individuals had sinned and, in so doing, marred the image of the Church. He called for a widespread expression of regret of such transgressions. John Paul returned the Church to a tradition of public confession which had largely died, over a thousand years ago.[2] Reasonable people still disagree over the effectiveness of John Paul's papacy; my aim here is not to canonize the man but to draw attention to the power of his apology, which could ultimately do more than anything else to lure "lapsed Catholics" back to the fold. That the apology did not seem immediately to draw back hordes of occasional Catholics might stem more from the unappealing symmetry of the apology than the gesture itself.

The Apology, the Pope, the World

On Sunday, 12 March 2000, Pope John Paul II presided over a pivotal Day of Pardon. He issued a formal apology for various transgressions committed by Catholics over the past two thousand years. In addition, he delivered a separate apology for Catholic anti-Semitism. Jews received special attention on that day because Jews had been particularly harmed. The very name "Day of Pardon" strikes me as unfortunate, for the title almost sounds as though the pope would be forgiving others, instead of asking forgiveness from them. Perhaps even worse, the title might suggest that the pope would be demanding that aggrieved groups pardon him.

At a solemn service in St. Peter's basilica, the pope asked forgiveness for the sins of Catholic people everywhere. By asking God's forgiveness, the pope was simultaneously trying to earn his fellow man's forgiveness as well. All Catholics were collectively guilty—not just ordinary parishioners, but clerics and cardinals as well. What seemed surprising and perhaps inopportune was the symmetry of John Paul's apology: He not only wanted forgiveness from harmed parties, but he wanted anyone who had ever harmed Catholics to apologize as well.

It must be said that John Paul opened himself willingly to criticism on several fronts. Some conservative Catholics complained that the apology undermined the church's authority, while others, including some Jewish leaders, contended the Pope had not gone far enough. Some wanted to hear more specific mention of the Church's failures, especially regarding Catholic attitudes toward Jews during the Second World War. Beyond that, the pope never entertained the possibility that the Church might err: John Paul reaffirmed the sanctity of "Mother Church" and stressed that while individual members can make mistakes, the collective Church always remains holy.

Although critics may contend that this crucial premise shifts moral responsibility from Church authorities to ordinary Catholics (along the lines of "One bad apple doesn't spoil the whole bunch"), still it remains that John Paul asked for forgiveness. It is always convenient for a person in a position of authority—say, a business manager—to pin responsibility for a mistake on an inferior. John Paul did not opt for that easy solution: He included himself and the Holy See in the problem, however ambiguously. This was all to the good, at least from the perspective of a disaffected Catholic who perceived the Church hierarchy as ever unwilling to admit fault.

Pope John Paul asked forgiveness of God for the errors committed by the Church's members. Implied in this entreaty was a request from real people who had been harmed. Before scores of bishops and cardinals, he said during his homily:

> We cannot not recognize the betrayal of the Gospel committed by some of our brothers, especially in the second millennium. We beg forgiveness for our guilt as Christians for the sins of the present. Faced with atheism, religious apathy, secularism, relativism, violations of the right to life, indifference towards the poverty endured by many nations, we can only ask what are our responsibilities.[3]

Next John Paul did something that may have been impolitic: He pointed out that Christians had been subjected to violence at the hands of others. "As we ask forgiveness for our sins, we also forgive the sins committed by others against us." In a sense, this was hardly a radical move, as John Paul was essentially following the script of the *Pater noster* (or "The Lord's Prayer"). And yet, the rhetorical turn may have unfortunately distracted attention from Catholic faults. Instead of saying on that important day, "Catholics have been responsible for terrible sins," John Paul ended up sounding as though he was making a much less noteworthy statement: "People have been responsible for terrible sins." It might have been more expedient for the pontiff to refrain from mentioning that aggrieved Catholics forgave others and focus instead on the central thread of Catholic guilt.

Seven of the Vatican's cardinals and bishops oversaw the confession of sins. Cardinal Bernardin Gantin, of Benin, West Africa, began the ceremony with a "confession of sins in general," followed by Germany's Cardinal Joseph Ratzinger, who read the confession of sins committed in the service of truth. "We recognize that even men of the church, in the name of faith and morals, have sometimes used methods not in keeping with the Gospel in the solemn duty of defending the truth." The lack of details, such as the Inquisition, did not necessarily undermine the pontifical gesture. It may have been simply impossible to ascertain all instances of wrongdoing and so it may have been prudent to speak in generalities, not privileging any particular

116 Catholic Culture in the USA

offenses over others. And yet, omitting details may have undermined the point of the apology. A high level of generality in an apology can minimize the seriousness of a specific offense. Instead of one person apologizing to another for having uttered a racial slur, for example, the person at fault may simply say, "I'm sorry you felt offended." That is to say that instead of apologizing and admitting fault, the person who uttered the racial slur simply regrets that the person to whom he spoke feels angry or uncomfortable.

Cardinal Roger Etchegaray of France then pronounced the "confession of sins which have harmed the unity of the Body of Christ," to which the pope added: "Merciful father, we urgently implore your forgiveness and we beseech the gift of a repentant heart so that all Christians, reconciled with you and with one another, will be able to experience anew the joy of full communion." It would be too easy to scoff at the professed wish for a repentant heart; I prefer to take John Paul at his word. Only hard-hearted skeptics will refuse to allow that John Paul was himself praying for a good heart, instead of hiding under a mantel of infallibility. And yet, given the Church's stance with regard to Protestant communities, the net effect of the French cardinal's apology seemed to amount to saying aloud, "We regret that Protestants insist on defiance."

Cardinal Edward Cassidy of Australia next read the "confession of sins against the people of Israel." Bishop Stephen Fumio Hamao of Japan in turn read the "confession of sins committed in actions against love, peace, the rights of peoples and respect for cultures and religions." The pope then responded, echoing the offense and begging pardon. In turn, Nigeria's Cardinal Francis Arinze read the "confession of sins against the dignity of women and the unity of the human race. . . . Let us pray for women, who are all too often humiliated and marginalized," he said. Pope John Paul affirmed that Christians had been guilty of racial and ethnic discrimination. Then Bishop François Xavier Nguyen Van Thuan of Vietnam read the last confession—"of sins in relation to the fundamental rights of the person." This apology covered a multitude of sins, including abortion and capitalism. The risk with these sub-apologies is that if the speaker does not emphasize that *Catholics* were doing the deeds in question, mea culpa becomes universal and applies to all people. Catholic wrongdoing is lost in the crowd.

As if to demonstrate his intention to live out the apology, the pope began to travel with his heart in his hand. The pope's trip to the Holy Land in March 2000 complemented the 12 March 2000 apology.

During his historic visit to Israel, the pope placed a written apology to the Jewish people in the Wailing Wall in Jerusalem. In time it became clear that John Paul did not focus exclusively on Jews: He would make similar efforts at ecumenical dialogue with the Orthodox Churches during his visits to Greece, Syria, and Ukraine in 2001 and at the Day of Prayer for Peace at Assisi in January 2002.

The apology at the heart of this chapter was not without precedent, for several bishops had issued public statements in the late 1990s admitting ecclesiastical guilt. The pope himself had taken various steps in the 1990s to convince the international Jewish community of the sincerity of his contrition over centuries of anti-Semitism. Contrition toward Jews was perhaps the impetus for the more global apology that ensued. It may have been Jews who prompted a pope to ask for forgiveness and consequently spark the interest of occasional Catholics.

Pope John Paul deserves credit, I think, for conducting an examination of conscience for an entire culture and then asking forgiveness for its mistakes. The act of confession led to a long document, "Memory and Reconciliation," released on 7 March 2000 by the Vatican's International Theological Commission (referred to in the rest of this chapter as "the commission"). According to the document, the Church remains holy, despite the sins of its children.[4] (This logic underlies the Catholic doctrine—*ex opere operato*—even though a priest may himself be sinful, his sinfulness does not taint the sacredness of the sacrament of the Eucharist.) The pope was pressing on resources in Catholic theology to do something new; he was not exactly inventing these ideas.

The Appeal of the Apology

In the same year as John Paul's apology, an American intellectual and practicing Roman Catholic attracted attention for accusing his Church of consistently refusing to admit wrongdoing. The enormous popular success of Garry Wills's 2000 book *Papal Sin* suggests that quite a few Catholics found the central argument of the work plausible or at least intriguing. Without empirical data, I rely on the assumption that many cultural Catholics in the United States sympathized with a view articulated by the Dominican nun Laurie Brink. Asked in 2008 what she would do if she were named pope, she replied, "I'd want a year of prayer and fasting for us and for the world, for the sins we committed, asking for forgiveness from those we've wronged and making reparation as a Church."[5] Although John Paul denounced the cultural Catholics of France in 1980 (as noted earlier), he may have appeased cultural Catholics throughout the West by admitting fault. Even though some critics insisted John Paul's apology did not go far enough—because it stated that only individual Catholics are capable of sin, not the Church itself—still it remains that the extraordinary gesture must have made it easier for distant Catholics to love what they had themselves seen as a defective Church.

A vivid example of how John Paul connected to cultural Catholics and inspired them is the American journalist Peggy Noonan.[6] Her 2005 work *John Paul the Great* stood apart from other biographies on John Paul because of the way in which she detailed his life in terms of its effect on her personally. She credits him with having brought her back to Roman Catholicism (even though, as a cultural Catholic, she had never really left). It seems reasonable to expect that John Paul would have attracted other cultural Catholics to return to Mass. Certainly some of the people who watched John Paul's funeral were cultural Catholics. About that funeral Peggy Noonan wrote:

> It was a phenomenon, certainly the biggest funeral in all human history, not only the four million who filled the streets, but the two to three *billion* people estimated to have watched or seen it on television. Two to three billion listened to the readings, experienced the Mass, and so it was the biggest Mass in human history. Two to three billion heard the eulogy.[7]

It would be simply wrong to suggest that crowds watched the pope's funeral because of his apology. I have no data to offer with regard to an increase of priestly vocations or an upsurge in Mass attendance since the death of John Paul II. Much more modestly, I argue only that a pope often described as conservative must surely have pleased some liberals by saying he was sorry.

Countless news stories subsequently proclaimed that John Paul II's act of repentance was unprecedented in church history. That was something of an overstatement. The International Theological Commission, whose study "Memory and Reconciliation: The Church and the Faults of the Past" laid the groundwork for the landmark prayer, presented a fuller picture. While "in the entire history of the Church there are no precedents for requests for forgiveness by the Magisterium for past wrongs," there have been rare occasions on which "ecclesiastical authorities—Pope, Bishops, or Councils—have openly acknowledged the faults of abuses which they themselves were guilty of."

For example, in a message to the Diet of Nuremberg on 25 November 1522, the reforming Pope Adrian (or Hadrian) VI acknowledged "the abominations, the abuses . . . and the lies" of which the "Roman court" of his time was guilty—a "sickness" extending "from the top to the members." Such sickness had been widely known. Adrian's predecessor, Leo X (whom Martin Luther called "Antichrist," among other things), was notorious for his excesses, and several members of the College of Cardinals had tried to poison him. Interestingly, Adrian, like John Paul II, was not Italian (he was Dutch), which might have accorded him some critical distance from the Roman See. The only other apology cited is much more recent.

Pope Paul VI, in his opening address at the second session of Vatican II, asked "pardon of God . . . and of the separated brethren [John XXIII's term for Orthodox believers]" who felt offended by the Catholic Church. Paul then declared himself ready for an apology from the Eastern Church. "In the view of Paul VI," the commission's study reads, "both the request for and offer of pardon concerned solely the sin of the division between Christians and presupposed reciprocity." Paul received his apology, in a sense, after he met with Greek Orthodox Patriarch Athenagoras in 1964; together, they lifted the mutual anathemas in place for one thousand years. Here we find evidence that an apology can actually heal wounds, even though Paul did not offer an apology for wrongdoing, but rather regret over wrongdoing. John Paul II's address also seemed to invite apologies for abuses Christians had suffered over the years, but as his address was much more inclusive than Paul's, he presumably didn't expect direct reciprocation from everyone mentioned. The risk of expecting or demanding reciprocity is that it can undermine an apology; much stronger is the apology issued without an expectation of reciprocity.

"Memory and Reconciliation" also examined Jubilee, which was first proclaimed under Pope Boniface VIII in 1300. At that time, "the penitential pilgrimage to the tombs of the Apostles Peter and Paul was associated with the granting of an exceptional indulgence for procuring, with sacramental pardon, total or partial remission of the temporal punishment due to sin." This first Jubilee evidently succeeded: up to 200,000 pilgrims thronged Rome throughout the year, which created a traffic jam the poet Dante used as a model for hell's travel arrangements in the *Inferno*. More significant problems resulted from the quest for indulgences, though. When pilgrims seeking forgiveness were denied access to holy sites by Muslim Turks in the late eleventh century, the Church launched a crusade. Special indulgences were then offered to anyone who participated. Thus, ironically, one of the main events for which the Catholic Church (as a whole) sought forgiveness in March 2000 was originally motivated, in part, by a quest (by Catholic individuals) to attain forgiveness.

"Memory and Reconciliation" certainly didn't address every confusing aspect of church history or of the idea of forgiveness. It did, however, explicitly address certain questions regarding John Paul II's public "purification of memory:" "Why should it be done? Who should do it? What is the goal and how should this be determined, by correctly combining historical and theological judgment? Who will be addressed? What are the moral implications? And what are the possible effects on the life of the Church and on society?"[8]

To determine these answers, the commission undertook a nuanced examination of collective conscience. Through biblical, historical, theological, and ethical inquiries, it attempted to determine what really happened in the Church's past, whether the Church or the supposedly Christian society was responsible, and whether the Christians involved knew they were doing wrong. The challenge was to steer a course between "an apologetics that seeks to justify everything and an unwarranted laying of blame, based on historically untenable attributions of responsibility."

Reasonable people may disagree over whether the apology was too vague, too sweeping, too limited, too late, or flat-out unnecessary, but they can't accuse it of being haphazard.[9] My view is that John Paul's apology *could* help—as few other gestures could—connect the Church to disaffected Catholics and the faithful of other religions. An examination of "Memory and Reconciliation" can help to clarify what makes for an effective apology.

Precedents and Context

This was not, as I've said, the first time a pope ever confessed fallibility. St. Peter, the first pope, confessed humbly on more than one occasion that he had been wrong, that he had made a mistake. This was, however, the first time a pontiff had admitted fallibility since Pius IX had formally ushered in the doctrine of papal infallibility in 1870. Although technically only two popes have ever invoked infallibility, most of the Western world (including quite a few "occasional

Catholics") believes that the pope always speaks as if he were infallible.

Nor was March 2000 exactly the first time John Paul himself made amends. In 1992, John Paul had apologized for the arrest of Galileo in 1633. He acknowledged that Galileo was wrongly censured in 1633 by the Inquisition for asserting that Earth is not the center of the universe. Before the 2000 apology, John Paul had already extended an olive branch to Jews by paying a visit to the synagogue of Rome in 1986 (some years earlier, John XXIII had his car stop once outside the synagogue to bless Jews who were leaving Sabbath services). The Vatican extended diplomatic relations to Israel in 1993, and in March 1998 the pope not only apologized for the failure of Catholics to help Jews during the Holocaust but also conceded that Christian anti-Semitism may have enabled the Holocaust. 1998 was the year of "We Remember," in which John Paul II expressed contrition for the failure of Catholics to offer more protection to Jews and for the fact that some took part in their persecution.

And it must be noted that, by the time of John Paul's March 2000 apology (in which he did not specifically mention the Holocaust), several other bishops had already issued apologies of their own. In 1997 French newspapers reported that the French bishops had convened at Vichy in order to formally ask forgiveness from Jews for Catholic silence in the face of anti-Jewish laws some fifty years earlier. *Le Monde* reported that the bishops went so far as to declare that the Roman Catholic liturgy of the Eucharist may have encouraged anti-Semitism. Six months later, in March 1998, Italian newspapers were the first to report of Joseph Cardinal Ratzinger's official apology to Jews. According to the *Corriere della Sera*, Ratzinger avowed that Catholic anti-Semitism played a role in the (Catholic) toleration of Nazi persecution of Jews."[10]

Not every apology from a bishop focused on Jews. In 1998, three years after he replaced Hans Groer, who had been accused of abusing young boys, Cardinal Christoph Schoenborn of Vienna apologized "for everything that my predecessors and other holders of Church office committed against people in their trust." Perhaps we can make out a Catholic pattern here, as Schoenborn's remark again raises the question of whether an apology has to be specific in order to work. It seems difficult to imagine aggrieved parties finding solace in Schoenborn's words, for their vagueness undermines the power of apology.

Of course, the Catholic Church is hardly alone in admitting guilt over something: Governments and private groups have also come clean about mistakes, and these occasions help us pinpoint moments of cultural change, if not outright transformation. On 18 March 1965, for example, the Sheriff of Montgomery County, Alabama apologized for routing six hundred civil rights demonstrators with horses and clubs. In 1983, Congress passed legislation providing an official apology and compensation to Japanese Americans interned in the Second World War. In 1970, at the site of the Warsaw ghetto, West German Chancellor Willy Brandt fell to his knees to express the guilt, sorrow, and responsibility of Germany for the Holocaust. The German state has publicly apologized for the Holocaust and, in 2003, funded a considerable monument in Berlin to those who perished in the Holocaust. US Senator Trent Lott apologized in 2002 for racist remarks he made at a party honoring Strom Thurmond. And in April 2005, the Prime Minister of Japan expressed grave remorse for Japan's actions in World War II.[11] The examples go on and on. The point of bringing them up is to underscore the potential of an apology not only to heal the aggrieved but also to inspire those who have become cynical.

It would be a stretch to suggest that the Southern Baptist Convention (USA) had been inspired by John Paul when they issued an apology in 1995 to all African-Americans and asked for their forgiveness. And yet the idea is not entirely far-fetched. In any event, these corporate apologies contrast with the highly personal apologies of American televangelists such as Jimmy Swaggart and Jim Bakker, whose sexual secrets toppled their respective ministries. Of course, plenty of other church leaders and politicians refuse to apologize for their transgressions (think of Ted Haggard, an American evangelist who maintained a two-year sexual relationship with a male prostitute, or Senator Larry Craig, who was arrested in the men's room of an airport after allegedly having propositioned an undercover policeman for sex).

Popular American twelve-step programs for those addicted to drugs or alcohol revolve around apology: we must make everything right with those we've harmed or offended. Apologies can work wonders, even—or especially—for the high and mighty. Even an insufficient expression of remorse can give hope for the future. In the United States, a country in which well over half of those who self-identify as Catholic support the ordination of women to the priesthood, ordinary believers were able to take some solace—admittedly not much—in John Paul's desire to recognize the inequality of the sexes in 2000. Although he allowed girls to participate as altar servers, he spelled out in 1994 his permanent opposition to the ordination of women. Four years later, he warned that theologians and others in authority who persisted in calling for women's ordination risked a "just penalty."

The pope surprised quite a few people when he issued an apostolic letter to women in June 1995 affirming their equality in marriage and the workplace and in intellectual achievements. He called for equal pay for equal work and lamented that too often women were valued more for their looks than their intelligence, skills, and sensitivity. He apologized for any role the church might have played throughout history in marginalizing women. Although John Paul refused to consider the possibility of female priests, one can perhaps read some regret or at least sensitivity in his refusal—at least if one views that refusal in the context of the relevant remarks about women in 1995 and March 2000.

Looming Problems

Benedict inherited some challenges when the College of Cardinals named him pope in April 2005. From an American perspective, no problem was more immediate than the priestly sex scandal.

The crisis, already well publicized by 2005, had erupted in January 2002 with the case of one accused priest in the Archdiocese of Boston. The scandal quickly spread throughout the United States and beyond. Within three years, hundreds of accused clergy had been removed from parish work in America. The US church said early in 2005 that it had paid at least $840 million for settlements with victims since 1950. By 2008, that sum had soared to two billion dollars.

It wasn't until January 2002 that the enormity of the situation began to unfold, when a Boston judge ordered the Catholic archdiocese to publicly release internal church documents about abusive priests. The public reaction resulted in efforts by state legislatures to strengthen laws against sexual abuse and criminal investigations across the United States. A conference of American bishops reported in February that there were 11,750 allegations of sexual abuse going back to 1950 involving 5,148 priests and deacons.

Bishops came under fire for protecting abusive priests, in some cases transferring them from parish to parish and state to state, where they molested again. As the scandal grew in magnitude, John Paul summoned American cardinals to an extraordinary closed-door meeting in the Vatican in April 2002. Days later, he publicly declared that there was "no place in the priesthood and or religious life for those who would harm the young." He called such abuse an "appalling sin" and a civil crime.[12] He apologized. Later, however, he roiled many American Catholics by promoting Cardinal Bernard Law of Boston to a plum position in Rome (at the basilica of Santa Maria Maggiore). Many Catholics in the archdiocese of Rome felt particularly betrayed, as they had demonstrated publicly and asked that Rome summarily fire Law. Law as well apologized.

Almost immediately after his election, Benedict XVI found himself accused of having protected priests guilty of sexually abusing children. In a letter sent to every Catholic bishop in 2001, he had ordered that all Church investigations into allegations of child sex abuse be carried out in secret. American lawyers argued that his definition of jurisdiction in such cases amounted to an obstruction of justice.[13] In his first papal visit to the United States, Benedict XVI apologized in 2008 explicitly and repeatedly for harm done to Catholic children abused by priests. He also acknowledged the pain and suffering endured by the families of the victims and all those whose confidence in the institutional Church had been shaken by the scandal. Benedict's predecessor and close friend John Paul had in a sense already shown him how to offer a sincere, if hedged, apology on camera.

American Catholics will continue to lament the damage wrought by this scandal for decades. Meanwhile, they struggle to figure out how to revere a spiritual tradition that veered off course during the pedophile revelations of 2002–2003.[14] That spiritual tradition sits in a culture that guides ordinary Catholics as to how to marry and how to mourn, what to do on Sunday and what not to eat on Friday, where to go when threatened with a dire illness and where to find God's principal representative on earth. The betrayal ordinary Catholics have internalized will surely transform the culture that reflects the hope and consolation of Catholics. John Paul's decision to apologize publicly and frequently may have been diplomatically brilliant and well timed; had he waited even two years to make the apology, it may have seemed less sincere.

Catholic–Jewish relations presented another looming problem for Benedict in 2005. Amos Luzzatto, president of the Union of Italian Jewish Communities, complained that there was a "contradiction between the penitence expressed by the church for so many sins against the Jews in the past and the beatification [of those who committed them]."[15] He was referring to Pope John Paul's decision to "beatify" (grant the title "blessed" to) Pope Pius IX in September 2000. (Pope John XXIII was beatified at the same time.) According to

Luzzatto, Pius IX (whose papacy began in 1846 and ended in 1878) restored restrictions on Jews in Rome, which was then under papal control.[16] John Paul's beatification of Pope Pius XII (also in 2000) had raised even more vocal objections from Jewish groups and Catholics sympathetic to them.

Benedict visited the death camp at Auschwitz in 2006 and stated, "It is my fervent prayer that the memory of this appalling crime will strengthen our determination to heal the wounds that for too long have sullied relations between Christians and Jews."[17] Indicating the vital link between himself and his predecessor, Benedict repeated the prayer that the late Pope John Paul II had used when he visited Jerusalem's Western Wall in 2000 and asked forgiveness from Jews for Christians who had persecuted them in past centuries. Benedict then added in his own words: "I now make his prayer my own."

It is significant that Benedict found time to enter a New York City synagogue in the course of his first, and rather brief, visit to the United States in 2008. Benedict knew that apologies sometimes work, and he must surely have hoped to boost or even mend the Church's reputation. In so doing, he also helped to change the Church's culture into a humbler, more honest force.

Political Sensitivities

Some members of the Catholic hierarchy openly criticized John Paul's round of apologizing. Surely John Paul knew that he would come in for chastisement from his own people. The example he set is worth noticing.

Benedict was asked to apologize in 2006, over an incident having nothing to do with his predecessor. While delivering a September address at the University of Regensburg, Germany, Benedict was understood to have equated Islam with violence, after he cited a medieval scholar who said that Islam brought things "evil and inhuman." He came under widespread attack from the Western media and issued a statement clarifying his intention. He did not exactly apologize for what he had said, but his statement seemed to take quite seriously the various demands that he make an apology to the international Muslim community.

Part of the problem no doubt stemmed from widespread suspicion in the West that Islam promoted violence. It is worthwhile to note the social context in which Benedict's comment was spoken. The arch-conservative American writer Ann Coulter, for example, made explicit a view later imputed (no doubt unfairly) to Benedict. In a 2004 interview with a British newspaper, she went so far as to state: "The question is not, 'Are all Muslims terrorists?' The question is, "Are all terrorists Muslims? And the answer is yes—every one I have to worry about.' "[18] It will not do to conclude that Benedict avoided the rhetorical excess of a far-right thinker. He came too close to endorsing what many non-Muslim Westerners on the right were rumored to think, and he realized the peril of his position. Through his response (which, again, was not exactly an apology), he tried to stop criticism in roughly the same way an apology often does. This phrasing suggests a lack of sincerity, I acknowledge.

It should not seem far-fetched to credit John Paul with having created a climate in which Benedict could more easily respond to demands for an apology. John Paul II could rise to such demands effectively. John Paul II never apologized for the church's position on the ordination of women or the morality of same-sex unions, however. This is to say that some Catholics—not just cultural Catholics—will understandably hold that the Church has more apologizing to do.

Onward and Upward

John Paul apologized to Jews, women, Orthodox Christians, and others for his Church's failings and sins against them throughout history. He apologized to Muslims for the Crusades, which ravaged the Holy Land from the eleventh through the thirteenth centuries. The attention from the international media on the occasion of the apology indicates the power the Vatican still enjoys and the importance of Catholic culture. In both the apology and the media attention lay the potential for an important cultural shift.

An apology may eventually change behavior or just perception, as we have seen. And stepping into the shoes of someone who apologized may make it easier for a strict disciplinarian to soften his stance. For example, Suzanne Morse, communications director for Voice of the Faithful, a 30,000-member group formed in the wake of the church's pedophilia scandals and which advocates a greater role for the laity in church governance, expressed some optimism at the election of Benedict XVI. "You don't necessarily know what a pope is going to do based on their experiences as a cardinal."[19] In his installation Mass on 24 April 2005, Benedict offered further reason for optimism. He declared his intention to reach out to those who are Catholic by baptism "but not yet in full communion with the Church" during the open-air Mass in St. Peter's Square. He also made clear his desire to "listen to the Church" rather than simply to lead it, as an old-fashioned autocrat might.[20]

Skeptics may continue to doubt the Church's contrition. Even they can see, though, the negative publicity John Paul risked in the apology. Bishop Piero Marini, who oversaw papal ceremonies, explained shortly before the 12 March 2000 ceremony that "given the number of sins committed in the course of 20 centuries, it [the apology] must necessarily be rather summary."[21] It is easy to interpret such sincerity snidely and to judge unfairly by assessing mistakes made long ago solely by contemporary standards. John Paul began the important work of apologizing for Catholic culture; others should now follow suit, exploring when, where, and how Catholics have abused their power to do good. John Paul perhaps allowed doubt about the Church's infallibility even as he enjoined faith and commitment. If he did that, he lifted the Church away from fanaticism and moved it closer to humility. Doubt does not necessarily undermine the papacy or the Sacred Congregation for the Doctrine of the Faith; doubt can help any leader anticipate and evaluate alternatives and, later, fine tune pronouncements if necessary. John Paul did at least *something* to lure cultural Catholics back to more regular participation in the Church. John Paul built a bridge to a crucial segment of American Catholicism.

Gone are the days when a pontiff was beyond criticism from his own people. John Paul made it difficult for Catholics ever again to pretend that their Church, the heart of their culture, lies beyond sin. John Paul made it easier for many alienated Catholics to agree with their church, to feel a part of a flawed but worthwhile family. I have used the journalist Peggy Noonan as example of John Paul's power to do just this, but it must be said that John Paul had brought her back to the fold *before* he issued the apology. Though the apology had nothing to do with her return, her admiration for him only seemed to grow in the years prior to his death. The point of discussing Noonan at all is to offer a specific example of how John Paul reached a self-avowed cultural Catholic.

I do not mean to suggest that Peggy Noonan is representative of cultural Catholics in the United States; no single person could be. Nor could any poll capture precisely the aggregate effect of John Paul's apology. Working out that effect is more of an art than a science. My point has been to focus on the question of what any pope *could* do to lure back the lapsed members of his flock; I cannot think of any better idea. Suddenly overturning the teachings on birth control, ordination of women, gay marriage, and embryonic stem cell research might well do more harm than good.

In her tribute to John Paul, Peggy Noonan moves directly from an articulation of awe at his funeral to a prediction by another American journalist, the television talk show host Laura Ingraham.[22] Ingraham, a convert to Catholicism, predicted to Noonan that John Paul's death would lead to "millions of conversions" (Ingraham was not talking about John Paul's apology). No poll or Catholic news source has indicated that this has happened.

Nor is there any empirical evidence that the apology reignited the piety of cultural Catholics. Does this mean that John Paul's apology fell flat? I don't believe it did; John Paul opened a window, much in the way that Pope John XXIII famously said he wanted to do at the outset of the Second Vatican Council. It is difficult to blame John Paul for those who didn't jump through the window, back into the pews. A poll might demonstrate that author James Carroll was one of many to take pride in John Paul's gesture:

> The moment I was most proud to be a Catholic was when John Paul II at the millennium insisted that we couldn't cross the threshold into the new century without a serious act of repentance for the failures of the Church.
>
> And Pope John Paul did that against the advice of his conservative inner circle. This man acknowledged the gravest failures of the Church, an instance of moral reckoning that, to consider another example, the United States of America has never come close to accomplishing.[23]

Even if the net effect of the apology did not lead to the elimination of cultural Catholicism in the United States (by transforming all cultural Catholics into orthodox Catholics), it is difficult to think of a more effective step another pope might have taken—apart from apologizing more straightforwardly, of course.

John Paul unleashed a wave of self-examination which may have made it easier for cultural Catholics to accept the eventual apologies of bishops in the priestly sex abuse scandal. What makes Noonan and Ingraham especially useful for my purposes is that both are political conservatives. It would be wrongheaded to assume that their political conservatism would automatically translate into ecclesiastical conservatism. That said, it does seem safe to imagine that these two conservatives may have figured among those rather less enthusiastic about the papal apology.

The point of this chapter ultimately is to suggest that it would be a mistake to portray Catholic culture exclusively as a grassroots phenomenon. It would be all to easy to portray pre-Vatican II Catholic culture in the United States as an example of "top-down" force and the post-Vatican II corollary as precisely the opposite. Change can still come from on high. Whether papal decisions find a receptive audience in the United States depends as much on the wisdom of a pope as on the sensitivity of Catholic people. While I applaud John Paul's gesture, I find the apology itself too ambiguous to have been effective. The symmetry on which the apology balanced interfered with the message; instead of focusing on and regretting harms done by Catholics, he chose to pull into the discussion the harm suffered by Catholics as well.

The ballet between pope and flock requires an awareness that defies quantification. The next chapter will demonstrate that the flock can sometimes work out apparent conflicts on their own. Just when it seemed that the Virgin Mary had become irrelevant to the lives of working women, Catholics found a way to update cultural understanding of her. The next chapter will complement this one by pointing to an important instance of "bottom-up" change in Catholic culture.

Chapter 6

What Would the Virgin Mary Do?

So far this book has focused on a broadly external division or choice between Catholic doctrine and Catholic culture. This chapter will turn to one of the most distinctive features of Catholic culture, devotion to the Virgin Mary. Through Mary's example we can glimpse not only willful amnesia on the part of educated Catholics who view Mary as largely passive but also the extent to which culture can change. Beyond that, the chapter will argue for the expediency of a cultural shift with regard to Mary.

Women in Western Europe and North America have made enormous social gains since 1960. Many women now possess a PhD, JD, MD, or MBA; increasingly often, such women oversee male colleagues in the workplace. These women may be on the pill and may regret not having more time to spend with their children at home. Some of these women may like to consider themselves serious Catholics as well. What relation with the Virgin Mary can professional women hope to have? A model of obedience and docility would not seem to have much relevance in the twenty-first century.

An updated profile of Mary would clarify what saintly women look like in a transformed social order and do much to enhance the confidence of Catholic women who work outside the home. Making Mary relevant today requires not a turn to something new but a return to something prominent in Mary's past. In heroic deeds credited to Mary, we'll find a feasible role model for twenty-first century girls and women as they march off to school, the office, or the gym.

Virgins in College

Efforts to follow Mary's example may surprise us by their creativity. One Pennsylvania college student invoked Mary's purity and angered many. Her case may compel us to see Mary in a new light.

Twenty-two year old Pennsylvania State University art student Christine Enedy provoked controversy in 1996 with a pair of works exhibited on campus under the auspices of the art department.[1] As part of her senior project, Enedy constructed a grotto in the form of a red vagina lined with black fur. The grotto held a statue of the Virgin Mary. Though it remained only briefly on view, the work angered some local Catholics, who questioned whether the University ought to adopt a policy against public desecration of religious symbols. Discussions of the incident in the local paper were picked up by national media, from where they came to the attention of the Catholic League's director William Donohue. Not content with reports that the work had been removed by the artist herself after consultation with the campus chaplain, Donohue sent out a missive asking the Catholic League's 250,000 members to write Penn State, demanding that Enedy be punished.

Enedy, a practicing Catholic, maintained in subsequent newspaper interviews that she had never intended her senior project to offend Catholics. She was quoted in the campus paper as saying, "It was never an issue of me against the Catholic Church. I was just trying to portray an image of the oppression of women in the church and the oppression of women in general." Enedy did not single out the Church for blame, she explained, but did indicate the scope of the Church's power by choosing a symbol near and dear to many Catholics. One might reasonably question how a fur-lined vagina symbolizes oppression, for some onlookers may have seen a different symbol: Mary standing guard over the prize of virginity. Even this interpretation, though, may have roiled conservative Catholics.

A few months later, Enedy presented another work in a student show on campus entitled "Twenty five years of Virginity . . . A Self-Portrait." It consisted of a quilt made of twenty-five pairs of women's panties, each with a red cross stitched on the crotch. Enedy saw this work as an opportunity to explain herself and the previous project, and to celebrate her cherished virginity in the face of a campus culture which had little sympathy for the traditional Catholic values she herself affirmed. Instead, this work simply re-ignited the controversy which later moved into the political arena, when a Pennsylvania state representative threatened to vote to withhold state subsidies to the University unless the work was removed from view. While the University administration refused to bend to this intimidation, the controversy became the occasion for a set of new guidelines urging greater dialogue among students and teachers with regard to the display of potentially controversial student art.

Once again Enedy insisted that angry Catholics had misinterpreted her work. Noting her desire to create a personal expression of her social struggle, she told a local reporter, "In olden times, women would take fabric from garments worn by their family members to make their quilts more personal. The first thing that came into my mind was my underwear, because it's very personal. The cross represents a chastity belt, something sacred." To another reporter she said, "All I wanted to do was something that pertained to me and would tell them who I am as a person. I am a Catholic and I am a virgin and that's that."

We might dismiss the Enedy case as mere grandstanding—she used what she found in her heritage bailiwick to make the loudest noise she could, attracting maximum attention. On the other hand, like black Catholics who profess that they prefer to pray to a black Madonna not to spite white Catholics but to feel Mary's presence more deeply, so might Christine Enedy be serious about remaining a virgin out of loyalty to a faith that prizes virginity. If the Virgin Mary were alive in the United States today, what would she do? How could she survive on an American college campus, especially a secular place like Penn State? On the one hand, it may seem impossible to imagine Mary stitching crosses on panties and then mounting a public display of them. On the other hand, it just might be that Mary didn't take offense of Enedy's expression of the Catholic values by which she lived.

Catholic women today, particularly well-educated ones, may struggle to take Mary as their example. Conscience may serve as a useful guide. Evelyn Waugh's memorable character Cordelia in *Brideshead Revisited* was kicked out of the Legion of Mary because the nuns considered her recalcitrant. The nuns had insisted that Cordelia put her shoes on one side of the bed before going to sleep every night, but Cordelia found the other side of the bed more convenient. Later, while reflecting on her dismissal from the club, an otherwise adorable Cordelia insisted to her older sister, "I don't believe the Blessed Mother gives two hoots if I put my shoes on the right or the left of my bed!"

The conscience of Waugh's fictional character directed her to show reverence to Mary in a non-mechanical way. It may be that Christine Enedy is a non-fictional example of the same thing.

Enedy's case should matter more to us not so much because she is real and Cordelia is not, but because Enedy was talking about purity and chastity, whereas Cordelia was talking about obedience. Roman Catholics, it is fair to say, are not ready to adopt a relaxed tone when talking about Mary's purity and chastity. Well and good, but, once more, it may still be that the Virgin approved of Enedy's postmodern devotion. For centuries, Catholic theologians have dug in their heels and insisted that Mary remained a virgin during and after childbirth; she died a virgin. Curiously enough, nothing in Enedy's devotion opposes that unyielding tenet in Catholic theology.

Enedy went on to finish college and pursue a life of her own, much as other graduates do. Not so long ago, she might have been sent to a Magdalene asylum to perform slave labor in a laundry. Peter Mullan's 2002 film *Magdalene Sisters* saddened audiences on several continents with its frank portrayal of the brutality waiting for young girls who dared to flirt or wear their skirts a bit too high. Frances Ferguson's academic study of this dark corner of Catholic culture can hardly fail to move readers who contemplate the thousands of wasted lives and the baffling number of Catholic communities which supported and ignored this brutality.[2] Sex is no longer the sin it once was; throwing your life away should certainly qualify as one. Throwing someone else's life away is worse yet. The fate of so many previous Catholic women escaped Christine Enedy, who chose freely to praise Mary. The victims of the Magdalene asylums on various continents had no choice but to imitate Mary in one very narrow way.

Previous Views of Mary

We don't know much about Mary's biography; the Gospels tell us surprisingly little. Scholars have observed that Catholics take a good deal on faith when it comes to Mary. It could be that Catholic leaders simply molded her image in such a way as to justify the prevailing gender dynamics of earlier times, which is effectively to say the subjugation of women. In any event, it does seem that Catholic leaders favored a passive and obedient exemplar. Catholics also depended on her body in a curious way. This dependence on the corporeality of

Mary might conjure up sensual images of a woman who enjoys her body, but in fact precisely the opposite happened.

Mary is not simply a spirit. Her body is a matter of great importance to those who love her. Debates over her perpetual virginity and bodily assumption into heaven are perhaps understandable, as doubting Thomas refused to believe that the man before him was Christ, resurrected from the dead, until the stranger allowed Thomas to inspect his body. Christ's body made all the difference, and Christ allowed his body to be used to facilitate belief. Christ's human body made it easier for ordinary humans to see themselves in him, and Mary's human body bridges a similar gap. (Unlike Jews or Muslims, Christians believe that their God took human form. Because of the Christian belief that Jesus redeemed it, it could be argued that the human body is particularly important for Christians.)

Moreover, we can hardly blame Mary's many admirers for their curiosity about her appearance. Expectations for Mary have always been high, and mortals have assumed that Mary is an actual work of art. After seeing the Virgin in a grotto in 1858, for example, Bernadette Soubirous fielded questions from French authorities about Mary's looks, of all things (Mary also spoke at Lourdes, remember). Priests showed the young girl various paintings of the Virgin by the great masters (for example, Leonardo, Raphael, Botticelli, Dürer) and asked her which was the most accurate. Aghast, Bernadette exclaimed, "My dear mother, how they slander you!" The eventual saint instead insisted that the local statue of the Virgin was a perfect likeness. Accuracy in regard to Mary's appearance also mattered when the Virgin appeared to St. Catherine Labouré in 1830 in Paris; Mary instructed St. Catherine to have a model cast in the Virgin's image. Depictions of the Virgin had already been circulating for centuries in parts of North America; artistic renditions of the remarkably attractive woman who appeared to Juan Diego on the back of a peasant cloak in 1531 were familiar to many Catholics long before 1830.

From Bernadette's testimony we can infer that Mary is permanently young, Caucasian, and serenely beautiful—even by today's standards. No Catholic has to look far for a statue of Our Lady of Lourdes, and most Catholics implicitly assume a likeness between the statue and the Blessed Mother. This is one of the people Catholics will recognize immediately after death. Catholics believe that after the Second Coming of Christ, everyone in heaven will have a body. For now, though, the only two beings in heaven with bodies are Jesus and Mary.

Although neither Luther nor Calvin challenged Mary's perpetual virginity, and despite the fact that Islam greatly honors her, Mary does not seem to appear to Protestants or Muslims. Mary became a problem in the twentieth century, to the extent that she was perhaps too Catholic. The minds at work in the Second Vatican Council saw fit to downplay Mary's role in the Catholic Church. Some Protestant leaders had complained that the prominence of statues to Mary in Catholic churches gave the impression that she was a deity. Partly in response to Protestant objections, the documents of Vatican II instructed parishes around the world to tone down the devotions to Mary. Church authorities had their way for about two decades, in so far as Mary fell from emphasis in much parish life. Popular love for Mary eventually stirred up renewed enthusiasm for her.[3] She seems to speak to perennial human need, which is not to say there aren't lingering problems of a different sort.

Some contemporary scholars complain that Mary is simply passive. In *Alone of All Her Sex*, Marina Warner classifies the types of images of the Virgin Mary around which devotion to the Blessed Mother has clustered: Virgin, Queen, Bride, Mother, and Intercessor. Warner, who grew up Catholic, dislikes the long tradition of exalting Mary, for the reason that idealizing Mary supposedly diminishes the value of ordinary women. No one can hope to live up to that image, according to Warner and some others, and so we'd be better off without it, or perhaps by placing it in a very different context (that is, a legend). In her study, Warner depicts Mary in her role as an occasionally active intercessor. Warner does portray a fairly active Virgin, if only in the spheres of midwifery and child-rearing. "For while Mary provides a focus for the steeliest asceticism, she is also the ultimate of fertility symbols," Warner concludes.[4] On the basis of Warner's book, contemporary Catholic women may quite reasonably find Mary an unsatisfactory role model.

Garry Wills, one of the influential Catholic intellectuals in the early twenty-first century, objected to enthusiastic devotion to Mary as well, albeit for a very different reason. His reason, curiously enough, had to do with scriptural accuracy. He argued in *Papal Sin* that Catholics have gone overboard with devotion to the Virgin Mother. Following the liberal, twentieth-century Catholic theologian Yves Congar, Wills contended that Catholics had uprooted the Holy Spirit from its traditional perch in the Holy Trinity and inserted the Virgin in its place. Wills found important allies in Raymond Brown, a modern Catholic theologian, and no less than Augustine himself. Wills also noted that

Thomas Aquinas, a lynchpin of the Catholic moral tradition, had argued forcefully against the immaculate conception of Mary back in the thirteenth century. The institutional Church overruled Aquinas's objection. The cumulative effect of these references alerts us to the malleability of Mary's public image.

It's not that Wills, himself a committed Catholic, dislikes Mary. It's that he sees her proper role as working in the foxholes with believers, not towering over them. Wills favors the Gospel according to Luke ultimately. That's where Catholics can orient themselves to Mary most authentically:

> Luke teaches us, then, how to pray to Mary—or, rather, with her. Not as to a queen or empress (the last thing suggested anywhere in the gospels), but as with our sister in the Spirit, a witness to God's power, not the wielder of it. Hers is a profound dignity, far from the hollow and bombastic titles heaped on her so that she might preside over papal structures of deceit.[5]

Wills urges Catholics to use the pronoun "she" to refer to the Holy Spirit in order to reinforce the feminine analogue of the deity. Such a move would contain the apparent psychological need to find a feminine aspect somewhere in the Trinity and therefore discourage untoward adulation of Mary.

Despite a post-Vatican II falling-off of devotions like novenas and rosaries in much of the laity, the hierarchy is more Marianized than ever, and private apparitions to women and children result in waves of emotional outpouring. At the center (that is, the Holy See) and the periphery (that is, conservatives), Marian devotion thrives. The popularity of Mary demonstrates that lay Catholics never needed to be told to revere Mary. They already wanted to.

Previous views of Mary, in sum, may tell us something useful about longstanding enthusiasm for praising Mary. In a religion in which people learned that their daily sexual desires were deeply sinful, committed believers looked for role models after whom they could fashion their own conduct. Seeing someone else pull off such a difficult act helped convince them that they could do it too. Projection is the operation of expelling feelings or wishes the individual finds wholly unacceptable—too shameful, too obscene, too dangerous—by attributing them to another. It is a prominent mechanism, for example, in anti-Semites, who find it necessary to transfer feelings of their own that they consider low or dirty onto Jews, and then "detect" those feelings in them. Catholics needed a figure on whom they could pin their highest hopes, a figure immune to the very forces Catholics yearned to eject from themselves. Previous views of Mary, it seems fair to conclude, said at least as much about the people who held them as they did about Mary herself.

Mary, Woman of Color

Catholics of color appear more comfortable discussing racial problems now than ever before. Here as well, Mary has a role to play. It turns out she has long stood ready to meet people of color on their own terms, sympathizing with those who have understandably felt excluded. Mary can be white, and Mary can be black.

The Madonna of Montserrat is known as La Moreneta, "the little black one." According to legend, the statue was found by shepherds in 888 CE, in a cave where it had lain not quite since St. Peter had brought it to Spain in 50 CE. The significance of the statue stems in part from the ability of Mary to be herself even as her skin color changes. Along the same lines, the most revered sacred image in Central Europe, an icon said to have been painted by St. Luke, is the "Black Madonna" of Czestochowa. "The blackened face of the Virgin in that icon was the result of smoke, but it has nevertheless had the salutary effect of stimulating and sanctioning the process of what Pope John Paul II, a special devotee of the Virgin of Czestochowa, has called 'acculturation,' particularly liturgical and artistic acculturation."[6] Believers may chuckle at the historical accident and at the same time find solace in the veil under which Mary's image lurked, conveniently disguised.

Given the troubled history of black/white social relations into which they were born, it's not so surprising that African-American Catholics have sometimes protested that the predominantly white Church makes them feel excluded. A few parishes have taken to painting white church statues of the Virgin Mother black. While some black Catholics have applauded the move, the paintings have not been without controversy. In Brooklyn, home to more black Catholics than any other diocese in the United States, a black priest once went so far as to order a white nun to change the skin color of the Virgin displayed in front of a predominantly black church.[7] If they claim to feel more comfortable that way, then it must be true that some black Catholics maintain a better prayer relation with Mary when they kneel before a black statue of her or peer at it from a distance.

The bride in the Song of Songs says: "Black am I and beautiful." Far from an awkward textual reference to be reconciled with the rest of Catholic belief about Mary (Catholics believe that references to the Mother of God are scattered throughout the Hebrew Bible, particularly in the book of Isaiah), Catholics can draw on this reference and on the veneration of various dark Madonnas to make black Catholics feel more part of the family. Of course, the Virgin of Guadalupe may serve the same function for Latinos living in the United States. Her skin in various copies of her image is invariably brown. If that artistic depiction were accurate, the Mary Catholics of color may currently need was there all along, just waiting to be asked for help.

Mary, a Feminist?

Today the big question is not so much Mary's color as her brio. That she takes orders from the Holy Trinity does not mean that she cannot have independent ideas of her own. Is she a feminist? The question comes down to whether Mary is largely or exclusively passsive. A feminist, generally speaking, is someone who rejects the traditional script of women obeying men mechanically, dutifully.

John Paul II devoted himself entirely to the Virgin Mother, proclaiming as much in his motto "Totus tuus" ("All yours"). What John Paul II tried to do was demonstrate that Mary always had been the active force that many of the faithful wanted her to be in the late twentieth century. As Father Andrew Greeley put it in *The Mary Myth*, "The high tradition of Mariology is compatible with a theory of the role of women which emphasizes the freedom, independence, strength, passion and responsibility of maternity."[8] That much is fine and good, but what about freedom and independence apart from motherhood?

Many Catholic (and certainly non-Catholic) women saw John Paul as the opposite of women-friendly. Birth control and abortion—matters central to women's reproductive freedom—stood out as primary reasons for this view. There was another issue at stake, also quite important. On 30 May 1994, John Paul II promulgated an apostolic letter affirming the Roman Catholic ban on women priests as "closed to debate" and "definitively held by all the Church's faithful." Cultural Catholics disagreed in great numbers with this teaching and so seemed to find themselves disqualified from the category "the

Church's faithful." A group of Canadian women who stormed the church of Sainte Marie, Reine du Monde in 2000 in Montreal, tossing stained tampons through the sacred space; these women disagreed that the pope was a feminist, or had women's best interests at heart.

By arguing that Pope John Paul II was a feminist, Mary Ann Glendon, a Harvard University law professor who became the first female president of the Pontifical Academy of Social Sciences, seems to be saying implicitly that Mary was a feminist, or that feminist ideals were consistent with Mary's image. It stands to reason that if the pope is a feminist, it is because Mary approves of his being a feminist. It does not automatically follow that Mary is herself a feminist, although it is possible. Glendon has remained optimistic about the marriage of modern women and traditional Catholicism, even despite institutional difficulties on how to manage this marriage.

In defending John Paul II, Glendon was making it easier to think of Mary as an active force. The US bishops had failed to bring out a pastoral letter on women, despite having tried for a full decade (from 1982 to 1992). After a series of revisions, the text ended in defeat in a floor vote. Not long after, in an essay entitled "The Pope's New Feminism," Glendon referred to the Catholic Church as "one of the world's most energetic champions of the freedom and dignity of women."[9] Glendon, who headed the Holy See Delegation to the 4th UN Women's Conference in 1995, credits Christianity with having helped women in the following ways (these ways have been noticed before, by others):

- A remarkable accomplishment of the early Church was to gain wide acceptance for the ideal of permanent monogamy in cultures where polygamy was common and men were permitted by custom to put aside their wives.
- Later, despite pressures from princes and merchants, the Council of Trent stood firm against marriages arranged without the consent of the spouses. Later still, continental European policies protecting mothers and children were influenced heavily by Catholic social thought.

The first accomplishment has perhaps become farcical, as critics allege that it's serial monogamy that is sometimes sanctioned by dubious annulments (mostly by the rich and prominent). Nonetheless, Glendon portrayed the Church as a tireless advocate for those whose voices are seldom heard in the corridors of power—refugee women, migrant

women, and mothers everywhere. Glendon pointed enthusiastically
to apostolic writings and Gospel passages in which Jesus departed
"radically" from the culture of his time in his friendships with women,
including public sinners. It is striking how many important conversa-
tions Jesus had with women, and how many of his most important
teachings were first confided to his women friends.

Against all challengers, then, Glendon, herself a woman, defended
John Paul II as a feminist. In *Mulieris Dignitatem* (1988), which
contains the theological basis for his messages to women, he labeled
discrimination against women as sinful, and repeatedly emphasized
that the Christian vision forbids the oppression of women. And in
an extraordinary letter to women on 29 June 1995, John Paul II
apologized for any sexism in the Church.

One of Glendon's central contentions was that John Paul II
"affirms the importance of biological sexual identity, but gives no
comfort to those who believe men's and women's roles are forever
fixed in a static pattern." Glendon praised John Paul for embracing
the cause of women's rights in specific terms. His Apostolic Letter to
Women prior to the 1995 Beijing Women's Conference articulated
"an urgent need" to reach equality in a variety of spheres: equal pay
for equal work, protection for working mothers, fairness in career
advancements, equality of spouses with regard to family rights, and
the recognition of everything that is part of the rights and duties of
citizens in a democratic State. Far from pressuring women to stay at
home all day, John Paul understood that many women simply had to
work and that they often endured discrimination and resentment
there.

John Paul II coined the term "new feminism" in his encyclical
Evangelium Vitae. He explained,

> In transforming culture so that it supports life, women occupy a
> place, in thought and action, which is unique and decisive. It
> depends on them to promote a "new feminism" which rejects the
> temptation of imitating models of "male domination," in order to
> acknowledge and affirm the true genius of women in every aspect of
> the life of society, and overcome all discrimination, violence, and
> exploitation (*Evangelium Vitae*, 99).

The pope recommended a new version of feminism, a compromise
between traditional views that stressed the importance of keeping
women in the home and new views of womanhood which emerged

in France and the United States in the 1970s. It stands to reason that, in endorsing the "new feminism," John Paul saw some important connection between it and the Virgin Mary.

John Paul II made it clear, many times, that the public sphere benefits from women's gifts, and that cultures should recognize distaff contributions to public life. Glendon's campaign may hold some merit, as it is possible to read in the words of John Paul something like encouragement for women to move into positions of influence outside the domestic sphere. What remains to be made explicit is how the Virgin Mary fits into this brave, new world in which women have emerged as corporate moguls and potentates.

Next Step: Overcoming the Vatican?

Anyone who prays to the Virgin Mary may struggle with the question of the extent of her power (Catholics do not believe that Mary is omnipotent) and her symbolic relation to living women. She can hardly be considered a minor player in the theatre of Catholic civilization, but she does seem quite meek. Would that be simply because she chose to adopt such a posture or because it was somehow pushed upon her? An answer to that question could help indicate just how active Mary might reasonably be portrayed by a world in which women gain more and more social power.

The way out of this conceptual problem might entail believing that Mary didn't stay at home so much because she wanted to, but because she had to; if she were alive today, she wouldn't have to stay at home (look at Catholic nuns), and so she might not; she might go to work outside the home, just as many women do today.

Alas, this view stands in conflict with what John Paul (through Cardinal Ratzinger) said in the summer of 2004. He seemed to blame working women for the gay marriage movement. On 31 July the Congregation for the Doctrine of the Faith, the Vatican's doctrinal watchdog agency, released a thirty-seven-page document titled "Letter to the Bishops of the Catholic Church on the Collaboration of Men and Women." The letter pulled no punches. "Radical feminism" had promoted a climate of hostility between men and women, it argued, and had led women to deny or play down their distinctive maternal and nurturing instincts. It had also spread confusion about gender that promoted tolerance of homosexuality. The alternative vision, according to the letter, was "the collaboration of men and women," meaning differences between the sexes should be seen as complementary rather than competitive.

Mary Ann Glendon called the document "essentially a critique of certain aspects of old-line "70s feminism" that had long since faded. Glendon said the document named but did not resolve a critical dilemma: how to respond to women's legitimate aspirations for full participation in social and political life, without harm to families, children, and the common good.

Here then emerges a central problem in cultural Catholicism today: How to include women who work in the corporate sector, stand passionately in favor of the equality of the sexes, and look to the Virgin Mary in the hope that she would show a way to have it all, without being a hypocrite? Confusion reigns in this area. Few Catholic women in North America will agree that their professional lives are to blame for the legal acceptance of gay marriage. If anything, working women might say that the struggles of gay and lesbian people have to do with social justice, not with feminism. One of the principal obstacles to seeing Mary as an action figure, however, has to do with ongoing ambivalence about feminist aspirations. What Mary has to do with these aspirations remains open to debate. Meanwhile, some professionally ambitious Catholic women choose to neglect Mary.

An End to Missed Opportunities

Rhapsodic emotions seem to follow Mary, even today. She maintains power in both the sacred and profane spheres. In November 2004, an American woman claimed her ten-year-old grilled cheese sandwich bore the image of the Virgin Mary and sold the item for $28,000 on eBay. GoldenPalace.com, an online casino, confirmed that it had placed the winning bid, and company executives said they were willing to spend "as much as it took" to own the ten-year-old half-sandwich (which was missing a chunk). Diana Duyser said she had taken a bite after preparing the sandwich ten years earlier and then spied a face peering at her. She then sealed the sandwich in a clear plastic box with cotton balls and kept it on her night stand. At the sale years later, she stated that the sandwich had never sprouted a spore of mold.

Each age will find a new way to celebrate Mary, perhaps even highly eccentric ways. Although the future remains unknown, the present is clear enough: Many woman want careers. How will Mary remain relevant to career women? That is a challenge for committed Catholics today. An obvious path is to emphasize aspects of Mary that have not received much notice before. In so doing, we can lay the foundation for a new—although not entirely different—personality profile, one more fitting with educated Western women who bring home a paycheck, not necessarily to a husband and children. This move can hardly be described as radical: John Henry Newman declared in the nineteenth century that Marian thinking must be repeatedly translated into contemporary forms if it is to continue to be meaningful. If we will take Mary as a model of human development at its best, we will have to focus on her creative powers in a way we have not before.

In the case of Mary, it seems that Catholics look for inspiration to live morally, to seek solace in times of turmoil, and then mold whatever inspiration they find to fit their present needs. Catholics may end up thwarting their own attempt to demonstrate through Mary that women can live piously. The danger is that Catholics are left with a trauma of inaccessibility, of unattainability. Mary simultaneously fosters and frustrates a desire for moral perfection. Her new action, her agenda for the twenty-first century, may be to serve as a guide, to lead us to greater understanding, to teach us something important: she never revealed more of herself than the world could understand at that time. It's not that Catholics failed to understand her previously, rather they weren't ready to understand more about her. When they are ready, they will see a new model of womanhood—a model that still shuns sin, but one that accommodates secular success and dovetails with political and corporate contributions.

As committed Catholics seek new evidence that Mary can respond to predicaments brought on by the new world of work, Catholics have good reason to hope that Mary will answer their call. Her answer, far from counsel to eschew the world of work in order to focus exclusively on the family, far from an exhortation to let your golden chances pass you by, may carry more nuance than previous messages. In that answer Catholics will discern a keen mind at work and a new direction for Catholic culture.

Chapter 7

Family Romances

> The Child is father of the Man
> —Wordsworth, "My Heart Leaps Up When I Behold"

Various psychological theories compete to explain why people believe in God, let alone remain Catholic. It's easy to dismiss the whole question by simply insisting that, with few exceptions, people follow the religion of their parents. While this largely accurate observation may indicate why a person refrains from switching to another religion, it doesn't explain why people would practice their faith with enthusiasm or, in the case of "occasional Catholics," somewhat mechanically. And so I examine three plausible accounts here, two endorsed by social psychologists generally (specifically, cognitive dissonance and terror management theory) and one more metaphorical but potentially much farther-reaching than these two: Freud's theory of family romances. Briefly put, Catholic children program themselves to mate with those of their own tribe (that is, to find appealing people who embrace the same religion that mother and/or father did). If Freud is right, an instinct developed in childhood unconsciously guides our spiritual and social choices.

Why we fall in love with a particular person and not another is a mystery. In the same way, why some people feel drawn to a religious tradition and others do not is a mystery as well (think of a child within a family who takes his religious training less seriously than a brother or sister). It will not do simply to conclude that some people have spiritual needs, and others do not. Within Christianity (both Catholicism and Protestantism), women generally exhibit more spiritual hunger, greater worship needs, than men.[1] This is not to suggest that Christian men tend to "fake it" in church; more often, Christian men shy away from church altogether. Why Muslim and Jewish men tend to be more devout than Christian men exceeds the scope of this chapter. I focus instead on those Catholics (male and female) who *do* care—especially those who can't quite articulate why.

Why does a Catholic identity matter to people of varying levels of commitment to the church? I find Freud's theory of "family romance" at least as useful as the more recent and potentially far-reaching idea of genetic predisposition, and so I will favor it over the other two psychological theories ("the God gene" is not a psychological theory).[2] We could apply Freud's theory of family romances to a variety of faith traditions, despite the fact that Freud does not explicitly see his theory as an explanation for the religious drive. Given the trauma of the 2002–2003 sex scandal in American Catholicism, Freud's theory might be particularly useful in explaining why Catholics might choose to stay in a faith that has disturbed or betrayed them.

A Sense of Belonging

Theology, doctrine, and tradition might retreat from our notice in the West if it weren't for living people who care about them. A certain critical mass of faithful in every generation breathes life into moral rules and tries to impose them on us. Apologists for the Church might simply credit the Holy Spirit for ecclesiastical longevity. Non-apologists, however, will insist on alternative explanations—explanations which do not necessarily rule out the Holy Spirit but which address human motivation from a less explicitly supernatural posture.

Social psychology can explain much of the sense of belonging underlying Catholic culture. The comfort of belonging to an altogether admirable tradition can account for some of the ambivalence of Americans who insist on a Catholic baptism, wedding, and funeral but who want little else to do with the Catholic Church. The raging progress of biotechnology has created a curiously new competition between religion and science (one has only to think of embryonic stem cell research here, and the Vatican's opposition to it early in the twenty-first century), and science has challenged many an American Catholic's loyalty to Rome. Still, the most powerful force of all might be simple indifference; perhaps none of the three theories described in this chapter account adequately for indifference. Indeed, the appeal of these theories makes indifference even harder to explain.

Social psychology explains individual behavior in terms of fulfilling two basic needs: maintaining self-esteem and understanding the world. What we really want from life comes down to these basic goals—to maximize pleasure and minimize pain. The self-esteem approach to social psychology claims that we act in ways which make it easier for us to like ourselves. The social cognition approach focuses on a drive to figure out the world around us. These two needs affect the way we experience what happens around us; how we make sense of the world significantly determines what we believe and how we will act. Social psychologists generally claim that all behavior (either of individuals or groups) can be understood in terms of these two principles.

The ramifications of self-esteem research can sometimes be surprising: According to one study, for example, a person's initials can even bear on his estimation of himself. In the United States, school grades of "D" or "F" indicate low academic performance and, perhaps, a relative lack of intelligence. Students with a first or last name beginning with "D" or "F" are more likely to under-perform academically in the United States.[3] It should not seem far-fetched to assert that individuals who closely identify themselves with a flailing institution (for example, an investment bank, a government, a baseball team, or a church) will also suffer self-esteem problems. Given the rapid erosion of moral prestige of the Catholic Church in America in the twenty-first century, we might expect a surge of Catholics either to cut ties to the Church or, more likely, to feel worse about themselves personally because their Church suffered such terrible media battering during the priestly sex abuse scandal.

Another important force in social psychology is conformity: group pressures shape the actions and beliefs of its members. Membership in a group can confer various benefits. Acceptance by other people increases our self-esteem and helps us cope with the difficulties we encounter in life. In order to preserve membership in a group, a member must conform to the social norms of the group. The social norms are the beliefs and ideals which all members of the group are supposed to share. Normative social influence prompts individuals to uphold certain beliefs in order to gain acceptance. Again, the need to maintain one's self-esteem pushes against the social processes which determine the direction our emotional lives take.

Conforming to the values of a group we admire uplifts us in both a social and emotional way. Social psychologists have pointed out a kind of narcissism at work here. According to the theory of implicit egotism, people prefer to live in cities and to work in occupations which begin with the letter of either their first or last name. Researchers conducted eleven studies in which they showed that Marys are over-represented in Maryland, as are Philips in Philadelphia and Georges in Georgia. Similarly, women disproportionately chose to live in cities whose names begin with "Saint" and then included the woman's own name (for example, St. Anne).[4] Given that our names come from our parents (that is, we don't choose them ourselves), it is not far-fetched to view this phenomenon of implicit egotism as related to the desire to please our parents. Parents will frequently praise their children, and children perhaps unconsciously return the favor by taking on some of the values of the parents—and certainly the religion.

We also show a tendency to bask in the reflected glory of successful people or groups.[5] Until the Second Vatican Council (1962–1965), the Catholic Church enjoyed a reputation of moral excellence in America. Sending a son or daughter to the seminary or convent brought great prestige to a family. Priests and nuns were generally beyond reproach; they commanded hearty respect in Catholic communities. Given the loss of moral prestige of the Catholic Church in the 2002–2003 scandal, this motive will apply less and less often. Fewer and fewer Catholics will want to ally themselves with the Church in order to bask in its reflected grandeur (although it is still possible to find Catholics who do).

Normative social influence is important to the discussion of religious beliefs because religions tend to sprout organized groups which require conformity. In principle, members of a church are expected to share the same beliefs. Religious leaders set the pace for members by prioritizing beliefs. Members of the church will demonstrate their faith and virtue publicly, so that targeted peers will accept appropriate values. More importantly, individuals who hold private beliefs which thwart the norms of their group will suppress these beliefs publicly and embrace the norm, out of a desire for acceptance. In some cases, a doubting or struggling individual will speak out publicly in order to bring himself in line with the group and to reduce nagging feelings of hypocrisy. This is termed counterattitudinal advocacy. Normative social influence can silence dissenting beliefs in a group and prompt individuals to revise beliefs according to the group's social norm.

When confronted by challenges to their beliefs, a group will respond with more ferocity than any individual member is likely to do.[6] Since individual members seek acceptance in the group, they will often only share the part of their opinion that fits into the norm of the group. The result of this self-censorship is that the members of the group give off more extreme viewpoints than they actually believe, and so the final consensus will be more extreme. The larger the group, the less responsible any individual will feel for the result of his or her decision. Thus, a group decision may evolve despite the disagreement of various individuals within the group; dissident members can go along with the group because they feel detached from the decision and feel normative pressure to conform. Ambivalent or conflicted Roman Catholics may respond to criticism or mockery of their church with a depth of conviction which does not mirror their personal commitment. If a Catholic's self-esteem is somehow bound up in her identity as a Roman Catholic, she may find a ready incentive to defend the church passionately—whether or not she feels "on board" with the church.

Before delving further into the principles of self-esteem and social cognition, it is important to acknowledge the cultural difficulty of maintaining belief in the omniscient, omnipotent, and loving God of Judaism and Christianity. Atheists have spoken out in the West at least since the Enlightenment. In the twenty-first century, they could be said to sound more antagonistic than ever (for example, Sam Harris, Richard Dawkins, and Christopher Hitchens). Three cultural shifts in the United States make it more difficult to understand how religious fervor mounts in America: (1) fear of death has declined significantly throughout Europe and North America (as Philippe Ariès has argued persuasively), reducing the dependence on religion for self-esteem; (2) the social power of religious groups has diminished, particularly with regard to science; and (3) the traditional nuclear family structure has been breaking down.[7]

A social psychologist might begin and end by weighing the relative benefits and burdens of religious belief. Virtually any religion can help an individual feel more secure in the world, but certain obstacles challenge the authority of religious claims. John Paul II apologized for harms caused by Catholics, an event on which I focused Chapter 5. As of yet, we lack data to prove that cultural Catholics are responding favorably to John Paul's overtures. If we accept the basic tenets of social psychology I've mentioned already, it would appear that cultural Catholics have good reason to respond sympathetically. Let's now delve a bit more deeply into these tenets to try to understand better psychological motives at work in cultural Catholicism.

Self-Esteem and Cognitive Dissonance

Fear of death will persist, no matter how technologically sophisticated a culture becomes. Likewise will occasional frustration with our limited knowledge of the natural world persist in a culture fascinated by scientific research. A religious group emphasizing mystery and human humility will maintain some appeal. As fear of terrorism spreads, the appeal of religion might be expected to increase, especially if it seems that enemy terrorists employ technology at least as well as we Americans do.

What social psychologists call cognitive dissonance also stems from the need to maintain self-esteem.[8] Cognitive dissonance refers to the potential conflict we feel when pulled between competing thoughts or beliefs. Discomfort threatens self-esteem to such an extent that an individual will try to reduce dissonance through any means. Reducing dissonance can take the form of changing beliefs so that they are no longer dissonant, changing behavior to reduce dissonance, or adding new beliefs which resolve or diminish the conflict. Most importantly, the discomfort which results from dissonance is strong enough to bring about irrational behavior and thinking. We can apply these insights either to individuals or to communities.

Terror management theory, a form of dissonance theory, claims that the ultimate threat to self-esteem is the idea of one's own death. Thinking about death will often lead to a yearning to feel connected to a culture and social groups: the "worldview defense." People reflecting on death will agree more readily with the dominant views of their culture, more eagerly self-identify as a member in the group, and show a propensity to feel antagonism toward members of other, conflicting social groups. A team of social psychologists linked mortality confrontation to cognitive dissonance by studying the difference a funeral home can make to a survey. Researchers found that people filling out a questionnaire tended to agree more readily with prevailing cultural values if they completed the questionnaire in front of a funeral home than people who filled out the same questionnaire farther away from the funeral home.[9] It seems that even slight references to mortality can influence individuals to conform to social norms and seek the reduction of cognitive dissonance by altering personal beliefs. Of course, terror is not a recent phenomenon: for many centuries, the inhabitants of small towns and even large cities feared attack by enemy armies.

Cognitive dissonance and terror management theories can compel us to embrace religious faith in spite of scientific counterevidence. Faith matters to plenty of people, no doubt in part because many religions promise an afterlife. Maintaining faith in an afterlife relieves the anxiety and dissonance that thinking about mortality can produce. Moreover, religious believers organize themselves into groups, so membership in a religious organization enacts and strengthens the worldview defense. Religion buoys people struggling to hold on to their self-esteem. Faith can also ease confrontation with the ultimate form of dissonance—death (and its concomitant separation from the family).

Science, on the other hand, quenches another human thirst, the need to master the natural world by figuring out how it works. We experience cognitive dissonance when we question our beliefs or when we lack understanding of something altogether. We want to be in control of ourselves and our environment, and so we are prone to exaggerating the accuracy of our knowledge about the world and create explanations for what we do not understand. Science both satisfies and feeds our desire for an accurate view of the world. What happens when scientific knowledge conflicts with religious beliefs? When scientific curiosity conflicts with beliefs which maintain self-esteem, self-esteem generally wins.

Those with the weakest religious beliefs can overcome dissonance simply by abandoning religion. This, of course, will only work for people with little faith in religion or those who depend on science for emotional support. At the beginning of the twenty-first century, 60 per cent of American scientists professed no religious belief, compared to a mere 6–8 per cent of the general American population. Clearly, beliefs which prop up our self-esteem are the most likely to overcome threatening evidence.

Family Romances

Now I turn to the final psychological theory I will explore in this chapter. The theories I have presented so far can help understand why Catholics remain Catholic; these theories stand on empirical data amassed by social psychologists. The final theory comes with no such pedigree.

Freud's theory of "family romance" holds that we carry from childhood to grave crucial impressions of and reactions to our parents. These memories, some of them unconscious, determine whom and how we love or hate. Every encounter with friend or foe, every clash with or submission to authority, reveals and testifies to the traces of family romance.

Freud placed great stock in childhood as a clue to individual behavior. In *Moses and Monotheism* Freud wrote,

> It has long since become common knowledge that the experiences of a person's first five years exercise a determining effect on his life, which nothing later can withstand. Much that deserves knowing might be said about the way in which these early impressions maintain themselves against any influences in more mature periods of life. . . . It may, however, be that the strongest compulsive influence arises from impressions which impinge upon a child at a time when we would have to regard this psychical apparatus as not yet completely receptive. The fact itself cannot be doubted; but it is so puzzling that we may make it more comprehensible by comparing it with a photographic exposure which can be developed after any interval of time and transformed into a picture.[10]

Freud goes on to say that by the age of two, children may well have already experienced events that they will remember, despite not having understood them. These memories, he held, will dictate what children eventually like and dislike; those memories will also determine with whom the child will fall in love.

We still know next to nothing of the mystery of falling in love or developing emotional attachments, as I've said. Willpower often disappoints us when we struggle to change how we feel. As poets and Hollywood screenwriters know, falling in love is irrational. Religious identity works more like love than science. A desire for immortality, to be reunited with dead loved ones, defies scientific ability to verify or describe it fully (although Freud made important inroads in this direction).

The reason for staying a Catholic, albeit a disgruntled or lapsed one, might come down to viewing the Church as a family and, that said, to desires, conflicts, and repression of and in the family. Because psychoanalytic interpretation favors an individual's perspective (as opposed to an institution's), this psychoanalytic interpretation is flawed from the start (although not necessarily more flawed than standard theories in social psychology).

In the brief essay "Family Romances" Freud suggests that the child's oedipal desires and disappointments spring from ideals and the stories which convey them.[11] As the child begins to realize that his parents are less wonderful than he had previously believed, disillusionment creeps in. The child then begins to fantasize that he has other parents somewhere else. His real parents, as opposed to the stand-ins he is currently stuck with, are every bit as wonderful as he used to think the stand-ins were. Wishful thinking doesn't recognize itself as such; instead, the child energetically denies what he fears is the truth. A second, sexualized state sets in. The boy's wish to be like or even to be the father combines with sexual rivalry. The father seems to own or at least rule over the mother, and so the boy must somehow get rid of him. The son either imaginatively conjures up a surrogate father or just becomes his own father (metaphorically speaking). Either way, the child has earned unimpeded sexual access to his mother.

Note that the father's "absence" (his fall from filial grace, or repudiation) triggers the child's imagination to find a satisfactory story, one that can keep the child's self-esteem intact. The family romance, then, is an attempt to rewrite origins, to replace the unsatisfactory fragments of a primordial past by a fiction capable of satisfying the demands of self-esteem. The child will later strive to overcome his guilt at having imagined such scenarios. The child will have to forgive himself for having eliminated his father or succumb to a possibly paralyzing neurosis. Forgiveness works in an analogous and parallel way: Through forgiveness, we don't erase the past, but we redeem it. We give ourselves hope by fundamentally changing the interpretive lens covering our past.

The guilt we feel over abandoning our father keeps nagging at us, keeps reminding us of where we "really" belong. It prompts us again and again to look for someone just like our mother or father, just a little better. It is this motivation, then, that keeps cultural Catholics Catholic. In *The Future of an Illusion*, among other places, Freud wrote: "Everything was the son–father relationship. God was the exalted father, and the longing for the father was the root of the need for religion."[12] If a son wants to become his father, then the Catholic devotion of the father will guide the son's life to some extent.

A biographical example will prove helpful here. Tony Hendra, a British writer, recounted the story of his life in a tribute to his one-time confessor and, along the way, illustrated the applicability of Freud's theory. In the best-selling *Father Joe*, Hendra explained that he gradually abandoned his biological father, both metaphorically and then literally (Hendra called one "my spiritual dad" and the other "my

actual dad").[13] At the funeral of his "actual dad," Hendra felt principally guilty:

> After the funeral I went down to Quarr [the abbey where his
> Benedictine confessor Joe lived]. It had been a while, and Father Joe
> was delighted to see me. Even at this mournful moment, we fell
> without thinking into an easy dialogue, like two old jazz musicians,
> picking up on each other's licks. Then it came home to me why I'd
> found it hard to weep for Dad. Despite our rapprochement and
> my pride in his artistic integrity, he'd never been as much my father
> as Father Joe. "My Two Dads" had been a defiant adolescent for-
> mulation, inaccurate despite the truth at its core. One man was far
> more my dad than the other—the one I thought of all the time, with
> alternating love and religion, with simultaneous guilt and anger and
> bafflement at the way bonds between men evolve.
>
> That was when I cried for Dad, because he must have known. He
> was a smart and sensitive guy. How lonely and desolate to discover
> that his firstborn—war-born—son had found another father. Worse
> still that he'd never had time to find a path to me, nor I to him. It
> was too late when I left home and too soon when he died.

This textbook case of Freud's theory hardly demonstrates the universal
applicability of family romances, and yet the story makes it more
difficult to pass over Freud as ridiculous. Although Freud cast sons
as the central players in the family romance, anyone trying to update
his theory should on principle be able to include daughters as well.

Hendra represents cultural Catholicism quite well; he strays from
the church but never leaves it, then marries another cultural Catholic,
with whom he decides to provide a Catholic education for their children. Hendra wrote of his adult self: "It had been years now since I'd
practiced my religion, but it was still a deep vein of my identity." It
is not difficult to find adult Catholics who come to similar conclusions
about their emotional lives. Consider this disclosure by Garry Wills,
one of the most productive intellectuals in the United States and a
vocal critic of the Catholic Church:

> We "born Catholics," even when we leave or lose our own church,
> rarely feel at home in any other. The habits of childhood are ten-
> acious, and Catholicism was first experienced by us as a vast set of
> intermeshed childhood habits—prayers offered, heads ducked in
> unison, crossing, chants, christenings, grace at meals; beads, altar,
> incense, candles; nuns in the classroom alternately too sweet and

too severe, priests garbed black on the street and brilliant at the altar; churches lit and darkened, clothed and stripped, to the rhythm of liturgical recurrences; the crib in winter, purple Februaries, and lilies in the spring; confession as intimidation and comfort (comfort, if nothing else, that the intimidations was survived), communion as revery and discomfort; faith as a creed, and the creed as catechism, Latin responses, salvation by rote, all things going to a rhythm, memorized, old things always returning, eternal in that sense, no matter how transitory.[14]

Wills's ruminations illustrate the wisdom of the indoctrination strategy "Get 'em while they're young!" Inculcating a religious sense or rhythm in a child is one of the best ways to insure that the child will remain faithful to the religion of the parent(s). Wills seems to bear out the accuracy of an observation William James had made decades earlier:

To intellectual Catholics many of the antiquated beliefs and practices to which the Church gives countenance are, if taken literally, as childish as they are to Protestants. But they are childish in the pleasing sense of "childlike,"—innocent and amiable, and worthy to be smiled on in consideration of the underdeveloped condition of the dear people's intellects.[15]

Education and modern technology can corrode the family romance, which will not necessarily last forever. The fragile family romance requires certain conditions, at least according to Freud. In another work, Freud challenged his readers to see the link between early childhood education and religious devotion:

Is it not true that the two main points in the programme for the education of children to-day are retardation of sexual development and premature religious influence? Thus by the time the child's intellect awakens, the doctrines of religion have already become unassailable.[16]

Freud certainly believed that attachment to traditional religious beliefs could be overcome through education and, if necessary, therapy.

Freud also speculated that for many members of his own class, the source of the family romance fantasy was the female servant working in the home:

Where does the material for creating the romance—adultery, illegitimate child, and the like—come from? Usually from the lower social circles of servant girls. Such things are so common among them that one is never at a loss for material, and it is especially apt to occur if the seductress herself was a person in service.[17]

Freud's theory of family romance of course focuses on men, and the source of their fantasies. A servant is inferior to Freud's target male not only by virtue of her sex but also her class. The theory conjures up images of power and domination. Freud would later abandon the notion of childhood seduction, choosing instead to promote the Oedipus complex.[18] It may seem quite unfair to blame maids and nannies as a class for luring men and boys into sexual misconduct, as these working women needed money and more likely than not worked hard for small salaries in morally legitimate occupations. That said, Freud was not the only intellectual of his day to consider maids and nannies a suspect class: "Maids and other female domestics, reported Hôpital, traditionally tried to excite young boys."[19]

Relatively few families will ever employ servants or nannies, and so relatively few men should be expected to conform to this aspect of the theory. Freud does not pretend to offer statistical proof of a man's emotional relationship to the female servants of his childhood days. I do not either, but I do note with interest a reference to broad cultural familiarity with the stereotype. When Britain's Prince Charles wed for the second time in 2004, the *New York Times* included in its coverage the following remark from the English journalist Tina Brown:

> Tina Brown, who is host of a talk show on MSNBC, noted that the bride looked quite a bit like the governess who raised Prince Charles as a boy, but explained that there was nothing abnormal about it. "Englishmen always marry their nannies," she stated briskly.[20]

And the American novelist Erica Jong summed up Jewish mating patterns in a similar way, drawing on Freud's theory:

> Marriage is sacred as long as you marry an Oedipal stand-in. Jewish adultery is an oxymoron. We read Updike for that. Jewish men who cheat end up like Woody Allen. In big trouble. Even Jewish lesbians are required to have silverware and bone china from Tiffany's. Jewish lesbians are required to fall in love with women who remind them of their mothers—and, in today's feminist times, are doctors or lawyers.[21]

Jong's levity rests on an intuition which Freud tapped. Whether Freud is plainly correct, whether his theory has become so familiar that we instinctively see patterns that aren't really there, I can't pretend to prove. It is enough here to note the accumulation of anecdotes around Freud's idea.[22]

Freud cast servants in other key roles in the formation of family romance fantasies. A child's observation of a liaison between a parent and a servant could provoke a fantasy of one of the sibling's illegitimacy. It could also awaken feelings of guilt over the wish to reproach the parent or console the opposite-sex parent. Freud toyed with these notions, again equating lower social status with lower morality, in another letter to Fliess:

> An immense load of guilt, with self-reproaches (for theft, abortion), is made possible by identification with these people of low morals who are so often remembered, in a sexual connection with father or brother, as worthless female material. And, as a result of the sublimation of these girls in fantasies, most improbable charges against other people are contained in the fantasies. Fear of prostitution (fear of being in the street alone), fear of a man hidden under the bed, and so one, also point in the direction of the servant girl.[23]

There is tragic justice in the circumstance that the family head's stooping to a maidservant is atoned for by his daughter's self-abasement. According to Freud, the father's or brother's dallying with the servants could bring on guilt and self-reproach in the daughter, who comes to associate sexuality with a social and familial delinquency. Such a scene observed by the young boy could in Freud's view also deepen Oedipal feelings for the mother who would have appeared to have been wronged by the father's indiscretion.

A family romance at its simplest is a fiction developed by children about imagined parents. Think of the *Illiad*, the *Odyssey*, and the *Aeneid* here, stories in which we argue for how special our parents (or ancestors) were. Family romance is not about abandoning the family, only improving (and thereby continuing) it. Family romance perpetuates the idea that a family is a good thing, that it can make us feel good about ourselves. In family romance we don't overthrow our personal identity, we refine it. New parents give us a new lease on life: Catholics learn that God is their father, Jesus their brother, and nuns and priests are servants of God. Such teachings lend plausibility to Freud's theory. Beyond that, celibate leaders (priests, brothers, and nuns) may fulfill the infant's wish that his parents no longer have sex. The language of "Father," "Sister," and "Mother Superior" connects Catholic experience quite strongly to the Freudian model, more so than the language of other religious communities does.

The web of earliest relations and most primitive of human bonds begins with a child's tie to his or her caretakers. This is the first love of any individual's existence. And what we call the first love or first awakening of adolescence isn't so much an awakening as it is a reawakening-of intense passions, first experienced beyond the reach of conscious memory and buried now, for the most part, in the distant, distorted, dreamlike world of infancy.

It was of course Freud who first drew attention to the potency and force of this early infantile love-attachment and to its grave significance for later psychological and sexual development. In a way this first love is an apprenticeship and a model for later love relations, the love-bonds formed in adulthood. Through this crucial first experience of emotional bonding we construct and reconstruct the family romance over and over, throughout a lifetime. We may replace a remote and unreachable parent with a remote and unreachable spouse. Parent and spouse may seem totally different kinds of people, but for those *in* that love relationship the emotional climate is the same.

The theory is not without its critics. Diana Meyers has undermined the recovered memory debate of the 1990s (according to which adults suddenly "remember" childhood sexual abuse) and tied it to the underlying influence of Freud's theory of family romance.[24] Meyers maintains that "both feminist therapists and advocates for victims of sexually abused girls have reason to develop alternatives to the family romance;" moreover, "it is time to displace the family romance and to replace it with tropes that support feminist emancipatory aims." Meyers subjects the entire recovered memory debate and its implications for Freudian theory to critical scrutiny. In the evolution of Freud's version of the family romance, the fantasy life of girls, according to Meyers, is viewed as dominated by fantasies of incestuous love, then incestuous seduction, then sadistic incest. Meyers aims to move beyond the recovered memory debate, which cannot help women determine whether or not they were victims of incest.

Family romances and patterns weave their way into fiction. D.H. Lawrence's classic *Sons and Lovers* fits Freud's theory nicely, as does Paul Hond's much later novel *Mothers and Sons*.[25] In one piece, "Repeat After Me," the American writer David Sedaris agonizes over using his family for raw material; he imagines training his sister's parrot to say: "Forgive me. Forgive me. Forgive me."[26] Freud's theory of family romances doesn't just provide grist for the mill of those who would unreflectively insist that most people simply follow the religion of their parents. Freud's theory gives us genuine insight into why.[27]

It is easy to dismiss Freud as ludicrously fanciful. It is troubling to accept Freud's beliefs that we sexually desire both our fathers and mothers and that we will spend the rest of our lives recreating the family dynamics we encountered in childhood and adolescence. And yet countless memoirs and autobiographies boil down to essentially that plot. Eugene Kennedy has argued that the Roman Catholic Church infantilizes its priests and that the proscription of a sex life creates an "unhealed wound" that makes grown men akin to children in the realm of sexuality.[28] Without invoking Freud's theory, Kennedy explains priestly abuse of children in terms similar to Freud's.

Further, contemporary scholars arguably continue to grasp for the kind of data it would take to prove Freud's theory of family romance definitively. The idea that the moral sense is an innate part of human nature does not strike all scholars as farfetched. The anthropologist Donald E. Brown, for example, compiled a list of human universals that includes a distinction between right and wrong; rights and obliga-tions; admiration of generosity; empathy; proscription of murder, rape and other forms of violence; and shame and taboos. Social psychologists such as Jonathan Haidt have suggested that group loyalty or appreciation for community is one of five "primary colors" of the human moral sense (along with harm, fairness, authority, and purity). Group loyalty differs from family romance and rivals Freud's provocative theory for explanatory power here. In a Web survey, Haidt found that conservative people tend to value group loyalty more than self-identifying liberals (who care more about fairness and harm).[29] Even those who prize social justice more than group loyalty, though, may evince strong religious impulses. And even those demon-ized by a religious community may still yearn to be a part of it. In the twenty-first century, when American families seem to dissolve regularly, "group loyalty" may be a better description for "family" (or for "family values" or even "family romance").

Always Our Children?

In the previous section, I considered why children might unconsciously strive to fashion Catholic lives for themselves: it is a force of habit. I have not considered the possibility that Catholic parents might reject their children and, in so doing, disrupt the family romance.

The bonds of family are famously strong, but Catholics sometimes need to be reminded of that supposedly obvious fact, witness the very reason for "Always Our Children," issued by the National Council of Catholic Bishops a few years before the priestly sex scandal broke.[30] So far we have considered the disappointment of children in their parents, now we will consider the inverse scenario. The American bishops were responding to Catholic parents who turned their backs on their own gay children. (To be fair, Catholic parents aren't the only ones who have shunned gay children.) In the twenty-first century, Roman Catholic bishops in the United States are advising parents of gay children to love and support their sons and daughters.

In a 1997 pastoral letter, Roman Catholic bishops reminded Catholic parents that homosexual orientation is not freely chosen and that therefore parents must not reject their gay children in a society already full of rejection and discrimination. "All in all, it is essential to recall one basic truth," the bishops wrote. "God loves every person as a unique individual. Sexual identity helps to define the unique person we are. God does not love someone any less simply because he or she is homosexual." The document was approved by the Administrative Board of the National Conference of Catholic Bishops in spite of internal dissension.

By the time the letter reached the media, almost every other church had already been struggling for two decades over gay ordination or efforts to ease church doctrine condemning homosexuality. The letter that tried to salve the wounds of aching Catholic families (drafts of earlier, more lenient, letters had been strenuously opposed by more traditional bishops) echoed the Roman Catholic position that homosexual sex is morally wrong. Although the bishops' letter in no way abandoned Catholic doctrine, it did allow for a little more nuance in intramural battles. More than anything, though, the document spoke to the pain of Catholic parents and to their readiness to repudiate children who confessed to being sexually active gays or lesbians. Catholic parents who repudiated gay children were following a germane family romance of their own.

The bishops urged parents to encourage their children to lead a chaste life—an unrealistic expectation perhaps, but at least a platform from which to keep some sort of conversation going. Somewhat exasperatingly, the bishops instructed parents that church rules should not be enforced at the expense of a relationship with their child. Parents might understandably have been confused by the bishops' missive, which cautioned parents away both from rejecting gay and lesbian children and embracing them wholeheartedly. Why gay and lesbian children would want to maintain contact with parents who steadfastly refused to think of them as moral people was not explained.

At first glace, family romance as a theory may account for much, but it cannot immediately explain the example of parents who reject their children. One could try to construct an argument that just as ambitious children can become disillusioned by less-than-perfect parents, so can committed Catholic parents become disillusioned by children considered by their religious tradition to be, if not intrinsically flawed, then intrinsically inclined to acts of grave sinfulness. Children have it easier in the Freud scenario, as it must be easier for them to imagine that their "real" (and really wonderful) parents will one day return than it is for adults to imagine that their "real" (and heterosexual) child will one day come back to them.

Some of the strength of Freud's theory of the family romance derives from our difficulty relinquishing beliefs, a difficulty for which we have ample psychological evidence.[31] Just as grown children may struggle to stop believing "truths" taught in childhood, so might the parents of those children struggle to stop believing what they learned about homosexuals when they were themselves children. Someone who grew up in the 1940s or 1950s may have been taught that gay people prey on children, haunt truck stops, and detest the Catholic Church. Catholic parents of gay children may put the Church before their "real children" and spin out fantasies of an imaginary, heterosexual substitute for the gay child. Abandoned children may internalize the disapproval of their distant parents and unconsciously seek out partners who will abuse them. In *Beyond the Pleasure Principle* Freud argued persuasively that the compulsion to repeat patterns of behavior can outweigh hedonistic pursuits (think of people who move from one abusive relationship to another).

Putting the Church before real people would later become a theme of the disastrous priestly sex scandal of 2002–2003. Various bishops knowingly endangered Catholic children by silently transferring known sex offenders to work in new parishes. Such bishops showed more ecclesiastical allegiance than human kindness. Keeping the family going, and keeping its reputation intact *à tout prix*, meant a great deal to certain bishops who could not, it seemed, brook disillusionment, family dissolution. The sex scandal of 2002–2003 transported American families from the realm of metaphor to real horror and astonishment.

Conversion = Death

Freud does not mention religion in "Family Romances," which is somewhat surprising, given how generally preoccupied he was with it in his writing. We can press on the central notion of murder in order to make room for religion in the theory of family romances. The disillusioned child may reinvent a parent (in order to appear nobler, more beautiful, or intelligent), but the child will not abandon or murder the parent. If the parent strongly self-identifies as, say, a Jew or a Catholic, then reinventing the parent as, say, a Lutheran or a Muslim, will effectively kill the parent. The child pulls back from this betrayal. When the child takes a spouse who resembles the gender-appropriate parent, the child unconsciously chooses a spouse who practices the religion of the parent he is vicariously marrying.

The depth of the parents' commitment counts for a good deal in Freud's theory. The link between the family romance and religious devotion would likely dissolve if the parents' religious enthusiasm waned. Perhaps one of the reasons the Vatican so deeply opposed communism was because it had understood the threat to something like the family romance. Children otherwise inclined to follow their parents' example (and unconsciously seek a mate just like one or both of them) could lose their feeling for Catholicism. That's not to say that Catholicism would necessarily be dead forever, only that the Church could suffer significant enough losses in the short term to compel the Church to protect its young through a war of words.

Cultural forces tend to keep us where we are. The Japanese recognize the emotion *amae*, which refers to a feeling of dependency similar to that which infants feel toward their mothers. The Japanese value this sentiment as a sort of glue that can bond individuals to each other and to hallowed institutions. The English language lacks an equivalent for this word; were we to have one, it might better explain the sense of loss which would attach to deserting the religion of our parents.

Our Family Forever

Of course, it is possible that God exists. If he does, then religious believers have a point when they insist that the Holy Spirit pulls them in the direction of one church or another. Social psychology, in the final analysis, may be unnecessary if God exists. But even if God exists, we on earth sometimes struggle to understand why so many people disagree about what he wants. And, beyond that, the veracity of the theory of family romances does not necessarily preclude God's existence—not at all.

Today, Freud's stress on the formative effect of the family romance perhaps seems less relevant amid endless deconstructions and permutations of the traditional family. His argument that society's repressions create unbearable suffering seems implausible in a society where permissiveness is creating new forms of suffering. But the family isn't gone yet, nor is our yearning to belong to a really good one. Our yearning, like our emotions, hardly qualifies as scientific—but that doesn't mean we should give up trying to understand unconscious motivation. A scientific theory can never fully grasp the haphazard ways in which we form our beliefs—Freud began from this premise.

As the divorce rate climbs and more and more Westerners speak publicly about abuse (emotional, physical, and sexual) suffered in their families, it might seem that children are unlikely to follow the example of their parents. Even if parental influence were declining, still it could be that the theory of the family romance holds sway. Perhaps the best application of that theory involves casting not the father in the father's role but the Roman Catholic Church itself. Cultural Catholics, on this reading, become disillusioned with their father but never let go of him. They just keep changing him, in order to keep him alive. Rough edges are smoothed away and embarrassing, anachronistic behavior is finessed away by imaginative explanations. The Church is both father and mother to all Catholics, including cafeteria Catholics.

A variety of applications of the theory keep it credible. No matter what blows the family has taken in the "tell-all" culture of television talk shows, Americans still privilege the family and so-called "family values." By arguing for the sanctity of the traditional Catholic family, the "nuclear family," the Church unwittingly supports Freud's theory of family romances. The stronger a family's commitment to Catholicism, the more likely it will be that nubile children will seek out or perhaps insist on a Catholic spouse. Freud's theory also makes it easy to understand why Catholic seminarians might fall in love with one another, as opposed to non-Catholic men in the outside world (referred to repeatedly in Michael Rose's *Goodbye, Good Men*), Catholic nuns with one another (see the various narratives in *Lesbian Nuns: Breaking Silence*) or former priests and former nuns with one another.[32] It's all in the family, or at least it used to be.

Postscript

Countless Americans insist on a Catholic baptism, wedding, and funeral but otherwise want little to do with the institutional Church. Some are just lazy. Others, though, sincerely worry about feeling hypocritical. Many Americans are torn between living the faith of their forebears, a faith with which they fundamentally disagree, and walking away entirely. I have called these Americans "cultural Catholics" and insist that they are worthy of notice. They are, in fact, part of a long, if previously undervalued, tradition of Catholics seeking opportunities to express their spiritual devotion. I tried in this book to begin to tell the story of cultural Catholics because they are an important part of the search for meaning occurring among all Americans today. They stand as the vanguard of the institutional church by pressing for a broadening of opportunities to plug oneself into a sacred community.

Cultural Catholicism must go back at least to the third or fourth centuries, where it would have begun gradually, as a more or less intuitive continuation of doctrinal beliefs. Life outside the institutional church took its cues from lessons learned inside. In time, cultural Catholicism became an "extra credit," optional experience. Practices such as pilgrimages and processions developed to deepen devotion.

Over time, this optional realm of activities came to rival orthodox ritual. As the clerical elite alienated the laity, the laity took more liberties to celebrate the faith independently (an obvious problem being that ordinary Catholics can't celebrate a Mass without a priest). Today, cultural Catholicism in North America or Western Europe sometimes seems equivalent to dissent or protest. A central "in addition to" aspect of the faith has taken on an "either/or" profile.

Kerry Kennedy's *Being Catholic Now* (2008) gathered spiritual biographies of high-profile Americans, many of whose Catholic identities were anchored in the "optional" realm. My book tried to take such testimonials seriously and anticipate a Catholic culture in which such misfits become dominant. Above all, I wanted to dispel the notion that Catholic nonobservance is to be explained simply as a function of laziness.

This speculative work, an essay, reflected upon a stream of emerging trends whose importance is frequently misunderstood. I praised cultural Catholicism as pointing the way toward the preservation of an old Church in a country fascinated by newness and rebellion. The British (and Catholic) intellectual G.K. Chesterton once quipped in the twentieth century, "In America, even the Catholics are Protestant." By this, Chesterton meant to emphasize the liberty and freedom of conscience which early American settlers prized and subsequently wove into the national culture. In my view, cultural Catholics act on their own, filling in the large gaps where the official church brandishes no particular instruction to specific details. From there, of course, cultural Catholics may continue on to frank disagreement with Catholic rules.

In recounting the broad transformation of a culture of obedience to ambivalence and outright dissent, I used the methodology of discourse analysis. My inquiry began in the occasional opposition between the teaching authority of the Church and the pull of secular society. Many scholars privilege an overarching causal explanation for doctrinal change or stasis: to oversimplify somewhat, some scholars emphasize the ways in which changes in the secular world are reflected in encyclicals and apostolic letters; others focus on change which occurs internal to ecclesiastical doctrine. By contrast, I took a holistic approach. I viewed cultural change as resulting from interactions among individual rights assertions, grassroots mobilization, scholarly production, and theological innovation.

I used one broad constraint in order to determine whether a religious belief or practice could be considered legitimately Catholic: the belief or practice must be associated with the supernatural elements actively endorsed by the Church (which usually means Christ, Mary, and the saints). Cultural Catholicism combines and recombines social contexts and theological arguments. At the core of cultural Catholicism burns a conviction that contemporary experience should count for more than it has done in theological pronouncements.

Catholic Culture in the USA explained some of the ambivalence with which many Catholics live their faith today, how they internalize an ancient spiritual tradition, how they argue over the best way to honor that tradition. This ambivalence will color the form of Catholicism most likely to spread in twenty-first century America—Latino and Spanish-speaking devotion. It stands to reason that education and prosperity will affect Spanish-speaking immigrants to the United States in roughly the same way as American secular culture transformed earlier immigrants from Europe and Ireland.

Cultural Catholics may endorse only one or two of the beliefs that demarcate traditional Catholicism. For cultural Catholics, the Church is less a set of rules than a series of experiences. Going through the rituals of Catholic baptism, First Communion, matrimony, and burial makes these people Catholic, not voting for pro-life political candidates or resolutely attending Mass every Sunday. This focus on experience, as in cultural Buddhism, is in keeping with the more generalized sense of spirituality growing among Americans, who increasingly report being "spiritual but not religious." Cultural Catholics favor a menu approach to their faith, as opposed to an all-or-nothing one. Families opt for a level of commitment which best suits their personal view of the Church. Far from straightforwardly preferring the secular world of science, rationalism, and MTV, cultural Catholics understand the strong appeal of the supernatural. It is (a very traditional) awe of the supernatural that keeps cultural Catholics spiritual, gives them hope, and saves them from hypocrisy. Cultural Catholics manage to reconcile their support for, say, stem cell research, the birth control pill, and gay marriage with their ancient faith.

It used to be that Christians who disagreed with the Catholic Church were called Protestants. Cultural Catholics are emphatically not Protestants, focused on maintaining a personal relationship with Christ. Cultural Catholics have a community—a community that just sort of happened, without being carefully planned and cultivated. Cultural Catholics differ from evangelical Protestants, another large group (they number approximately fifty million Americans) in important ways. Evangelicals tend to hold to four basic theological propositions, the first three of which may rub cultural Catholics the wrong way: the primacy of biblical authority, the necessity of conversion, the exclusivity of salvation through Jesus, and a mandate for activism in the world. Unlike evangelical Protestantism, cultural Catholicism does not thrive on its own sense of embattlement in a larger culture. Cultural Catholics tend to espouse secular culture, not condemn it. Cultural Catholics are often willing to accept the authority of bishops and the pope; in any event, cultural Catholics do not insist on the primacy of biblical authority. And cultural Catholics squirm at the idea that conversion to Catholicism (or even Christianity) is necessary for salvation.

Perhaps not surprisingly, "cultural Catholic" has become a sort of insult uttered by more devout Catholics who disapprove of the "buffet" attitude of their more lax brothers and sisters. Pejorative terms frequently capture some truths and are often successfully taken up by their targets as a badge of honor. I have used the term "cultural Catholicism" to denote Catholic experience outside the official structure of the Vatican; "cultural Catholicism" carries no negative connotation for me. I believe cultural Catholics have come to dominate Catholic culture in the United States.

Religious *Bona Fides*

It isn't just in Catholicism that the questions of identity and exclusivity present themselves.[1] A brief glance at other religious groups will reveal a common struggle to establish an adherent's *bona fides*.

Buddhists—particularly in America—have struggled with the same questions. Thomas Tweed has called cradle Buddhists "adherents" and has divided the converts to Buddhism into two groups: self-identifiers and "sympathizers." Various scholars of American Buddhism have concluded that Buddhists are those people who simply say they are Buddhists.[2] Hybridism is perhaps the defining problem with regard to American Buddhists; distance and time have played a similar, destructive role in Chinese-American identity and religions. Until 1893, when emigrants were given the official designation as *huaqiao* (Overseas Chinese), they were viewed as "sojourners," temporarily outside the middle kingdom until circumstances allowed them to return.[3] An even more useful example than these two might be Judaism. In 1983 the Reform movement, currently the denomination with which the plurality of American Jews identifies, formally rejected the traditional definition of Jewish identity by adopting a resolution accepting any child with at least one Jewish parent as a Jew—provided that child engaged in public acts of Jewish religious participation.

The schema I have offered here begs the overarching question of who is a Catholic. Apart from comparatively rare instances in which conservative Catholics will excoriate a pro-choice Catholic politician or Pope John Paul II's lament in 1980 that much of the French nation had drifted into cultural Catholicism, we don't find open accusations of this sort. The whole phenomenon of cultural Catholicism is interesting in part because it has yet to be fully articulated and therefore fully attacked. As of yet, no Catholic authority has explicitly assured the world that cultural Catholics can validly and assuredly claim a Catholic identity. Yet plenty of Catholics worry about the validity of their religious identity. "Catholics and non-Catholics alike wonder whether Catholics believe that they will lose their salvation for missing Mass on Sunday, refusing to fast on a specific fast day, or rejecting an officially defined Catholic doctrine, such as the Immaculate Conception of Mary."[4] Only an isolated or deceptive Catholic would disagree with the view that "Catholics seem to compete more and more with each other over what constitutes Catholic identity."[5]

To make matters even more difficult, it is necessary to point out that the very distinction between Catholic Christians and non-Catholic Christians is itself considered unfortunate by the teaching authority of the Church. Pope John XXIII (d. 1963) frequently stressed that what all Christians have in common is far more important than what divides them. Cultural Catholics would seem happy with distance, if not outright division, from other Christians and, especially, from the institutional Church. According to John (17:21), God wills the unity of all Christians. Cultural Catholics worry about the cost of this unity; something will have to give, and they hope the Church will move beyond certain supposedly outdated views. Most prominent on their list might be claims about what is "natural," particularly in the realm of sex.

I defended these "problem Catholics"—the earnest dissenters and the lazy. It would be impossible to draw a clear boundary between the problem groups, and so I tried to credit both the dissident and the lazy as having their hearts in the right place. One of my central claims in this book, as well as the launching pad for it, was that *people are Catholic to the extent they wish to be Catholic*. I offered what might be called a "maximizing" criterion of Catholicism, which is to say that I set the bar quite low. I invited on board all baptized Catholics who want to be part of the community. A "minimizing" criterion would exclude quite a few Catholics and would insist on at least professing to follow everything the Vatican decrees. A skeptic might assert that cafeteria Catholics are all about "moral minimalism"—doing the least possible in order to receive credit for still being Catholic. A more charitable critic might note that plenty of cafeteria Catholics speak from their conscience—that cafeteria Catholics disregard certain rules because they sincerely don't agree with those rules.

It's by no means only liberal outliers who take this view. Before becoming Pope John Paul II, Karol Wojtyla stated in the book *The*

Acting Person, "The one who voices his opposition to the general or particular rules of the community does not thereby reject its membership. Instead, he contributes to its growth."[6] The wisdom of this position grounded my argument in this book.

Cultural Catholics are keeping their faith alive in America. Concluding an exhaustive appraisal of Irish literature in 1995, Declan Kiberd speculated, "[T]he evidence would now suggest that the Irish may be about to jettison Catholicism as unsentimentally as they once disposed of their own language."[7] Say what you will against cultural Catholics in the United States, but recognize that, as a group, they have no intention of jettisoning their faith.

Notes

Preface
1   For a summary of this turmoil, see Amy Sullivan, *The Party Faithful: How and Why Democrats are Closing the God Gap* (New York: Scribner, 2008). For a brief account of the St. Louis archbishop who publicly opposed John Kerry, see Peter Slevin, "St. Louis Prelate aims to bring flock in line: Burke takes firm stance on social issues," *Washington Post*, 29 May 2007, p. A2. It seems fair to say that Burke opposes cultural Catholicism and wants it purged from the Church, leaving behind only orthodox believers.

Introduction
1   Austin Flannery, O.P., ed., "Pastoral Constitution on the Church," *Vatican Council II: The Conciliar and Post-Conciliar Documents* (Collegeville, IN: Liturgical Press, 1988), p. 958. This quotation comes from Part II, Chapter 2 of the *Constitution*. The notion of culture is developed further in the document *Gaudium et Spes*, also from Vatican II.

2   Joseph Cardinal Ratzinger, *Europe: Its Foundations Today and Tomorrow* was published in Italian by San Paolo in 2004.

3   Clifford Geertz, "Religion as a cultural system," *The Interpretation of Cultures* (New York: Basic Books, 1977).

4   See Leo Steinberg, *The Sexuality of Christ in Renaissance Art and in Modern Oblivion* (Chicago, IL: University of Chicago Press, 1996). Steinberg argues in this riveting book that Protestant reformers found artistic depictions of Christ's genitals or Mary's breasts distasteful and effectively shut down a practice which made sense in terms of Christian theology. The book implies, but does not attempt to establish definitively, that Catholics felt more comfortable with nudity than did the early Protestants.

5   See Edward Muir, *Ritual in Early Modern Europe* (Cambridge, MA: Cambridge University Press, 2005), Chapter 3. According to Muir, ". . . people represented their hopes and desires through the festive performances" (p. 94) and it seemed only natural to prepare for the forty-day

abstinence from meat and sex by throwing a wild party. In a bitter irony, new Protestants would sometimes use the Catholic practice to deride Catholics in parody: "During the Protestant Reformation in Germany and France, there were numerous occasions when carnivalesque travesty was employed to mock Catholicism" (p. 105).

6   James J. Kavanaugh, *A Modern Priest Looks at His Outdated Church* (New York: Trident Press, 1967).

7   Such courage or chutzpah extended beyond the Boston Catholics who publicly protested the Church's secrecy after the priestly sex scandal of 2002–2003. See, for example, Dan Warner, "Catholic Group Will Hold Fort Myers Rally in an Effort to Have More Say in Church," *News-Press* (Southwest Florida), 16 January 2009. The January rally in Florida featured the president of the University of Rochester as its lead speaker. The rally took place in an Episcopal church.

8   Although I do not support such an idea, I do, however, note the potential benefit of a public degradation ritual for Catholics who have strayed too far from orthodoxy. On these rituals, see Harold Garfinkel, "Conditions of Successful Degradation Rituals," *American Journal of Sociology* 61 (1956): 420–24.

9   Eamon Duffy, *The Stripping of the Altars: Traditional Religion in England c. 1400–c. 1580* (New Haven, CT: Yale University Press, 1992), p. 480.

10 Elaine Pagels, *The Origin of Satan* (New York: Random House, 1995), p. 47.

11 Michel de Montaigne, "Travel Journal," *The Complete Works of Montaigne*, trans. D.J. Frame (Stanford: Stanford University Press, 1967), p. 944.

12 Thomas Ferraro, "An interview with Camille Paglia," in Thomas Ferraro, ed., *Catholic Lives/Contemporary Culture: The South Atlantic Quarterly*, Summer 1994. The essays collected in this periodical may lack methodological rigor but, taken together, represented perhaps the richest account of Catholic culture in the United States at end of the twentieth century. For an interesting account of Catholic culture in Italy, see Jeff Pratt, "Catholic Culture," in *Italian Cultural Studies: An Introduction*, ed. David Forgacs and Robert Lumley (New York: Oxford University Press, 1996), pp. 129–43. Pratt offers a model for understanding cultural Catholicism in terms of social anthropology.

13 Michael Novak, *No One Sees God: The Dark Night of Atheists and Believers* (New York: Doubleday, 2008).

14 It is not difficult to find histories of American Catholicism. Historians and sociologists sometimes break down this community's history into four phases: (1) the republican era (1790–1852); (2) the immigrant phase (1850–1924); (3) the maturing phase (1924–1960); and (4) the Post-Vatican II age (1960–present). See, for example, James Jennessey,

S.J., *American Catholics: A History of the Roman Catholic Community in the United States* (New York: Oxford University Press, 1981). See also Thomas Bokenkotter, *A Concise History of the Catholic Church* (New York: Doubleday Image Books, 1990). My study focuses on the Post-Vatican II age.

15 Samuel P. Huntington, *Who Are We?: The Challenges to America's National Identity* (New York: Simon & Schuster, 2004).

16 Emile Durkheim, *The Elementary Forms of the Religious Life* (1915), trans. Joseph Swain (Glencoe, NY: Free Press, 1974).

17 David Kertzer, *Ritual, Politics & Power* (New Haven, CT: Yale University Press, 1988), p. 69.

Chapter 1: Who Are Cultural Catholics?

1 Kerry Kennedy, *Being Catholic Now: Prominent Americans Talk about Change in the Church and the Quest for Meaning* (New York: Crown, 2008).

2 Frank J. Prial, "Pope Chides French Over State of Church," *New York Times*, 2 June 1980, p. A3.

3 Kenneth Woodward and Andrew Nagorski, "A Blast from the Inquisitor," *New York Times*, 31 December 1984.

4 E. J. Dionne, Jr., "America and the Catholic Church: Conflicts with Rome and within," *New York Times*, 24 December 1986, p. A1. Of course, the Church has hosted other intramural battles over the centuries. During Augustine's lifetime, for example, the Donatists accused the Catholic Church in North Africa of being traitors to the faith. At the same time, this faction asserted that ministers could not validly administer the sacraments. Some of these intramural battles led to schisms. For a history of full-blown rifts, see David Christie-Murray, *A History of Heresy* (Oxford: Oxford University Press, 1991).

5 E. J. Dionne, Jr., "No Room for Dissent," *Washington Post*, 31 May 2005, p. A17.

6 Peter J. Boyer, "The Deliverer: A Pizza Mogul Funds a Moral Crusade," *New Yorker*, 19 February 2007. Monahan also contributed a vignette to Kennedy's volume *Being Catholic Now*.

7 Between these two categories we might perhaps wedge a third, those who march to the beat of a different drummer. In his 1988 work *Tomorrow's Catholics, Yesterday's Church* (New York: Harper & Row, 1988), Eugene Kennedy argued for two different cultures in American Roman Catholicism. Those in the "organizational culture of the institutional church" looked to the Council of Trent for spiritual and ecclesiastical answers. Roman Catholics in the second culture heard a different drummer and followed him. Such Catholics "do not accept the controlling, authoritarian style of institutional bureaucrats as an adequate or healthy substitute for generative authority." What Kennedy refers to as a

culture of "the Church as a community of vital believers," I refer to as "cultural Catholics." See Kennedy, p. xiii.

8   Thomas Bokenkotter, *A Concise History of the Roman Catholic Church* (Garden City, NY: Doubleday, 1977), pp. 273, 277.

9   I have said that this book focuses on the United States, but this question of whether a person or a nation can cease to be Catholic admits of non-American examples. The editor-in-chief of the French newspaper *Le Monde*, Frederic Lenoir, declared in January 2007 that France was "no longer a Catholic country." A poll published in the newspaper revealed that 51 per cent of the country's population described themselves as Catholics—down from 80 per cent in the early 1990s and 67 per cent in 2000.

10 Michael Cuneo, *The Smoke of Satan: Conservative and Traditionalist Dissent in Contemporary American Catholicism* (New York: Oxford University Press, 1997), p. 19.

11 Joan Didion, *The Year of Magical Thinking* (New York: Knopf, 2006), p. 149.

12 See J. Shaw, "The late seventeenth and eighteenth centuries," in Richard Harries and Henry Mayr-Harting, eds, *Christianity: Two Thousand Years* (Oxford: Oxford University Press, 2001), pp. 162–91, especially pp. 178–86.

13 Gerald O'Collins and Mario Farrugia, *Catholicism: The Story of Catholic Christianity* (New York: Oxford University Press, 2003), p. 329.

14 Alan Schreck, *Catholic & Christian: An Explanation of Commonly Misunderstood Catholic Beliefs* (Cincinnati, OH: Servant Books, 2004), p. 34. This book bears an *imprimatur*.

15 See *Dignitatis Humanae* (1965), the declaration on religious freedom. In *Gaudium et Spes* (1965), also from Vatican II, the Council defined conscience as follows:

> In the depths of his conscience, man detects a law which he has not laid upon himself but which he must obey. Its voice, ever calling him to love and to do good and to avoid what is evil, tells him inwardly at the right moment: do this, shun that. For man has in his heart a law inscribed by God. His dignity lies in observing this law, and by it he will be judged. His conscience is man's most secret core and his sanctuary. There he is alone with God, whose voice echoes in his depths. By conscience, in a wonderful way, that law is made known which is fulfilled in the love of God and one's neighbor.

16 Christian Smith, *Soul Searching* (New York: Oxford University Press, 2005). Various other sociological surveys have documented the crisis in Catholic identity. See Andrea Williams and James D. Davidson, "Catholic conceptions of faith: A generational analysis," in *Sociology of Religion* 57/3 (1996): 273–89; or Michele Dillon (work already cited).

17   Andrew M. Greeley, *The Catholic Imagination* (Berkeley, CA: University of California Press, 2001). (It might be objected that Greek, Russian, and other Orthodox Christians share the same range of seven sacraments.)

18   See Andrew M. Greeley, *American Catholicism Since the Council: An Unauthorized Report* (Chicago, IL: Thomas More Press, 1985), pp. 61–5.

19   See, for example, the Pew Foundation's 2008 *Religious Landscape Survey*.

20   David Lodge, *Thinks*—(New York: Penguin, 2001), pp. 28–9.

21   John Grogan, *The Longest Trip Home: A Memoir* (New York: William Morrow, 2008).

22   Kennedy, *Being Catholic Now*, p. 104.

23   John Lanchester, *Family Romance* (London: Faber, 2007), p. 333.

24   Ludwig Wittgenstein, *Philosophical Investigations*, trans. G.E. Anscombe (Oxford: Basil Blackwell, 1988), secs. 65–6.

25   See, for example, Jean-Luc Barré, *Jacques and Raissa Maritain: Beggars for Heaven*, trans. Bernard E. Doering (South Bend, IN: University of Notre Dame Press, 2005) and Stephen Schloesser, *Jazz Age Catholicism: Mystic Modernism in Postwar Paris, 1919–1933* (Toronto: University of Toronto Press, 2005). Maritain's wife converted to Catholicism from Judaism. The Maritains seemed to attract to their band of Catholics especially homosexuals and alcoholics.

26   Jack Wertheimer, "What is a Jewish family? The radicalization of rabbinic discourse," in Don S. Browning and David A. Clairmont, eds, *American Religions and the Family: How Faith Traditions Cope with Modernization and Democracy* (New York: Columbia University Press, 2007), p. 161.

27   See Randall Kennedy, *Sellout: The Politics of Racial Betrayal* (New York: Pantheon, 2008). Malcolm X polarized the underlying distinction in a 1963 speech: House Negroes had worked as slaves within white households and generally sided with whites; Field Negroes had worked outside the house before the emancipation of the slaves and tended to oppose whites. See also Sudhir Venkatesh, *Gang Leader for a Day: A Rogue Sociologist Takes to the Streets* (New York: Penguin, 2008), p. 16. Venkatesh polls young African-Americans in Chicago who inform him that they are all "niggers," for "African Americans" live in the suburbs and wear ties to work. These impoverished African-Americans placed themselves on a lower social tier than upwardly mobile African-Americans in the way that cultural Catholics will sometimes do when comparing themselves to pious or orthodox Catholics.

28   Peter Steinfels, *A People Adrift: The Crisis of the Roman Catholic Church in America* (New York: Simon & Schuster, 2003).

Chapter 2: European Origins

1   Elliott Horowitz has highlighted the similarity of Jewish and Catholic practice in the sphere of public piety: that of the confraternal processions

in early modern Venice. See his "Processions, piety, and Jewish confraternities," in Robert C. Davis and Benjamin Ravid, eds, *The Jews of Early Modern Venice* (Baltimore, MD: Johns Hopkins University Press, 2001), pp. 231–48.

2   See Danièle Hervieu-Léger, "'What scripture tells me': Spontaneity and regulation within the Catholic charismatic renewal," in David Hall, ed., *Lived Religion in America: Toward a History of Practice* (Princeton, NJ: Princeton University Press, 1997), p. 22.

3   For an account of what some of these processions looked like from the outside, see Robert Darnton, *The Great Cat Massacre and Other Episodes in French Cultural History* (New York: Basic, 1984), pp. 106–41; or Reofilo F. Fuiz, "Elite and popular culture in late fifteenth-century Castilian festivals," in Barbara A. Hanawalt and Kathryn L. Reyerson, eds, *City and Spectacle in Medieval Europe* (Minneapolis, MN: University of Minnesota Press, 1994). For a somewhat cursory example "from the inside," see Craig Harline, *The Burdens of Sister Margaret: Inside a Seventeenth-Century Convent* (New Haven, CT: Yale University Press, 2000), pp. 155–58. For other examples "from the inside," although not of a procession per se, see Daniel Bornstein, ed., *Life and Death in a Venetian Convent: The Chronicle and Necrology of Corpus Domini 1395–1436* (Chicago, IL: University of Chicago Press, 2000) or Jeanne de Jussie, *The Short Chronicle: A Poor Clare's Account of the Reformation*, trans. Carrie F. Klaus (Chicago, IL: University of Chicago Press, 2006). For an overview of the influence of processions in social culture, see Natalie Zemon Davis, "From popular religion to religious cultures," in Steven Ozment, ed., *Reformation Europe: A Guide to Research* (St. Louis: Center for Reformation Research, 1982), pp. 321–42.

4   Here I borrow from the entry for "Corpus Christi," in Richard McBrien, ed., *The New Catholic Encyclopedia* (San Francisco: Harper-Collins, 1995). The liturgical guidelines for the procession long associated with the feast are found in the *Ceremonial of Bishops*, nos 385 through 394 and *Holy Communion and Worship of the Eucharistic Outside of Mass*, nos 101 through 108.

5   For a history of the feast, see Mimi Rubin, *Corpus Christi: The Eucharist in Late Medieval Culture* (Cambridge, MA: Cambridge University Press, 1991). See especially pp. 199, 204, 243.

6   Alta Macadam, *Blue Guide: Umbria* (London: A & C Black, 2000), p. 135.

7   Saint Rosa is a "local hero" in Viterbo. For an overview of the emotional appeal of saints to ordinary people, see Peter Brown, *The Cult of the Saints: Its Rise and Function in Latin Christianity* (Chicago, IL: University of Chicago Press, 1980). For another, particularly detailed, example, see Robert Orsi, *The Madonna of 116th Street: Faith and Community in Italian Harlem, 1880–1950* (New Haven, CT: Yale University Press, 1985).

8   See Robert Orsi, "Snakes Alive," in *Between Heaven and Earth: The Religious Worlds People Make and the Scholars Who Study Them* (Princeton, NJ: Princeton University Press, 2005). For a helpful account of popular longing for connection with something transcendent, see George S. Williamson, *The Longing for Myth in Germany: Religion and Aesthetic Culture from Romanticism to Nietzsche* (Chicago, IL: University of Chicago Press, 2004).

9   See Keith Thomas, *Religion and the Decline of Magic* (New York: Scribner's, 1971), pp. 48–50. See also Ioan P. Couliano, *Eros and Magic in the Renaissance*, trans. Margaret Cook (Chicago, IL: University of Chicago Press, 1987). Of particular interest is the argument in this second book that magic gave birth to modern psychology and the link between magic and sexual desire. Sexual desire has a great deal to do with religious drives as well.

10 Solidarity on two opposing sides can polarize marchers and spectators. Writing about the annual celebrations of Corpus Christi Day in sixteenth century France, Natalie Davis notes that public processions highlighted the day. The parade route passed before both Catholic and Protestant homes. Catholics would hang lavish decorations from the windows, but Protestants would not. Protestants would sometimes pelt Catholic marchers with stones. Catholics pelted Protestants during their own processions. See Davis, "The reasons of misrule: Youth groups and charivaris in sixteenth-century France," *Past and Present* 50 (1971): 41–75.

11 These quotations come from the PBS Web site (www.pbs.org), which uses these quotations to advertise its documentary on the St. Patrick's Day parade.

12 For more on Halloween as a secular parade of sacred provenance, see Nicholas Rogers, *Halloween: From Pagan Ritual to Party Night* (New York: Oxford University Press, 2002).

13 See Beverly J. Stoeltje, "Festival," in Richard Bauman, ed., *Folklore, Cultural Performances, and Popular Entertainment* (New York: Oxford University Press, 1992).

14 Wayne A. Meeks, *The First Urban Christians: The Social World of the Apostle Paul* (New Haven, CT: Yale University Press, 1983), p. 149. I have termed such planned escapes from the self "raving" and analyzed the dynamic in *Bad for Us: The Lure of Self-Harm* (Boston, MA: Beacon Press, 2004).

15 The literature on crowd mentalities and the sheer joy of being part of a mass of people is extensive. See especially George Rude, *The Crowd in the French Revolution* (Oxford: Oxford University Press, 1959).

16 Umberto Eco has argued persuasively for this interpretation of Mardi Gras. See his *Carnival!*, ed. Thomas A Sebeok (New York: Mouton, 1984). On Luther's opposition to this Catholic tradition, see Bob Scribner, "Reformation, carnival and the world turned upside down," *Social*

History 3, no. 3 (1978): 303–29. On Brazilian carnival, see Victor Turner, "*Carnaval* in Rio: Dionysian drama in an industrializing society," in Frank Manning, ed., *The Celebration of Society: Perspectives on Contemporary Cultural Performance* (Bowling Green, OH: Bowling Green University Popular Press, 1982), pp. 103–24. For an analogy to sports in the United States, see Richard Lipsky, *How We Play the Game: Why Sports Dominate American Life* (Boston, MA: Beacon, 1981) or Louis Kutcher, "The American sports event as carnival: An emergent norm approach to crowd behavior," *Journal of Popular Culture* 16, no. 4 (Spring 1983): 34–41.

17   On the elasticity of this identity, see Michele Dillon, *Catholic Identity: Balancing Reason, Faith, and Power* (Cambridge, MA: Cambridge University Press, 1999); and David Gibson, *The Coming Catholic Church* (San Francisco: HarperCollins, 2004). See also Charles R. Morris, *American Catholic: The Saints and Sinners Who Built America's Most Powerful Church* (New York: Times Books, 1997).

18   Explaining the point of Renaissance processions, Edward Muir has written, "The constructed dynamics of processions created ritual-specific ways of seeing, which can be described as follow. First, contemporary optical theories suggested that the viewers of rituals were brought under the influence of what they saw through a profusion of material or spiritual emanations. Or, to put it in their terms, through the radiation of species. A ritual, especially an ecclesiastical or official procession, attempted to irradiate viewers with beneficent spiritual or authoritarian influences. One of the sources of the reputed capacity of public processions to create social harmony, therefore, was their ability to maximize the radiation of beneficial species broadly through the troubled atmosphere of the community" (p. 130). See his essay "The eye of the procession: Ritual ways of seeing in the Renaissance," in Nicholas Howe, ed., *Ceremonial Culture in Pre-Modern Europe* (South Bend, IN: University of Notre Dame Press, 2007), pp. 129–53.

19   See Emile Durkheim, *The Elementary Forms of the Religious Life* (New York: Free Press, 1926), p. 249.

20   For studies of religious trances, see Vincent Crapanzano, *The Hamadsha: A Study in Moroccan Ethnopsychiatry* (Berkeley, CA: University of California Press, 1973); Vincent Crapanzano and Vivian Garrison, eds, *Case Studies in Spirit Possession* (New York: Wiley, 1977); or I.M. Lewis, *Ecstatic Religion: An Anthropological Study of Spirit Possession and Shamanism* (Harmondsworth: Penguin Books, 1971).

21   See, for example, Aaron Ben-Ze'ev, *The Subtlety of the Emotions* (Cambridge, MA: MIT Press, 2000), p. 406.

22   James Shapiro, *Oberammergau: The Troubling Story of the World's Most Famous Passion Play* (New York: Vintage, 2001), p. 57. The Shapiro book reached the market roughly three years before the American media

began to anticipate the Gibson film. The play found itself criticized before the Second Vatican Council and, for similar reasons, Gibson's film also came under fire. As Shapiro writes, "By the late nineteenth century a backlash against the play's aura as an innocent and pure expression of faith was probably inevitable" (p. 127).

23 For scholarly reflections on Gibson's film, see Timothy K. Beal, ed., *Mel Gibson's Bible: Religion, Popular Culture, and "The Passion of the Christ"* (Chicago, IL: University of Chicago Press, 2005).

24 See Sarah McFarland Taylor, *Green Sisters: A Spiritual Ecology* (Cambridge, MA: Harvard University Press, 2007). Some eco-nuns, for example, see activities such as conserving water, paper, and electricity as "social sacraments" (p. 96). For some sisters, ". . . moments of resource-using personal care and hygiene became moments for contemplation and spiritual reflection" (p. 97).

25 In his homily at Fatima on 13 May 1982, Pope John Paul II said, "The Church has always taught and continues to proclaim that God's revelation was brought to completion in Jesus Christ, who is the fullness of that revelation, and that 'no new public revelation is to be expected before the glorious manifestation of the Lord' ('Dogmatic Constitution on Divine Revelation,' no. 4). The Church evaluates and judges private revelations by the criterion of conformity with that single public revelation." It is not a foregone conclusion that all Catholics understand this point, which is to say that some Catholics may believe that Mary provides the world with new revelations.

Chapter 3: Baptisms, Weddings, and Funerals

1 Several academic theories of ritual compete for explanatory power. For a trenchant argument in favor of the view I endorse, David I. Kertzer, *Ritual, Politics, and Power* (New Haven, CT: Yale University Press, 1988), especially Chapter 4. According to Kertzer, "Durkheim formulated what has become the most influential theory of social cohesion, emphasizing the key role played by ritual in producing and maintaining solidarity" (p. 61).

2 For a useful overview of not just baptism but also marriage and death, see John Bossy, *Christianity in the West, 1400–1700* (Oxford: Oxford University Press, 1985). See also Shulamith Shahar, *Childhood in the Middle Ages* (New York: Routledge, 1990), which includes an historical discussion of baptism.

3 Milan Kundera, *The Unbearable Lightness of Being* (New York: Perennial Library, 1987), p. 99: "People in Italy or France have it easy. When their parents force them to go to church, they get back at them by joining the Party (Communist, Maoist, Troskyist, etc.)."

4 The next few paragraphs come largely from the *HarperCollins Encyclopedia of Catholicism*, ed. Richard McBrien (San Francisco: HarperSanFrancisco, 1995), pp. 133–37.

5   For a riveting account of a resurrection cult devoted to succoring the souls of unbaptized infants, see Silvano Cavazza, "Double death: Resurrection and Baptism in a seventeenth-century rite," in Edward Muir and Guido Ruggiero, eds., *History from Crime* (Baltimore, MD: Johns Hopkins University Press, 1994), pp. 1–31. This example drives home the depth of suffering parents endured after an infant who had not yet been baptized died.

6   David Kertzer has set out this dramatic story in *The Kidnapping of Edgardo Mortara* (New York: Knopf, 1997). In the late twentieth century, the American writer William F. Buckley, Jr. and his wife used to baptize unwitting non-Catholic guests to their home. See Garry Wills, "Daredevil," *The Atlantic*, July/August 2009, p. 104.

7   It was the proposed canonization of Pope Pius IX that renewed this criticism shortly before John Paul II's death. Mortara descendents not surprisingly took the position that Piux IX was not a saint, because he had kidnapped a child and tortured its parents.

8   Tim Naumetz, *The Gazette* (Montreal), 15 July 2005, p. A1. See also Deborah Gyapong, "Same-sex marriage may impact Baptism," *Western Catholic Reporter*, 22 August 2005 (online version).

9   See the *Los Angeles Times*, 14 January 2005.

10 *Martin Luthers Werke*, 67 vols. (Weimar: Herrmann Bohlaus Nachfolger, 1883–1997), vol. 6, p. 533. Quoted in Richard Marius, *Martin Luther: The Christian between God and Death* (Cambridge, MA: Belknap Press of Harvard University Press, 2000), p. 254. I borrow here from Marius' discussion on pp. 254–56.

11 See Antony Kosnick et al., *Human Sexuality: New Directions in American Catholic Thought* (New York: Paulist Press, 1977) for a fuller discussion of Aquinas's role in Catholic thinking about sex. The work of a commission of the Catholic Theological Society of America, this report represented a comprehensive reevaluation of Catholic sexual morality.

12 Peter Coleman, *Christian Attitudes to Marriage: From Ancient Times to the Present* (London: SCM Press, 2004), p. 149.

13 Edward Schillebeeckx, *Marriage: Human Reality and Saving Ministry* (London: Sheed and Ward, 1965), vol. 1, pp. 203–04, vol. 2, p. 167. Quoted in Coleman, p. 168–69.

14 See Jack Goody, *The Development of the Family and Marriage in Europe* (Cambridge, MA: Cambridge University Press, 1983); Christopher Brooke, *The Medieval Idea of Marriage* (Oxford: Oxford University Press, 1989); Georges Duby, *The Chivalrous Society*, trans. Cynthia Postan (Berkeley, CA: University of California Press, 1980); David Herlihy, *Medieval Households* (Cambridge, MA: Harvard University Press, 1985).

15 See Mary Anne Glendon, *Abortion and Divorce in Western Law:*

American Failures, European Challenges (Cambridge, MA: Harvard University Press, 1987).

16 On the evolution of marriage in the United States, see Nancy Cott, *Public Vows: A History of Marriage and the Nation* (Cambridge, MA: Harvard University Press, 2000) and E.J. Graff, *What is Marriage For? The Strange Social History of Our Most Intimate Institution* (Boston, MA: Beacon Press, 1999).

17 For a moving account of child abandonment, see John Boswell, *The Kindness of Strangers: The Abandonment of Children in Western Europe from Late Antiquity to the Renaissance* (New York: Pantheon, 1988) and Anna-Maria Tapaninen, "Motherhood through the wheel: The care of foundlings in late nineteenth-century Naples," in Perry Willson, ed., *Gender, Family and Sexuality: The Private Sphere in Italy, 1860–1945* (New York: Palgrave Macmillan, 2004), pp. 51–70.

18 For an exhaustive account of annulments, see John T. Noonan, Jr., *The Power to Dissolve: Lawyers and Marriages in the Roman Curia* (Cambridge, MA: Belknap Press of Harvard University Press, 1972).

19 John P. Beal, ed., *New Commentary on the Code of Canon Law* (New York: Paulist Press, 2000), pp. 1296–1323.

20 Philippe Ariès, *The Hour of Our Death*, trans. Helen Weaver (New York: Knopf, 1981).

21 According to Craig M. Koslofsky, it was in the area of funeral rituals that the Protestant Reformation most clearly changed Christian practice. He analyzes the cultural affects of Luther's opposition to Purgatory in *The Reformation of the Dead: Death and Ritual in Early Modern Germany, 1450–1700* (New York: St. Martin's Press, 2000). See also Richard K. Fenn, *The Persistence of Purgatory* (Cambridge, MA: Cambridge University Press, 1995).

22 Edward Muir, *Ritual in Early Modern Europe* (Cambridge, MA: Cambridge University Press, 2005), p. 58.

23 See Samuel C. Heilman, *When a Jew Dies: The Ethnography of a Bereaved Son* (Berkeley, CA: University of California Press, 2001), p. 31. See also Sherwin Nuland, "Foreword," in *Jewish Insights into Death and Mourning*, ed. J. Riemer (New York: Schocken, 1995). For an explanation of the Jewish practice of sitting shiva, see Heilman, pp. 119–54. For an exploration of both the ritual and social dimensions of Jewish mourning as it is represented in biblical texts, see Saul M. Olyan, *Biblical Mourning: Ritual and Social Dimensions* (New York: Oxford University Press, 2004).

24 This list comes from the *New Catholic Encyclopedia*, 2nd ed. (2005), vol. 6, p. 33.

25 To watch a Tridentine Mass with the explanations of a narrator, see *The Most Beautiful Thing This Side of Heaven: An Introduction to the Rubrics of the Tridentine Mass* (Coalition Ecclesia Dei, 1991). For an

overview of the sacrament of Mass, see Austin Flannery, O.P., ed., *Vatican Council II: The Conciliar and Post Conciliar Documents* (Collegeville, IN: Liturgical Press, 1992), pp. 161–79.

26   See John Bossy, *Christianity in the West, 1400–1700.*

27   Emile Durkheim, *The Elementary Forms of the Religious Life* [1915], trans. Joseph Swain (Glencoe: Free Press, 1974), p. 230.

28   See Ian Herbert, "Church split feared as Pope backs return of 'Anti-Semitic' Latin Mass," *The Independent* (London), 8 July 2007. Many lay and intellectual Catholics criticized Benedict XVI in February 2009 when he lifted the excommunications of four bishops from the Society of St. Pius X, including one bishop who had denied the Holocaust. President Angele Merkel of Germany publicly challenged Benedict to "clarify" his position on the Holocaust after embracing Bishop Richard Williamson.

29   Kertzer, pp. 157–58.

30   Kertzer, p. 167.

31   Kertzer, pp. 83, 97.

32   Brad S. Gregory, *Salvation at Stake: Christian Martyrdom in Early Modern Europe* (Cambridge, MA: Harvard University Press, 1999), p. 301. Gregory continues in a corresponding footnote, "Popes between Gregory XIII and Urban VIII seem to have permitted veneration of the martyrs as saints without drawing attention to the fact. In so doing, they avoided the politically sensitive issue of canonization without contesting the faithful's response to their new heavenly advocates."

33   See Silvano Cavazza, "Double death: Resurrection and Baptism in a seventeenth-century rite," in Edward Muir and Guido Ruggiero, eds., *History from Crime* (Baltimore, MD: Johns Hopkins University Press, 1994), p. 1.

Chapter 4: A Brief Sketch of Catholic Dissent in the United States

1   Jay P. Dolan, *In Search of an American Catholicism: A History of Religion and Culture in Tension* (New York: Oxford University Press, 2002), pp. 199–203. For other versions, see Daniel Donovan, *Distinctively Catholic: An Exploration of Catholic Identity* (Mahwah, NJ: Paulist, 1997) and Darrell Jodock, ed., *Catholicism Contending with Modernity* (Cambridge, MA: Cambridge University Press, 2000).

2   Eamon Duffy, *Saints and Sinners: A History of the Popes* (New Haven, CT: Yale University Press, 1997), p. 342.

3   Catholic priests were not allowed to take part in such public, ecumenical services. It should be pointed out that Catholics weren't the only exclusive parties. The Revered David Benke, a member of the Lutheran Church-Missouri Synod, found himself censured for having taken part in a 9/11 interfaith ceremony at Yankee Stadium in New York City. Members of this denomination are not allowed to pray in public with

anyone from another faith, even Lutherans of other denominations. See Stephanie Simon, "Lutherans Accused of 'Idolatry'," *Washington Post*, 2 December 2001, p. A9.

4 Thomas C. Fox, *Sexuality and Roman Catholicism* (New York: Braziller, 1995), p. 332.

5 This and other encyclicals can be found (and searched through easily) on the Vatican's Web site: www.vatican.va.

6 Curran ruminated on this event in Gregory Baum, ed., *Journeys: The Impact of Personal Experience on Religious Thought* (New York: Paulist Press, 1975), pp. 87–116. See especially pp. 103–07.

7 Quoted in John T. Noonan, *The Morality of Abortion: Legal and Historical Perspectives* (Cambridge, MA: Harvard University Press, 1970), pp. 18, 23.

8 Remarriage after divorce had long been prohibited until the abandoned spouse died. This was in order to avoid the sin of adultery. John T. Noonan, Jr. points out that Catholic doctrine allowed a Catholic convert in the ancient world to exit a marriage to a non-Catholic in order to marry a Catholic. Noonan views this change in marriage laws as significant. See "Development in moral doctrine," in *Theological Studies* 54 (1993): 662–77. Noonan writes, "The implication, teased out in patristic times, is that the convert can commit what otherwise would be adultery and bigamy and enter a second marriage in the Lord." Noonan's intriguing article highlights the fact that Catholic morals can and do change.

9 Mary Ann Glendon, *Abortion and Divorce in Western Law: American Failures, European Challenges* (Cambridge, MA: Harvard University Press, 1987), p. 66.

10 See Arthur Jones, "Her 1979 Plea Unanswered: Sister Theresa Kane Champions Women's Roles in Catholic Church," *National Catholic Reporter*, 8 September 2000.

11 John Fialka, *Sisters: Catholics, Nuns, and the Making of America* (New York: St. Martin's Press, 2003), p. 1. For a general overview of Catholic feminism in America, see Mary J. Henold, *Catholic and Feminist: The Surprising History of the American Catholic Feminist Movement* (Chapel Hill, NC: University of North Carolina Press, 2008).

12 Chris L. Jenkins and Michelle Boorstein, "Virginia Catholics Pushed to Support Same-Sex Marriage Ban," *Washington Post*, 30 October 2006, p. B1.

13 William N. Eskridge and Darren R. Spedale, *Gay Marriage: For Better or For Worse?* (New York: Oxford University Press, 2006), p. 219. This section largely summarizes their study.

14 Matthew Engel, "Supreme Court Bans Execution of Low-IQ Convicts," *The Guardian* (London), 21 June 2002.

15 Julian Borger, "US Becomes Last Country to End Death Penalty for Under-18s," *The Guardian* (London), 2 March 2005.

16   See, for example, John T. McGreevy, *Parish Boundaries: The Catholic Encounter with Race in the Twentieth-Century Urban North* (Chicago, IL: University of Chicago Press, 1996).

17   Jo Ann Kay McNamara, *Sisters in Arms: Catholic Nuns through Two Millennia* (Cambridge, MA: Harvard University Press, 1996).

18   Gregory D. Black, *The Catholic Crusade Against the Movies, 1940–1975* (Cambridge, MA: Cambridge University Press, 1997), p. 104.

19   For an usual and particularly compelling example of early twentieth-century discrimination against Latinos, see Linda Gordon, *The Great Arizona Orphan Abduction* (Cambridge, MA: Harvard University Press, 1999). Particularly interesting is the way that race trumped religion in the minds of early twentieth-century Americans.

20   Moises Sandoval, *On the Move: A History of the Hispanic Church in the United States* (Maryknoll, NY: Orbis Books, 1990), pp. 80, 144. Quoted in Dolan, *In Search of an American Catholicism*, pp. 219–20. See also Robert A. Burns, O.P., *Roman Catholicism after Vatican II* (Washington, DC: Georgetown University Press, 2001), pp. 118–25.

21   Pastoral in *Origins* 14, no. 18 (18 October 1984), p. 281. Quoted in Jay Dolan, *In Search of an American Catholicism*, p. 220.

22   Jayasri Majumdar Hart, *Sisters of Selma: Bearing Witness for Change* (PBS, 2007). For a scholarly treatment of nuns struggling against American racism, See Amy L. Koehlinger, *The New Nuns : Racial Justice and Religious Reform in the 1960s* (Cambridge, MA: Harvard University Press, 2007).

23   See John Connelly, "Catholic Racism and Its Opponents," *Journal of Modern History* 79 (December 2007): 813–47.

24   See, for example, *Edwards v. Aguillard* (1987) or *Smith v. Board of School Commissioners of Mobile County* (1987).

25   John Paul II, "Truth Cannot Contradict Truth," Address to the Pontifical Academy of Sciences, 22 October 1996. This document is available on the Vatican's Web site.

26   Christoph Schoenborn, "Finding Design in Nature," *New York Times*, 7 July 2005, p. A23.

27   Joseph Cardinal Ratzinger and Jürgen Habermas, *Dialectics of Secularization: On Reason and Religion*, ed. Florian Schuller, trans. Brian McNeil, C.R.V. (San Francisco: Ignatius Press, 2006), pp. 69–70.

28   On this, see John Portmann, *Sex and Heaven: Catholics at Bed and at Prayer* (New York: Palgrave Macmillan, 2003).

29   See Michael Paulson, "Keating to Quit Board on Sex Abuse; Stands by His Criticism of Some Bishops' Secrecy," *Boston Globe*, 16 June 2003, p. A1.

30   Daniel J. Wakin, "Refusing to Recant, Keating Resigns as Church Panel Chief," *New York Times*, 17 June 2003. Keating fought for his own

vision of what the Catholic Church is: "The Church," he said in a letter, is "a home to Christ's people." "It is not a criminal enterprise," Mr. Keating stated. "It does not condone and cover up criminal activity. It does not follow a code of silence. My remarks, which some bishops found offensive, were deadly accurate. I make no apology."

31   The information and statistics in this section come from John T. Allen, "USCCB Day Two: Bishops Tackle Stem Cells, In Vitro Fertilization," *National Catholic Reporter*, 13 November 2007.

32   This information circulated widely in the early twenty-first century. For a solid and scholarly account of it, see Cynthia B. Cohen, *Renewing the Stuff of Life: Stem Cells, Ethics, and Public Policy* (New York: Oxford University Press, 2007).

33   Most of the history in this section comes from John Allen, in the work previously cited.

34   See, for example, Jeremy Laurance, "A Clump of Cells? Or a Living Being with a Soul?," *The Independent* (London), 26 March 2008 and especially Steve Connor, "Parkinson's: The Breakthrough," *The Independent* (London), 24 March 2008.

35   "Poll: Most Catholic MDs Dissent from Church Teachings," *Catholic World News*, 26 April 2005.

Chapter 5: A Pope's Apology

1   Michelle Martin, "Shrine to be built for abuse survivors," *The Catholic Virginian*, 3 January 2005, p. 14.

2   I summarize the rise of private confession or the "manual tradition" in *A History of Sin* (Lanham, MD: Rowman & Littlefield, 2007), Chapter 2.

3   During the month of March 2000, the Catholic News Service published a variety of articles on this topic. I have culled the information in this section from various Catholic News Service articles.

4   See the document on the Vatican's Web site: www.vatican.va.

5   Kerry Kennedy, *Being Catholic Now: Prominent Americans Talk about Change in the Church and the Quest for Meaning* (New York: Crown, 2008), p. 135.

6   Noonan has elsewhere identified herself and her parents with cultural Catholicism: "My parents weren't particularly interested in the Church and didn't really like it. They were culturally Catholic but not practitioners of their religion. However, on Sundays they'd say, 'Go to church.' " Playing off of the very distinction between *bona fide* Catholic and inauthentic Catholic at the heart of my book, Noonan also wrote, "I became a *true* Catholic at age forty. I always felt the tug of my religion, my faith, but I'd swim in and out of connection for many years. In some ways, it was so strongly in me, but in many ways it wasn't convenient to live a Catholic life, or to come back to basics." See Kerry Kennedy, *Being*

Catholic Now, p. 242. The upshot of Noonan's personal narrative suggests that "true Catholics" are better than cultural Catholics.

7   Peggy Noonan, *John Paul the Great: Remembering a Spiritual Father* (New York: Viking, 2005), p. 222.

8   These questions come directly from "Memory and Reconciliation."

9   For another overview of John Paul II's act, see John Cornwell, "Contrition and the Jews," in *The Pontiff in Winter: Triumph and Conflict in the Reign of John Paul II* (New York: Doubleday, 2004), pp. 188–95. A Catholic journalist who publicly criticized John Paul, Cornwell concludes, "Once again, John Paul had revealed his talent for making a theatrical gesture of outreach in what looked like the opposite direction."

10 See *Le Monde*, 22 September1997, p. 1; see also *Corriere della Sera*, 16 March 1998, p. 15. This section borrows from John Portmann, *Sex and Heaven: Catholics in Bed and at Prayer* (New York: Palgrave Macmillan, 2003), pp. 93–4.

11 "Koizumi Apologizes for Past, Says to Meet Hu on Saturday," *New York Times*, 22 April 2005.

12 "Advocacy Group Leaders to Protest Cardinal Law," *New York Times*, 10 April 2005.

13 Jamie Doward, "Pope 'obstructed' sex abuse inquiry," *The Observer* (London), 24 April 2005.

14 Melinda Henneberger, "Vatican Weighs Reaction to Accusations of Molesting by Clergy," *New York Times*, 3 March 2002, p. A30.

15 Larry B. Stammer, "A Tragic Youth Laid the Foundation for Karol Wojtyla's Life of Compassion," *Los Angeles Times*, 3 April 2005. Much of this section comes from Stammer's piece.

16 Rupert Shortt, *The Guardian* (London), March 2000.

17 "Pope Condemns Holocaust Denial," *New York Times*, 12 February 2009.

18 Sholto Byrnes, "Ann Coulter," *The Independent* (London), 16 August 2004.

19 Dean E. Murphy, "For America's Divided Catholics, A New Disagreement," *New York Times*, 20 April 2005.

20 See Ian Fisher and Laurie Goodstein, "At Installation Mass, New Pope Strikes a Tone of Openness," *New York Times*, 24 April 2005.

21 Alessandra Stanley, "A Sweeping Apology for Church Errors: Pope Asks Forgiveness for Church Errors over 2,000 Years," *New York Times*, 6 March 2000.

22 Noonan, *John Paul the Great*, p. 223.

23 Kennedy, *Being Catholic Now*, p. 64.

Chapter 6: What Would the Virgin Mary Do?

1   This section comes from Eleanor Heartney, *Postmodern Heretics: The Catholic Imagination in Contemporary Art* (New York: Midmarch Arts Press, 2004), pp. 146–48.

2   Frances Finnegan, *Do Penance or Perish: Magdalen Asylums in Ireland* (Oxford: Oxford University Press, 2004). Although Finnegan focuses on Ireland, she points out that Ireland was not the only country to allow or welcome the Sisters of Mercy to run such laundries.

3   See Charlene Spretnak, *Missing Mary: The Queen of Heaven and her Re-Emergence in the Modern Church* (New York: Palgrave Macmillan, 2004).

4   Marina Warner, *Alone of All Her Sex: The Myth and the Cult of the Virgin Mary* (New York: Vintage, 1983), p. 274.

5   Garry Wills, *Papal Sin: Structures of Deceit* (New York: Doubleday, 2000), p. 217.

6   Jaroslav Pelikan, *Mary Through the Centuries: Her Place in the History of Culture* (New Haven, CT: Yale University Press, 1996), p. 79.

7   David Barstow, "A Catholic Parish Finds Its Black Voice; Priest in Brooklyn Helps Reconcile Racial and Religious Identities," *New York Times*, 6 February 2000, p. A29. According to the Office of Black Ministry, at least 80 of the diocese's 218 parishes were then predominantly black. But there were only five black pastors in the diocese, which comprises Brooklyn and Queens. See also Joyce Shelby, "Pilgrimage Honors Special Madonna," *Daily News* (New York), 19 April 1998, Suburban, p. 3.

8   Andrew Greeley, *The Mary Myth: On the Femininity of God* (New York: Seabury Press, 1977), p. 165.

9   MaryAnn Glendon, "The Pope's New Feminism," *Crisis* 15 (March 1997): 28–31.

Chapter 7: Family Romances

1   See Peter Steinfels, "One Writer is on to Something, Even if Not Everything" (review of David Murrow's *Why Men Hate Going to Church*), *New York Times*, 4 June 2005.

2   Dean Hamer, *The God Gene: How God is Hardwired into Our Genes* (New York: Doubleday, 2004).

3   Leif Nelson and Joseph P. Simmons, "Moniker Madness: When Names Sabotage Success," *Psychological Studies* (December 2007).

4   B.W. Pelham, M.C. Mirenberg, and J.T. Jones, "Why Susie Sells Seashells by the Seashore: Implicit Egotism and Major Life Decisions," *Journal of Personality and Social Psychology* 82 (2002): 469–87.

5   R.B. Cialdini, R.J. Borden, A. Thorne, M.R. Walker, S. Freeman, and L.R. Sloan, "Basking in reflected glory: Three (football) field studies," *Journal of Personality and Social Psychology* 34 (1976): 366–75.

6   See, for example, Yohsuke Ohtsubo, Charles E. Miller, Nahoko Hayashi, and Ayumi Masuchi, "Effects of group decision rules on decisions involving continuous alternatives: The unanimity rule and extreme decisions in mock civil juries," *Journal of Experimental Social Psychology* 40 (2004): 320–31.

7   See Philippe Ariès, *Western Attitudes Toward Death: From the Middle Ages to the Present*, trans. Patricia Ranum (Baltimore, MD: Johns Hopkins University Press, 1975). Remember that in the chapter "European antecedents" of my book, I referred to Protestant changes to prevailing burial customs in the sixteenth century, changes which made death seem more distant, less immediate.
8   See especially Leon Festinger, *A Theory of Cognitive Dissonance* (New York: Harper & Row, 1957).
9   J. Greenberg, T. Pyszcynski, and S. Soloman, "The causes and consequences of the need for self-esteem: A terror management theory," in R.F. Baumeister, ed., *Public Self and Private Self* (New York: Springer Verlag, 1986), pp. 189–212.
10 Sigmund Freud, "Moses and monotheism," in Donald Capps, ed., *Freud and Freudians on Religion: A Reader* (New Haven, CT: Yale University Press, 2001), p. 74. For a collection of testimonials to this effect by Catholic writers, see Marilyn Sewell, *Resurrecting Grace: Remembering Catholic Childhoods* (Boston, MA: Beacon Press, 2001).
11 Sigmund Freud, "Family romances," in *The Standard Edition of the Complete Psychological Works of Sigmund Freud*, ed. James Strachey, IX (London: Hogarth Press, 1953–1974), pp. 235–44.
12 Sigmund Freud, *The Future of an Illusion*, trans. James Strachey (New York: Norton, 1961), p. 28.
13 Tony Hendra, *Father Joe: The Man Who Saved My Soul* (New York: Random House, 2005), pp. 133, 164, 158.
14 Garry Wills, *Bare Ruined Choirs* (Garden City, NY: Doubleday, 1972), pp. 15–6, 19.
15 William James, *The Varieties of Religious Experience* (New York: Penguin Classics, 1985), p. 461.
16 Sigmund Freud, *The Future of an Illusion*, trans. James Strachey (New York: Norton, 1989), p. 60.
17 *The Complete Letters of Sigmund Freud to Wilhelm Fliess, 1887–1904*, trans. and ed. Jeffrey Moussaieff Masson (Cambridge, MA: Belknap Harvard, 1985), p. 317. Quoted in Nancy Locke, *Manet and the Family Romance* (Princeton, NJ: Princeton University Press, 2001). This section has benefited from Chapter 3 of Locke's book.
18 Family romance differs from his so-called seduction theory, the claim that all neuroses are the result of a brother's, a servant's, a father's sexual abuse of a child. The theory seemed inherently implausible, and Freud abandoned it in the late 1890s.
    The energy assumptions in the seduction theory were problematic. If the only energy involved was strangulated affect from long-past external trauma, why didn't the symptom successfully use up that energy and so clear itself up? Further, he came to see that fantasy could have the same effects as memory of actual events. What was repressed was not

memories, but desires. He came to see the repetition of symptoms as fueled by internal, in particular sexual, energy.

19   Dr. Hôpital, "Quelques mots sur les exhibitionistes," *Annales-médico-psychologiques* 21 (1905): 224. Quoted in Angus McClaren, *The Trials of Masculinity: Policing Sexual Boundaries, 1870–1930* (Chicago, IL: University of Chicago Press, 1997), pp. 203–04.

20   Alessandra Stanley, "For American Royal Watchers, Wink-Wink, Nudge-Nudge," *New York Times*, 10 April 2005. At the start of the twenty-first century, the most popular screen adaptation of an American musical remained *The Sound of Music* (which was based loosely on a true story). In the film, a governess becomes first a highly sexualized servant (even though she's a would-be Catholic nun), then the wife of the aristocratic man who owns the house. Surely Freud was on to something important when he discussed the eroticization of domestic servants.

21   Erica Jong, "How I got to be Jewish," in *Who We Are: On Being (and Not Being) a Jewish American Writer*, ed. Derek Rubin (New York: Schocken, 2005), p. 103.

22   See Lynn Hunt, *The Family Romance of the French Revolution* (Berkeley and Los Angeles: Univeristy of California Press, 1992). Hunt uses Freud's theory to describe the images of the familial order underlying revolutionary politics. In a wide-ranging account using novels, engravings, paintings, speeches, newspaper editorials, pornographic writing, and revolutionary legislation about the family, Hunt shows that politics were experienced through the grid of the family romance, the fantasy of being freed from one's family and joining one of higher social standing.

23   Freud to Fliess, "Draft L," enclosed with letter of 2 May 1897, *Complete Letters*, p. 241.

24   Diana Meyers, *Gender in the Mirror: Cultural Agency and Women's Agency* (New York: Oxford University Press, 2002), pp. 78, 80. Chapters 4 ("The family romance: A Fin-de-Siecle tragedy) and 5 ("Lure and allure: Mirrors, fugitive agency, and exiled sexuality") are the conceptual and discursive central chapters of the book. Chapter Four focuses on implications for girls.

25   Paul Hond, *Mothers and Sons* (New York: Random House, 2005).

26   David Sedaris, *Dress Your Family in Corduroy and Denim* (Boston, MA: Little, Brown, 2004).

27   In a book reflecting on why he left Catholicism for Judaism, Stephen Dubner concluded: "In the end I came to understand that all religion, like all politics, is local. We believe as we do because of the families we are born into, the teachers we learn with, the dark-if-night fears and candle-bright desires that flit between our minds and hearts." *Turbulent Souls: A Catholic Son's Return to His Jewish Family* (New York, 1999), p. 15.

28   Eugene Kennedy, *The Unhealed Wound: The Church and Human Sexuality* (New York: St. Martin's Press, 2001).

29   See "Moral psychology and the misunderstanding of religion." Published on www.edge.org, 9 September 2007, http://www.edge.org/3rd_culture/haidt07/haidt07_index.html.

30   The letter can be found on the Vatican's Web site: www.vatican.va.

31   L. Ross, M.R. Lepper, and M. Hubbard, "Perseverance in self-perception and social perception: Biased attributional processes in the debriefing paradigm," *Journal of Personality and Social Psychology* 32 (1975): 880–92. In an experiment from 1975, individuals received praise regarding how well they had performed a task. The feedback was deliberately skewed, false. When individuals later learned that they had in fact performed the task poorly, they continued to believe in their ability and to predict that they would perform well the next time.

32   Michael Rose, *Goodbye, Good Men: How Liberals Brought Corruption into the Catholic Church* (Washington, DC: Regnery, 2002). Rosemary Curb and Nancy Manahan, eds., *Lesbian Nuns: Breaking Silence* (Tallahassee, FL: Naiad Press, 1985). Richard A. Schoenherr, *Goodbye Father: The Celibate Male Priesthood and the Future of the Catholic Church* (New York: Oxford University Press, 2002).

Postscript

1   See, for example, Robert Wuthnow, *Loose Connections: Joining Together in America's Fragmented Communities* (Cambridge, MA: Harvard University Press, 1998) and Wade Clark Roof, *Spiritual Marketplace: Baby Boomers and the Remaking of Religion* (Princeton, NJ: Princeton University Press, 1999).

2   See Thomas Tweed, "Who is a Buddhist? Night-stand Buddhists and other creatures," in Martin Baumann and Charles Prebish, eds, *Westward Dharma: Buddhism Beyond Asia* (Berkeley, CA: University of California Press, 2002), pp. 17–33.

3   Gungwu Wang, *The Chinese Overseas: From Earthbound China to the Quest for Autonomy* (Cambridge, MA: Harvard University Press, 2000), p. 9. Quoted in Jeffrey F. Meyer, "Confucian 'Familism' in America," in Don S. Browning and David A. Clairmont, eds, *American Religions and the Family: How Faith Traditions Cope with Modernization and Democracy* (New York: Columbia University Press, 2007), p. 173.

4   Schreck, p. 32.

5   Dugan McGinley, *Acts of Faith, Acts of Love: Gay Catholic Autobiographies as Sacred Texts* (New York: Continuum, 2004), p. 90.

6   Karol Wojtyla, *The Acting Person*, trans. Andrzej Potocki (Dordrecht, Boston, and London: Reidel, 1979; original Polish edition, 1969), p. 286.

7   Declan Kiberd, *Inventing Ireland: The Literature of the Modern Nation* (Cambridge, MA: Harvard University Press, 1995), p. 650.

Bibliography

Allen, John L. "USCCB Day Two: Bishops Tackle Stem Cells, In Vitro Fertilization." *National Catholic Reporter*, 13 November 2007.

Ariès, Philippe. *The Hour of Our Death*. Trans. Helen Weaver. New York: Knopf, 1981.

Ariès, Philippe. *Western Attitudes Toward Death: From the Middle Ages to the Present*. Trans. Patricia Ranum. Baltimore, MD: Johns Hopkins University Press, 1975.

Barré, Jean-Luc. *Jacques and Raissa Maritain: Beggars for Heaven*. Trans. Bernard E. Doering. South Bend, IN: University of Notre Dame Press, 2005.

Baum, Gregory, ed. *Journeys: The Impact of Personal Experience on Religious Thought*. New York: Paulist Press, 1975.

Baumann, Martin and Charles Prebish, eds. *Westward Dharma: Buddhism Beyond Asia*. Berkeley, CA: University of California Press, 2002.

Beal, John P., ed. *New Commentary on the Code of Canon Law*. New York: Paulist Press, 2000.

Beal, Timothy K., ed. *Mel Gibson's Bible: Religion, Popular Culture, and "The Passion of the Christ."* Chicago, IL: University of Chicago Press, 2005.

Ben-Ze'ev, Aaron. *The Subtlety of the Emotions*. Cambridge, MA: MIT Press, 2000.

Black, Gregory D. *The Catholic Crusade Against the Movies, 1940–1975*. Cambridge: Cambridge University Press, 1997.

Bokenkotter, Thomas. *A Concise History of the Roman Catholic Church*. Garden City, NY: Doubleday, 1977.

Bornstein, Daniel, ed. *Life and Death in a Venetian Convent: The Chronicle and Necrology of Corpus Domini 1395–1436*. Chicago, IL: University of Chicago Press, 2000.

Bossy, John. *Christianity in the West, 1400–1700*. Oxford: Oxford University Press, 1985.

Boswell, John. *The Kindness of Strangers: The Abandonment of Children in Western Europe from Late Antiquity to the Renaissance*. New York: Pantheon, 1988.

Boyer, Peter J. "The Deliverer: A Pizza Mogul Funds a Moral Crusade." *New Yorker*, 19 February 2007.

Brooke, Christopher. *The Medieval Idea of Marriage.* Oxford: Oxford University Press, 1989.

Brown, Peter. *The Cult of the Saints: Its Rise and Function in Latin Christianity.* Chicago, IL: University of Chicago Press, 1980.

Browning, Don S. and David A. Clairmont, eds. *American Religions and the Family: How Faith Traditions Cope with Modernization and Democracy.* New York: Columbia University Press, 2007.

Burns, Robert A., O.P. *Roman Catholicism after Vatican II.* Washington, DC: Georgetown University Press, 2001.

Cavazza, Silvano. "Double Death: Resurrection and Baptism in a Seventeenth-Century Rite." In *History from Crime*, eds Edward Muir and Guido Ruggiero. Baltimore, MD: Johns Hopkins University Press, 1994, pp. 1–31.

Cialdini, R.B., R.J. Borden, A. Thorne, M.R. Walker, S Freeman, and L.R. Sloan, "Basking in Reflected Glory: Three (Football) Field Studies." *Journal of Personality and Social Psychology* 34 (1976): 366–75.

Christie-Murray, David. *A History of Heresy.* Oxford: Oxford University Press, 1991.

Clark, Wade Roof. *Spiritual Marketplace: Baby Boomers and the Remaking of Religion.* Princeton, NJ: Princeton University Press, 1999.

Cohen, Cynthia B. *Renewing the Stuff of Life: Stem Cells, Ethics, and Public Policy.* New York: Oxford University Press, 2007.

Coleman, Peter. *Christian Attitudes to Marriage: From Ancient Times to the Present.* London: SCM Press, 2004.

Connelly, John. "Catholic Racism and Its Opponents." *Journal of Modern History* 79 (December 2007): 813–47.

Cornwell, John. *The Pontiff in Winter: Triumph and Conflict in the Reign of John Paul II.* New York: Doubleday, 2004.

Cott, Nancy. *Public Vows: A History of Marriage and the Nation.* Cambridge, MA: Harvard University Press, 2000.

Couliano, Ioan P. *Eros and Magic in the Renaissance.* Trans. Margaret Cook. Chicago, IL: University of Chicago Press, 1987.

Crapanzano, Vincent. *The Hamadsha: A Study in Moroccan Ethnopsychiatry.* Berkeley, CA: University of California Press, 1973.

Cuneo, Michael. *The Smoke of Satan: Conservative and Traditionalist Dissent in Contemporary American Catholicism.* New York: Oxford University Press, 1997.

Curb, Rosemary and Nancy Manahan, eds. *Lesbian Nuns: Breaking Silence.* Tallahassee, FL: Naiad Press, 1985.

Darnton, Robert. *The Great Cat Massacre and Other Episodes in French Cultural History.* New York: Basic, 1984.

Davis, Natalie Zemon. "From Popular Religion to Religious Cultures." In *Reformation Europe: A Guide to Research*, ed. Steven Ozment. St. Louis: Center for Reformation Research, 1982.

Davis, Natalie Zemon. "The Reasons of Misrule: Youth Groups and Charivaris in Sixteenth-Century France." *Past and Present* 50 (1971): 41–75.

Didion, Joan. *The Year of Magical Thinking*. New York: Knopf, 2006.

Dillon, Michele. *Catholic Identity: Balancing Reason, Faith, and Power*. Cambridge, MA: Cambridge University Press, 1999.

Dionne, E.J., Jr. "America and the Catholic Church: Conflicts with Rome and Within." *New York Times*, 24 December 1986, p. A1.

Dionne, E.J., Jr. "No Room for Dissent." *Washington Post*, 31 May 2005, p. A17.

Dolan, Jay P. *In Search of an American Catholicism: A History of Religion and Culture in Tension*. New York: Oxford University Press, 2002.

Donovan, Daniel. *Distinctively Catholic: An Exploration of Catholic Identity*. Mahwah, NJ: Paulist, 1997.

Dubner, Stephen. *Turbulent Souls: A Catholic Son's Return to His Jewish Family*. New York: HarperCollins, 1999.

Duby, Georges. *The Chivalrous Society*. Trans. Cynthia Postan. Berkeley, CA: University of California Press, 1980.

Duffy, Eamon. *Saints and Sinners: A History of the Popes*. New Haven, CT: Yale University Press, 1997.

Duffy, Eamon. *The Stripping of the Altars: Traditional Religion in England c. 1400–c. 1580*. New Haven, CT: Yale University Press, 1992.

Durkheim, Emile. *The Elementary Forms of the Religious Life* [1914]. Trans. Joseph Swain. Glencoe, NY: Free Press, 1974.

Ehrenreich, Barbara. *Dancing in the Streets: A History of Collective Joy*. New York: Metropolitan, 2006.

Eskridge, William N. and Darren R. Spedale. *Gay Marriage: For Better or For Worse?* New York: Oxford University Press, 2006.

Fenn, Richard K. *The Persistence of Purgatory*. Cambridge, MA: Cambridge University Press, 1995.

Ferraro, Thomas. "An Interview with Camille Paglia." In *Catholic Lives/Contemporary Culture: The South Atlantic Quarterly*, ed. Thomas Ferraro, Summer 1994.

Festinger, Leon. *A Theory of Cognitive Dissonance*. New York: Harper & Row, 1957.

Fialka, John. *Sisters: Catholics, Nuns, and the Making of America*. New York: St. Martin's Press, 2003.

Finnegan, Frances. *Do Penance or Perish: Magdalen Asylums in Ireland*. Oxford: Oxford University Press, 2004.

Flannery, Austin, O.P., ed. *Vatican Council II: The Conciliar and Post-Conciliar Documents*. Collegeville, IN: Liturgical Press, 1988.

Fox, Thomas C. *Sexuality and Roman Catholicism*. New York: Braziller, 1995.

Freud, Sigmund. "Family Romances." In *The Standard Edition of the Complete Psychological Works of Sigmund Freud*, ed. James Strachey, IX. London: Hogarth Press, 1953–1974, 235–44.

Freud, Sigmund. *The Future of an Illusion*. Trans. James Strachey. New York: Norton, 1961.

Freud, Sigmund. "Moses and Monotheism." In *Freud and Freudians on Religion: A Reader*, ed. Donald Capps. New Haven, CT: Yale University Press, 2001.

Fuiz, Reofilo F. "Elite and Popular Culture in Late Fifteenth-Century Castilian Festivals." In *City and Spectacle in Medieval Europe*, eds Barbara A. Hanawalt and Kathryn L. Reyerson. Minneapolis, MN: University of Minnesota Press, 1994.

Garfinkel, Harold. "Conditions of Successful Degradation Rituals." *American Journal of Sociology* 61 (1956): 420–24.

Geertz, Clifford. *The Interpretation of Cultures*. New York: Basic, 1977.

Gibson, David. *The Coming Catholic Church*. San Francisco: HarperCollins, 2004.

Glendon, Mary Ann. *Abortion and Divorce in Western Law: American Failures, European Challenges*. Cambridge, MA: Harvard University Press, 1987.

Glendon, Mary Ann. "The Pope's New Feminism." *Crisis* 15 (March 1997): 28–31.

Goody, Jack. *The Development of the Family and Marriage in Europe*. Cambridge: Cambridge University Press, 1983.

Gordon, Linda. *The Great Arizona Orphan Abduction*. Cambridge, MA: Harvard University Press, 1999.

Graff, E.J. *What is Marriage For? The Strange Social History of Our Most Intimate Institution*. Boston, MA: Beacon, 1999.

Greeley, Andrew M. *American Catholicism since the Council: An Unauthorized Report*. Chicago, IL: Thomas More Press, 1985.

Greeley, Andrew M. *The Catholic Imagination*. Berkeley, CA: University of California Press, 2001.

Greeley, Andrew M. *The Mary Myth: On the Femininity of God*. New York: Seabury Press, 1977.

Greenberg, J., T. Pyszcynski, and S. Soloman, "The Causes and Consequences of the Need for Self-Esteem: A Terror Management Theory." In *Public Self and Private Self*, ed. R.F. Baumeister, 189–212. New York: Springer Verlag, 1986.

Gregory, Brad. S. *Salvation at Stake: Christian Martyrdom in Early Modern Europe*. Cambridge, MA: Harvard University Press, 1999.

Grogan, John. *The Longest Trip Home: A Memoir*. New York: William Morrow, 2008.

Hamer, Dean. *The God Gene: How God is Hardwired into Our Genes*. New York: Doubleday, 2004.

Harline, Craig. *The Burdens of Sister Margaret: Inside a Seventeenth-Century Convent.* New Haven, CT: Yale University Press, 2000.

Heartney, Eleanor. *Postmodern Heretics: The Catholic Imagination in Contemporary Art.* New York: Midmarch Arts Press, 2004.

Heilman, Samuel C. *When a Jew Dies: The Ethnography of a Bereaved Son.* Berkeley, CA: University of California Press, 2001.

Hendra, Tony. *Father Joe: The Man Who Saved My Soul.* New York: Random House, 2005.

Henold, Mary J. *Catholic and Feminist: The Surprising History of the American Catholic Feminist Movement.* Chapel Hill, NC: University of North Carolina Press, 2008.

Herlihy, David. *Medieval Households.* Cambridge, MA: Harvard University Press, 1985.

Hervieu-Léger, Danièle. "What Scripture Tells Me': Spontaneity and Regulation within the Catholic Charismatic Renewal." In *Lived Religion in America: Toward a History of Practice,* ed. David Hall. Princeton, NJ: Princeton University Press, 1997.

Hond, Paul. *Mothers and Sons.* New York: Random House, 2005.

Horowitz, Elliott. "Processions, Piety, and Jewish Confraternities." In *The Jews of Early Modern Venice,* eds Robert C. Davis and Benjamin Ravid. Baltimore, MD: Johns Hopkins University Press, 2001.

Hunt, Lynn. *The Family Romance of the French Revolution.* Berkeley and Los Angeles: University of California Press, 1992.

Huntington, Samuel P. *Who Are We? The Challenges to America's National Identity.* New York: Simon & Schuster, 2004.

James, William. *The Varieties of Religious Experience.* New York: Penguin Classics, 1985.

Jennessey, James, S.J. *American Catholics: A History of the Roman Catholic Community in the United States.* New York: Oxford University Press, 1981.

Jodock, Darrell, ed. *Catholicism Contending with Modernity.* Cambridge, MA: Cambridge University Press, 2000.

Jong, Erica. "How I Got to be Jewish." In *Who We Are: On Being (and Not Being) a Jewish American Writer,* ed. Derek Rubin. New York: Schocken, 2005.

Jussie, Jeanne de. *The Short Chronicle: A Poor Clare's Account of the Reformation.* Trans. Carrie F. Klaus. Chicago, IL: University of Chicago Press, 2006.

Kavanaugh, James. J. *A Modern Priest Looks at His Outdated Church.* New York: Trident Press, 1967.

Kennedy, Eugene. *The Unhealed Wound: The Church and Human Sexuality.* New York: St. Martin's Press, 2001.

Kennedy, Eugene. *Tomorrow's Catholics, Yesterday's Church.* New York: Harper & Row, 1988.

Kennedy, Kerry. *Being Catholic Now: Prominent Americans Talk about Change in the Church and the Quest for Meaning.* New York: Crown, 2008.

Kennedy, Randall. *Sellout: The Politics of Racial Betrayal.* New York: Pantheon, 2008.

Kertzer, David. *The Kidnapping of Edgardo Mortara.* New York: Knopf, 1997.

Kertzer, David. *Ritual, Politics & Power.* New Haven, CT: Yale University Press, 1988.

Koslofsky, Craig M. *The Reformation of the Dead: Death and Ritual in Early Modern Germany, 1450–1700.* New York: St. Martin's Press, 2000.

Kosnick, Antony et al. *Human Sexuality: New Directions in American Catholic Thought.* New York: Paulist Press, 1977.

Kundera, Milan. *The Unbearable Lightness of Being.* New York: Perennial Library, 1987.

Kutcher, Louis. "The American Sports Event as Carnival: An Emergent Norm Approach to Crowd Behavior." *Journal of Popular Culture* 16, no. 4 (Spring 1983): 34–41.

Lanchester, John. *Family Romance.* London: Faber, 2007.

Lewis I. M. *Ecstatic Religion: An Anthropological Study of Spirit Possession and Shamanism.* Harmondsworth, England: Penguin Books, 1971.

Lipsky Richard. *How We Play the Game: Why Sports Dominate American Life.* Boston, MA: Beacon, 1981.

Locke, Nancy. *Manet and the Family Romance.* Princeton, NJ: Princeton University Press, 2001.

Lodge, David. *Thinks.*—New York: Penguin, 2001.

Macadam, Alta. *Blue Guide: Umbria.* London: A & C Black, 2000.

Marius, Richard. *Martin Luther: The Christian between God and Death.* Cambridge, MA: Belknap Press of Harvard University Press, 2000.

Masson, Jeffrey Moussaieff, ed. and trans. *The Complete Letters of Sigmund Freud to Wilhelm Fliess, 1887–1904.* Cambridge, MA: Belknap Harvard, 1985.

McBrien, Richard, ed. *The New Catholic Encyclopedia.* San Francisco: HarperCollins, 1995.

McClaren, Angus. *The Trials of Masculinity: Policing Sexual Boundaries, 1870–1930.* Chicago, IL: University of Chicago Press, 1997.

McGinley, Dugan. *Acts of Faith, Acts of Love: Gay Catholic Autobiographies as Sacred Texts.* New York: Continuum, 2004.

McGreevy, John T. *Parish Boundaries: The Catholic Encounter with Race in the Twentieth-Century Urban North.* Chicago, IL: University of Chicago Press, 1996.

McNamara, Jo Ann Kay. *Sisters in Arms: Catholic Nuns through Two Millennia.* Cambridge, MA: Harvard University Press, 1996.

Meeks, Wayne A. *The First Urban Christians: The Social World of the Apostle Paul.* New Haven, CT: Yale University Press, 1983.

Meyers, Diana. *Gender in the Mirror: Cultural Agency and Women's Agency.* New York: Oxford University Press, 2002.

Montaigne, Michel de. *The Complete Works of Montaigne.* Trans. D.J. Frame. Stanford, CA: Stanford University Press, 1967.

Morris, Charles R. *American Catholic: The Saints and Sinners Who Built America's Most Powerful Church.* New York: Times Books, 1997.

Muir, Edward. "The Eye of the Procession: Ritual Ways of Seeing in the Renaissance." In *Ceremonial Culture in Pre-Modern Europe,* ed. Nicholas Howed, 129–53. South Bend, IN: University of Notre Dame Press, 2007.

Muir, Edward. *Ritual in Early Modern Europe.* Cambridge, MA: Cambridge University Press, 2005.

Nelson, Leif and Joseph P. Simmons, "Moniker Madness: When Names Sabotage Success." *Psychological Studies* (December 2007).

Noonan, John T., Jr. "Development in Moral Doctrine." In *Theological Studies* 54 (1993): 662–77.

Noonan, John T., Jr. *The Morality of Abortion: Legal and Historical Perspectives* Cambridge, MA: Harvard University Press, 1970.

Noonan, John T., Jr. *The Power to Dissolve: Lawyers and Marriages in the Roman Curia.* Cambridge, MA: Belknap Press of Harvard University Press, 1972.

Noonan, Peggy. *John Paul the Great: Remembering a Spiritual Father.* New York: Viking, 2005.

Novak, Michael. *No One Sees God: The Dark Night of Atheists and Believers.* New York: Doubleday, 2008.

Nuland, Sherwin. "Foreword." In *Jewish Insights into Death and Mourning,* ed. J. Riemer. New York: Schocken, 1995.

O'Collins, Gerald and Mario Farrugia. *Catholicism: The Story of Catholic Christianity.* New York: Oxford University Press, 2003.

Ohtsubo, Yohsuke, Charles E. Miller, Nahoko Hayashi, and Ayumi Masuchi. "Effects of Group Decision Rules on Decisions Involving Continuous Alternatives: The Unanimity Rule and Extreme Decisions in Mock Civil Juries." *Journal of Experimental Social Psychology* 40 (2004): 320–331.

Olyan, Saul M. *Biblical Mourning: Ritual and Social Dimensions.* New York: Oxford University Press, 2004.

Orsi, Robert. *The Madonna of 116th Street: Faith and Community in Italian Harlem, 1880–1950.* New Haven, CT: Yale University Press, 1985.

Orsi, Robert. "Snakes Alive." In *Between Heaven and Earth: The Religious Worlds People Make and the Scholars Who Study Them,* ed. Robert Orsi. Princeton, NJ: Princeton University Press, 2005.

Pagels, Elaine. *The Origin of Satan.* New York: Random House, 1995.

Pelham, B.W., M.C. Mirenberg, and J.T. Jones. "Why Susie Sells Seashells by the Seashore: Implicit Egotism and Major Life Decisions." *Journal of Personality and Social Psychology* 82 (2002): 469–87.

Pelikan, Jaroslav. *Mary Through the Centuries: Her Place in the History of Culture*. New Haven, CT: Yale University Press, 1996.

Portmann, John. *Bad for Us: The Lure of Self-Harm*. Boston, MA: Beacon Press, 2004.

Portmann, John. *A History of Sin*. Lanham, MD: Rowman & Littlefield, 2007.

Portmann, John. *Sex and Heaven: Catholics at Bed and at Prayer*. New York: Palgrave Macmillan, 2003.

Pratt, Jeff. "Catholic Culture." In *Italian Cultural Studies: An Introduction*, eds David Forgacs and Robert Lumley. New York: Oxford University Press, 1996.

Ratzinger, Joseph Cardinal. *Europe: Today and Tomorrow*. San Francisco: Ignatius, 2007.

Ratzinger, Joseph Cardinal and Jürgen Habermas. *Dialectics of Secularization: On Reason and Religion*. Ed. Florian Schuller. Trans. Brian McNeil, C.R.V. San Francisco: Ignatius Press, 2006.

Rogers, Nicholas. *Halloween: From Pagan Ritual to Party Night*. New York: Oxford University Press, 2002.

Rose, Michael. *Goodbye, Good Men: How Liberals Brought Corruption into the Catholic Church*. Washington, DC: Regnery, 2002.

Ross, L., M.R. Lepper, and M. Hubbard, "Perseverance in Self-Perception and Social Perception: Biased Attributional Processes in the debriefing Paradigm." *Journal of Personality and Social Psychology* 32 (1975): 880–92.

Rubin Mimi. *Corpus Christi: The Eucharist in Late Medieval Culture*. Cambridge, MA: Cambridge University Press, 1991.

Rude, George. *The Crowd in the French Revolution*. Oxford: Oxford University Press, 1959.

Schloesser, Stephen. *Jazz Age Catholicism: Mystic Modernism in Postwar Paris, 1919–1933*. Toronto: University of Toronto Press, 2005.

Schoenborn, Christoph. "Finding Design in Nature." *New York Times*, 7 July 2005, p. A23.

Schoenherr, Richard A. *Goodbye Father: The Celibate Male Priesthood and the Future of the Catholic Church*. New York: Oxford University Press, 2002.

Schreck, Alan. *Catholic & Christian: An Explanation of Commonly Misunderstood Catholic Beliefs*. Cincinnati, OH: Servant Books, 2004.

Scribner, Bob. "Reformation, Carnival and the World Turned Upside Down." *Social History* 3, no. 3 (1978): 303–29.

Sedaris, David. *Dress Your Family in Corduroy and Denim*. Boston, MA: Little, Brown, 2004.

Shahar, Shulamith. *Childhood in the Middle Ages*. New York: Routledge, 1990.

Shapiro, James. *Oberammergau: The Troubling Story of the World's Most Famous Passion Play*. New York: Vintage, 2001.

Shaw, J. "The Late Seventeenth and Eighteenth Centuries." In *Christianity: Two Thousand Years*, eds Richard Harries and Henry Mayr-Harting. Oxford: Oxford University Press, 2001.

Slevin, Peter. "St. Louis Prelate Aims to Bring Flock in Line: Burke Takes Firm Stance on Social Issues." *Washington Post*, 29 May 2007, p. A2.

Smith, Christian. *Soul Searching: The Religious and Spiritual Lives of American Teenagers*. New York: Oxford University Press, 2005.

Spretnak, Charlene. *Missing Mary: The Queen of Heaven and Her Re-Emergence in the Modern Church*. New York: Palgrave Macmillan, 2004.

Stanely, Alessandra. "For American Royal Watchers, Wink-Wink, Nudge-Nudge." *New York Times*, 10 April 2005.

Steinberg, Leo. *The Sexuality of Christ in Renaissance Art and in Modern Oblivion*. Chicago, IL: University of Chicago Press, 1996.

Steinfels, Peter. "One Writer is on to Something, Even if Not Everything." Review of *Why Men Hate Going to Church*, by David Murrow. *New York Times*, 4 June 2005.

Stoeltje, Beverly J. "Festival." In *Folklore, Cultural Performances, and Popular Entertainment*, ed. Richard Baumand. New York: Oxford University Press, 1992.

Sullivan, Amy. *The Party Faithful: How and Why Democrats are Closing the God Gap*. New York: Scribner, 2008.

Tapaninen, Anna-Maria. "Motherhood through the Wheel: The Care of Foundlings in Late Nineteenth-Century Naples." In *Gender, Family and Sexuality: The Private Sphere in Italy, 1860–1945*, ed. Perry Willson, 51–70. New York: Palgrave Macmillan, 2004, pp. .

Taylor, Sarah McFarland. *Green Sisters: A Spiritual Ecology*. Cambridge, MA: Harvard University Press, 2007.

Thomas, Keith. *Religion and the Decline of Magic*. New York: Scribner's, 1971.

Turner, Victor. "*Carnaval* in Rio: Dionysian Drama in an Industrializing Society." In *The Celebration of Society: Perspectives on Contemporary Cultural Performance*, ed. Frank Manning, 103–24. Bowling Green, OH: Bowling Green University Popular Press, 1982.

Warner, Marina. *Alone of All Her Sex: The Myth and the Cult of the Virgin Mary*. New York: Vintage, 1983.

Wertheimer, Jack. "What is a Jewish Family? The Radicalization of Rabbinic Discourse." In *American Religions and the Family: How Faith Traditions Cope with Modernization and Democracy*, eds. Don S. Browning and David A. Clairmont. New York: Columbia University Press, 2007.

Williams, Andrea and James D. Davidson. "Catholic Conceptions of Faith: A Generational Analysis." *Sociology of Religion* 57/3 (1996): 273–89.

Williamson, George S. *The Longing for Myth in Germany: Religion and Aesthetic Culture from Romanticism to Nietzsche*. Chicago, IL: University of Chicago Press, 2004.

Wills, Garry. *Bare Ruined Choirs*. Garden City, NY: Doubleday, 1972.

Wills, Garry. *Papal Sin: Structures of Deceit*. New York: Doubleday, 2000.

Wittgenstein, Ludwig. *Philosophical Investigations*. Trans. G.E. Anscombe. Oxford: Basil Blackwell, 1988.

Woodward, Kenneth and Andrew Nagorski, "A Blast from the Inquisitor." *New York Times*, 31 December 1984.

Wuthnow, Robert. *Loose Connections: Joining Together in America's Fragmented Communities*. Cambridge, MA: Harvard University Press, 1998.

Index